CW01465186

GENERATION Y

Presented by
Vallentine Mitchell
Publishers

To Dor
Our first grandson
With love

Generation Y

Generation Snowflake?

Tamar Almog and Oz Almog

VALLENTINE MITCHELL

LONDON • CHICAGO, IL

First published in 2019 by Vallentine Mitchell
First edition published in Hebrew by Modan Publishing House, Israel

Catalyst House,
720 Centennial Court,
Centennial Park, Elstree WD6 3SY, UK

814 N. Franklin Street
Chicago, Illinois
IL 60610 USA

www.vmbooks.com

Copyright © 2019 Tamar Almog and Oz Almog

British Library Cataloguing in Publication Data:
An entry can be found on request

ISBN 978 1 912676 05 7 (Cloth)
ISBN 978 1 912676 06 4 (Paper)
ISBN 978 1 912676 07 1 (Ebook)

Library of Congress Cataloging in Publication Data:
An entry can be found on request

All rights reserved. No part of this publication may be reproduced in any form or by any means, electronic, mechanical, photocopying, reading or otherwise, without the prior permission of Vallentine Mitchell & Co. Ltd.

Printed by 4Edge Ltd, Hockley, Essex

Contents

1

Introduction

Background

We were born in Haifa and spent our childhood and our teen years atop Mount Carmel, home to Haifa's 'nobility'. We met in the Scouts and the Hebrew Reali School and fell in love at the age of seventeen. We got married in the early 1980s, immediately after our military service, and before starting a family we went on the big trip to the Far East. Social and political unrest in Israel was at its peak at the time and there was a feeling in the air that everything we once took for granted was being undermined. The innocence of old was starting to dissipate, and the country was on the verge of entering the post-national and global age. We loved and cherished the moral code bestowed upon us by our Israeli-born parents and by our teachers, but felt disillusioned and aspired to be better than them, in every possible way.

In the mid-1980s we had two children. We raised them according to the values of Zionism, but our upbringing approaches were already influenced by more western models of critical thinking, feminism and empathy for the individual's needs and hardships. We spent the period's most dramatic events together: a meteoric economic development on the one hand (malls, trips abroad, computers, cellphones and more), and instability and lack of security on the other hand (terrorist bombings, rocket attacks, political turmoil and tensions, the collapse of the education system etc.)

We got our BAs, MAs and Ph.Ds side by side and entered the world of academia at about the same time; Oz specialized in the sociology of Israeli society while Tamar focused on alternative education. In 1997, *The Sabra – A Profile* was released and seven year later, *Farewell to Srulik – Changing Values Among the Israeli Elite (2004)*. The books, which dealt with Israel's young, 'wasp' class were written by Oz, but the writing process was collaborative and included endless conversations and preliminary discussions. Our mutual work stemmed not only from the nature of our relationship and shared profession, but also from the fact that these are actually indirect autobiographies: the collective story of our generation – the Israeli interim generation.

About five years ago, having reached the age of fifty and after a long career in university, our professional conversations started to take on a new tone. We found ourselves complaining about our students, time and time again. We noticed that the institutions around us were ignoring an increasingly troubling problem. Academic quality had been deteriorating with each passing year and we felt as if we were working for an institution that was gradually trading higher education for selling degrees in bulk. When we were young, we assumed that following the rapidly developing technology and the deepening of the democratic culture, generation gaps would soon be a thing of the past. Turns out we were wrong. In many ways, the gap between our generation and our parents' generation is smaller than the gap between our generation and our children's generation.

We would constantly ask ourselves: maybe we're overreacting? Perhaps we suffer from the typical syndrome of older people who are appalled by 'kids these days'? We started to read books, articles and online conversations that focused on contemporary young people. We suddenly discovered that our feeling was not subjective or random, and that there is a universal phenomenon here, coming into play in various fields. They really are 'not like us'. How different are they? How does this manifest itself? Why did this happen? And what are the repercussions of this change? We decided to answer these questions in our research, which is in many ways the third chapter of an ongoing private study of our lives.

The Book's Impact in Israel

Jewish-Israeli society has always been very fond of its youth and has expressed a great deal of interest in their lifestyle, worldviews and aspirations. This has been due to the Jewish peoples' communal and familial nature, the enthusiasm towards the new Israeli natives who embody the vision of the 'New Jew', and the fact that Israel is a nation of immigrants where young people surpass their parents in adapting to their new homeland.

Furthermore, the State of Israel has been embroiled in a historic battle against mortal enemies and the nation's main burden of defence has always been placed on the young fighters' shoulders. The prestige of military service next to the idolization of fallen brethren have similarly intensified the mythological status and image of Israeli Sabras and increased the fascination around them.

Israel's fast-paced development in the past four decades in the fields of economics, technology, media, science and politics has changed the cultural DNA of its citizens. Israel was one of the first countries to embrace the computer revolution and in fact became digitally oriented before many western countries. It is therefore only natural for many to wonder what it is exactly that distinguishes Israeli millennials, who were born into the computer revolution and grew up in a society of abundance, which absorbs a multitude of new cultural influences.

The Hebrew edition of our book was published in Israel at a time when public debate about the younger generation made its return in full force. This was mainly due to the staggering addiction to smartphones, the surprising impact of social media and the housing and high cost of living crisis that led to the social protest of the summer of 2011. However, a deeper reason lurked in the background: the feeling among many of the older Israelis that something big was happening around them. That 'something' was millennials' induction into adulthood. For the first time ever, young millennials and the older generations interacted with each other on a daily basis – in the army, in academia, in the workplace and in pastime activities. Much like in other countries around the world, this interaction in Israel exposed wide generational gaps and stirred new awkward situations, anxieties and tensions.

When our book about the Israeli Generation Y was published in Israel in early 2016, it immediately attracted vast media and public attention. Reports about the comprehensive study had appeared before the book was even published, but an extensive interview we gave for the weekend supplement of *Yedioth Ahronoth* – the largest circulated newspaper in Israel – went viral, generating thousands of shares and comments on websites and social media sites as well as dozens of reviews and articles in mainstream media: television, radio, print and online. The culmination of this trend was a television documentary series on Channel 10 that dealt with this generation's characteristics as portrayed in our study. The term 'Generation Y', which at the time was only known to few people in Israel, became a common phrase in Israeli discourse and the generational gap became a widely talked about issue on countless forums.

The book also had a practical impact. Hundreds of public and private institutions invited us to speak about the findings and their consequences and try to come up with possible solutions for the challenges that arose from the study. Many organizations started to develop new recruitment and employment programmes tailored to the new generation.

The success of the book – which has become a bestseller in Israel – could be attributed to three main reasons: (a) at the time, this was the world's most comprehensive study about millennials, trying to create a general profile of the generation. Most people who responded to the study claimed it perfectly described how they felt about their friends/children employees /co-workers and generally about young people around them. Many youngsters were grateful that 'finally someone is telling these "old folks" who we are and why we don't play by their rules'. (b) The book deals with a socio-historical phenomenon in real time and does not succumb to political correctness. (c) The study deals with a new generation whose impact on the image and future of the State of Israel is likely to be dramatic. Not only do these youngsters indirectly challenge the Zionist vision, they also influence and continue to influence the very nature of Israel and its future. In effect, millennials all around the world have been changing the rules of the social game and leading humanity towards a new cultural age.

The Twilight Age

We're currently living in a period of transition – a twilight age, in which long-standing social conventions and structures no longer fit as they used to, with a growing need to construct upgraded systems befitting the spirit of the times. Social and private bodies and organizations are feeling their way towards the future, weighing options, experimenting, making mistakes and correcting themselves as they go. Many of the people who make decisions on the strategic level are shaping a policy based on social axioms whose grasp on reality is fading. They aren't properly aware of the fact that the past few years have produced a young generation with a different cultural language, different codes of behaviour and new aspirations, inspired by the environment in which they were raised. The Tents Protest in the summer of 2011, led by embittered young people, demonstrated the ever-growing generation gap and deepening problems that transpired due to an obsolete social structure that doesn't meet the changing needs. This is a period that requires bold, in-depth introspection that would include studying millennials' characteristics and needs.

When we embarked on this study, we assumed that the current young generation is changing the nature of Israeli culture in many aspects: the interpersonal relationships, interfamily relationships, aspirations and basic goals in life, leisure culture, work culture and more. But we couldn't have possibly imagined how deep the change is and the difficulties and functional crises it creates in all systems of life, from schools to the army, higher education, employment and economic systems.

Generations in a Society

In the mid-1700s, with the rise of the Industrial Revolution and the Age of Enlightenment in Europe, the distinction and recognition of different cognitive and social patterns based on age groups emerged for the first time. Rapid developments in technology had made it so youths in modern society were raised in different technological and spiritual environments than their parents, creating significant intergenerational gaps and tensions for the first time in history. Over time, the generation gap became one of the signs of the new age.

Generation study experts all agree that it's hard to pinpoint the division of history into generations, and furthermore, to define the exact traits that distinguish one generation from the other. Nonetheless, it seems this division – albeit somewhat arbitrary – greatly contributes to understanding the historic development of worldviews and lifestyles.

It is also widely agreed by most researchers that the generational consciousness is often moulded in a single upsurge – by sudden, traumatic social events such as wars or economic crises. This creates a sense of a shared destiny and etches the collective memory.

However, a common denominator and generational consciousness is also formed in a gradual evolutionary manner. The 'silent' generational revolution is mostly formed by the constant flow of technological (in the fields of economy, medicine, entertainment, etc.) and intellectual innovations (new theories and ideas), which in turn lead to changes in consumption habits, artistic taste and social perceptions.

When a distinct generational group is formed, it usually gets a catchy nickname, which becomes its sociological ID, like Baby Boomers or Flower Children.

Ever since the concept of a generation became a key term in western media and social studies and the arts, many attempts have been made to perform a periodization of generations throughout history. Naturally, this segmentation is schematic and has soft borders. Many people fall under intermediate areas and belong in two categories, due to their date of birth as well as their cultural attribution. There are also minor differences between different western countries regarding generational periodization, resulting from different formative experiences.

Generations in Israel

Israeli society has been through multiple perilous events, which have produced high generational turnover. The fact that war breaks out here (more or less) every decade, has created a situation in which youngsters (mostly the ones who fought as soldiers and junior officers in the line of fire) went through a different melting pot than their parents and developed a unique generational consciousness. The collective sacrifice of the War of 1948 is fundamentally different from the power trip of Operation Kadesh, the messianic gospel of the Six-Day War, the rift of Yom Kippur War, the identity crisis of the Intifada and the embarrassment and helplessness of the first and second Lebanon wars. Generations in Israel can be divided as follows:

Palmach and Early-Israel Generation
(Millennials' Grandparents)

These are the creators of the Sabra model – born in the 1920s, 30s and 40s, who were born in Israel or emigrated to Israel at an early age (they share several basic characteristics with the Silent Generation and Baby Boomers in the western world). The formative experiences of their mutual biography took place during the British Mandate, the fight for Jewish autonomy (resistance movements) and the birth of the nation: the Holocaust in Europe, emigration to Israel, the formation of generation gaps among immigrant families (the tension between Holocaust refugees and refugees from Arab nations and their children), the War of Independence, growing up under the early Sabra social frameworks (youth movements, gymnasiums, Kibbutzim, etc.) and Zionist education, mass immigration, the emergence of ethnic cleavages in Israeli society, the period of austerity, the Sinai Campaign, the Six-Day War and War of Attrition (in which they fought as senior commanders or in reserve duty).

Many members of this generation, who are now millennials' grandparents, are frustrated and disappointed by the current reality in Israel. This feeling is due to the contrast between the age of innocence and the current age of cynicism, the lack of perspective and disproportion – typical of a group raised in a bubble, unable to understand social processes, and the griping and grievance typical among older generations around the world. However, this is also an expression of the ever-growing differences between generations, some of which are greatly disturbing for older people (and rightfully so).

Israeli Generation X
(Millennials' Parents)

Born in the late 1950s and 60s, they share some similarities with Generation X in the western world. This generation institutionalized the sexual and feminist revolutions, invented and developed the Yuppie model and established hi-tech industry and digital communications. The term Generation X became common thanks to a popular book called *Generation X: Tales for an Accelerated Culture* by Douglas Coupland in 1991, in which he describes the anxiety among Generation X and its feeling of not belonging.

This generation was mostly born and raised in Israel, with one foot in youth movements and the other in the laptop. Their parents raised them according to national-Zionist codes while they raised their own children according to more universal values. As aforementioned, this generation's metamorphosis was described extensively in the book *Farewell to Srulik – Changing Values Among the Israeli Elite*.

The formative experiences in their shared biography include: intergenerational tensions in immigrant families, Zionist-pioneering upbringing, the Six-Day War (as children), the War of Attrition, the Yom Kippur War, the First Lebanon War (they fought in these wars either as young soldiers or junior commanders), the political shift and rise of the Likud, expansion and surfacing of social rifts, the media revolution, the backpacking experience (they were first to head out to the Far East and South America), the rise of the computer and hi-tech (most pioneering entrepreneurs in this industry come from this generation) and the inception of the post-Zionist age (this generation led the critical approach in all fields).

The Interim Generation
(Generation XY)

These are young people born in the 1970s, i.e. in the period between Generation X and Generation Y. This category was introduced during the study, when it became clear to us that there is a group that represents an interim model – with one foot in Generation X's values and lifestyle while the other foot is in Generation Y's values and lifestyle.

Post-Sabra Generation
(Israeli Generation Y)

The term Generation Y corresponds with Douglas Coupland's *Generation X*, marking the biological and cultural heirs of Generation X. In the early 2000s, the term Generation Y became common in US media, gradually spreading to other countries. This generation has received many definitions and nicknames: Millennials, the Internet Generation, the Global Generation, the Non-Rebellious Generation, the Me Generation, the Lost Generation and more.

Israeli millennials are a group of young secular Jews born between 1980-1995 and currently in their first decade as independent adults. Since their formative experiences are similar to those of young people around the world, they share similarities with their contemporaries in western countries.

They came of age during the days of commercial channels, the revolution of personal computers, the internet and mobile phones, the development of feminist culture, civil rights and individualism, the Iraq missile attack, the assassination of Yitzhak Rabin, the economy of wealth and entrepreneurship, suicide bombings and the war on terror, the leadership crisis, the leisure and entertainment revolution, the normalization of travelling abroad, the rise of a wide middle class comprised of both Ashkenazi and Mizrahi Jews (narrowing ethnic gaps), the Second Lebanon War and operations to eradicate terrorism in the West Bank and Gaza. This generation's impact on Israeli society is tremendous, and its social profile raises some tough questions.

Post-millennial Generations

It's hard to tell when a new generation with different characteristics will be formed. For now, a tentative generational label has been given to two age groups, whose social DNA has yet to be examined:

Generation Z: people born in the mid-1990s to 2009. These are the millennials' younger siblings.

Generation Alpha: people born in 2010 onward, some to millennial parents.

Research Population

On the eve of Israel's 65th Independence Day (2013), Israel's population amounted to roughly eight million people. Our study focuses on young, non-religious men and women from the Jewish sector.

It should be noted that our study does not include young people from the Arab, Druze, ultra-Orthodox or National-Religious sectors, for three reasons: 1) we couldn't encompass all sectors in Israeli society and chose to focus on the largest, most influential sector; 2) the social class we studied is the most similar to dominant classes in the western world (it is also the most influenced by western culture); 3) we assume (among others based on our conversations with people from non-secular Jewish sectors), that most of Generation Y's characteristics exist in other sectors as well. However, since these are conservative sectors, the millennial influence is likely to be more moderate.

The non-religious Jewish sector population is comprised of around 3.4 million people born in Israel or living in it for at least twenty years, as well as about one million new immigrants (who emigrated to Israel in the past twenty years). Therefore, the total traditional-secular population in Israel is some 4.5 million.

Our study's population is comprised of ages 21 (after military service) to 35 (born in 1980), i.e. fifteen annual cycles. According to calculation based on data from the Central Bureau of Statistics, each cycle includes about 57,500 people. This means that the study's population includes about 860,000 young people, most of whom have graduated from high school.

Research Method

The study was based on a combination of empirical methods – both quantitative and qualitative. Most of the information was obtained through focus groups, polls, comprehensive interviews with millennials from different background and with the people who come in close contact with them: parents, teachers, counsellors, commanders, lecturers, employers and specialists in different fields (economy, security, education, entertainment, psychological and employment consultancy etc.). We also analyzed texts from various sources: blogs, forums, Facebook pages, newspaper articles, online comments, novels, poems and songs, slang words and phrases, plays, television shows, videos and films. We also used participant observations in youngsters' zones (residential and recreational areas, workplaces, universities and colleges, backpacking centres and more) as well as thousands of photographs taken by us and other photographers.

Since this age group has similar characteristics in many countries, we were also able to use hundreds of published scholarly and popular articles and books as well as thousands of reports and statistics published by foreign media and scientific platforms.

In order to validate our findings and conclusions, we uploaded chapters of the research to the internet, as drafts, immediately after writing them. This allowed us to receive feedback from the public in real time, make additions and corrections and calibrate the study's findings as it progressed. Our interviews on various media outlets increased exposure to the study's interim results and gave us more feedback from readers, listeners and viewers. We also held meetings with groups of young people (mainly students) and high-ups from a variety of fields in the public and private service: senior security forces officials, HR managers and CEOs in the business field, couples and parenting counsellors, administrative and academic staff in institutions of higher education, high school teachers and principals, psychologists, social workers and more. These meetings, which usually incorporated a lecture on the study's findings, allowed us to get the lay of the land, receive criticism and demonstrations and clarify facts and insights. It took about three years to conduct and write the study; it's been a gruelling yet fascinating journey.

Such an integrative study – both quantitative and qualitative – that outlines Generation Y's overall characteristics and lifestyle – has never been performed around the world, let alone in Israel. This makes our study the first of its kind.

The book you are reading now is essentially a summary of the research report. In order to make the material more accessible to the general public, we edited the original text and omitted the full scientific apparatus: references, statistics, citations, graphics and charts, photos and bibliographies. The full scientific report can be found (in Hebrew) either on the internet or in universities libraries.

The Art of Broad-Strokes

One of the obvious questions of a generational study is: what kind of general trends can we derive from our findings, or to what extent do the characteristics we found actually represent the entire demographic at hand? The answer to this question is complex and inconclusive. As specified above, the sensors we used in the study were diverse and intended to crosscheck testimonies and confirm hypotheses, unmediated impressions and gut feelings as much as possible. We didn't admit a generational characteristic into writing before we felt we were on solid ground in terms of the evidence collected.

Nevertheless, it should be noted that most research tools in this study are essentially qualitative; this is what the science world refers to as 'soft research'. Furthermore, our findings are 'soft' because we have analyzed a very large demographic entity (hundreds of thousands of people), which includes countless nuances and exceptional subgroups.

Our empirical goal is a modest one: we tried to identify general trends and characteristics, which have a real (prominent, non-accidental) presence in the lives of young seculars in Israel. In that respect, the exact statistic numbers are not as important. We also tried focusing on characteristics that seemed unique compared to generations that came before.

We don't go as far as to claim that every young, secular, Jewish man or woman in Israel behaves according to all of the generational characteristics we've outlined. The profile of each and every person obviously depends on particular influences (upbringing and education, social environment, socio-economic status and more), and local influences occasionally beat the general influences of the times.

Therefore, our study deals with the most common and prominent characteristics. i.e. ones that came up time and time again in a variety of fields. What is the weight of each characteristic we've outlined when typifying Generation Y's profile? We don't have an empiric answer as of now and it's doubtful if one is even necessary. Because at the end of the day, the individual characteristics are not the point, but rather the cultural jigsaw puzzle they create when combined.

How are Millennials Different from Previous Generations?

It's important for us to emphasize to the readers that the study does not focus on the question of whether and how millennials are different from their parents. Our goal was to illustrate this generation's worldview and lifestyle in detail. That's also why we chose a wide research setting and strove to identify generational characteristics in the fields of employment, leisure habits, family, relationships, politics, education and more.

It's clear that the real scale for intergenerational comparison is over a period of time. In other words, comparing the values and lifestyles of previous generations, when they were the same age as millennials, with the values and worldviews of young people today. We don't have empirical tools to do that, because a generational study like ours has never been conducted before. The most comprehensive studies about the Baby Boomers (Palmach and early-Israel generation) and Generation X (The Revolution and Lebanon War Generation) appear in Oz's books, *The Sabra – A Profile* and *Farewell to Srulik – Changing Values Among the Israeli Elite*. But these studies were conducted mostly by analyzing texts and maintain a retrospective view. Our research, on the other hand, has been done in real time – at the period of the formation of the Y Generation and includes a wider range of research tools and data: quantitative and qualitative as well.

Comparisons between millennials and previous generations are actually implied and more understandable to the people who experienced both periods, i.e. veteran Israelis over the age of fifty. For instance, there is no study that looked into how many workplaces young people changed jobs during the 1970s and 1980s in the decade following their military service. Today we know that young people at these ages tend to change three to nine jobs over the course of a decade. Therefore, we can only assume (based on intuition, common sense and interviews with employers and manpower professionals from older generations), that this is a real turning point in the employment market and is actually a deep cultural change, which creates a generational difference. In other words, we are leaving it up to the readers to decide for themselves, using the data we present them, how different young millennials are from young people from previous periods.

One of the most interesting, and to a great extent, one of the most surprising findings in our polls is actually the similarity between millennials and their parents when it comes to their basic worldview (fundamental values). This phenomenon could be explained with how everyone – young and old – is exposed to the same media that surrounds us, and the tight and open relationships within the typical Israeli family. This is why the changing spirit of the times (social codes) is evident among all age groups.

The values shared by parents and their children are also due to the fact that parents in Israel (and practically across the western world) tend to align with their children. Furthermore, Israel, much like other western countries, is a very mobile society (allowing social mobility) and the study has proven that in such families, it is the young people who usually set the tone.

However, it seems that the code of values that embodies our time is more prominent and dynamic among the younger population – which was born into it and developed it. In other words, this period's young people don't have the cultural 'brakes' or the 'inhibitions' of someone raised according to the old code, i.e. the pre-digital-consumerist-global age. In this context, we can say: even if we are all part of 'Generation Y', young people are more 'Y' than us. Thus, we can definitely consider the study of Generation Y more than a study of a generation but rather also a study of a new age in the making.

Even though we did not examine this empirically, we get the impression that the most fundamental differences between Generation X and their children, Generation Y, are expressed more in the practical level and less in theoretical value systems about right and wrong and what you should do with your life. For example, both Gen Y and Gen X are worn out by work and dream of 'breaking out of prison'. But while Gen Xers choose to stay in a stable workplace (usually until retirement), even if they are sick of it, millennials will be less hesitant to bail, even when they don't have any available alternatives.

One of the claims we heard in the meetings we held was that the study's findings are more age-oriented and less culture-oriented ('they'll grow up and change eventually'). One can assume that some of the young generation's characteristics will change as they grow older, as biological age and experience take their toll. However, there are quite a few generational traits created in early stages of the young people's lives. They've left such a deep imprint that a fundamental change is unlikely. And even if they do change, it will be from a certain starting point, for example when it comes to consuming stimuli and engaging with their surroundings. How will this generation's unique characteristics endure over time and lead to the creation of a new culture? Time will tell.

We feel it important to elaborate on another fundamental point: generational research deals with a very wide population that includes subgroups, and often the difference between said subgroups is bigger than the difference between one generation and the next. For example, the differences between genders, ethnic origins, socio-economic classes and even between a younger age group (21-27) and an older age group (28-35). Our study does not deal with these differences but rather with the widest common denominators, i.e. what's called in sociology, 'the generational core'.

Triumph of the Nerds – The Origins of Generation Y

Birth of the Yuppie

The big winners of the Second World War (the Soviet Union, UK and United States) used the victory's heroics to feed patriotic sentiment, although the mass killing and horror of the acts committed by the dictatorial mutation, next to the development of the Cold War, raised question marks in the democratic west over the State's authority and the intentions of its leaders. This doubt started a gradual, years-long process that softened the collective authority and limited the national credit, while individualistic orientation grew stronger.

The appearance of Generation Y, half a century later, is the pinnacle of this process and perhaps its dangerous radicalization to a certain degree.

The transition from the Machine Age to the Computer Age began around the late 1950s. It was only some three decades later, as the personal computer revolution started to take form, that globalization got on the express lane.

Whereas the hero and the engine of the Machine Age and nationalism was the patriot (the model it represents), the Computer and Globalization Age's hero and engine is the Yuppie.

Yuppie (short for Young, Urban, Professional) is a snide nickname that became popular in the United States ahead of the mid-1980s. It refers to upper middle-class people in their 20s and 30s who live in major metropolitan areas, have a college education and deal in free professions.

In its early stages, the term Yuppie was mostly used to criticize the extreme western materialism and careerism that it represented. But when personal computers invaded popular culture and when it turned out that startup heroes, armed with their laptops were turning into successful businesspeople, the term 'Yuppie' also received a more positive tone.

The Yuppie generation's emergence was a precursor to the age of an everchanging privatized, commercialized and hedonistic society. A society in which the individual has become more important than the collective, and freedom of choice has become the highest value.

The lifestyle of the Yuppies, who in turn became millennials' parents, teachers and bosses, was moulded by the following changes: waning traditional social frameworks – nationality, religion, ethnicity, extended family, place of residence; the increasing use of computer technologies; the rising importance of the professional career up to the point of workaholism; the intensifying materialist, consumerist and hedonistic code; the rise of democratic pluralism and decline of the buffers between nationalities, genders, races and ethnic groups; expansion of the metropolitan area at the expense of the periphery, the development of new options of mobility and flexibility in all aspects of life; the growing, expanding influence of the psychological worldview (self-awareness and openness).

The professional identity is placed high in the Yuppie's identity scale, often even above their national, religious or ethnic identity. You could say that Yuppies are attached to their work the same way that total patriots were attached to their homeland. But they are not enslaved to a specific workplace, like the nationalists, but rather to a more flexible and more mobile career. This mobility is made possible among others thanks to the development of tiny computers, smartphones, wireless internet and high-speed transport. Today's Yuppies don't just work at the office but also at home, in cafés, on the train, on planes etc. For millennials, the disengagement from the employment framework will make an amazing turnaround from addiction to a personal career into a rebellion against it.

A keyword in the Yuppie's world is diversity – in food, in clothing, in recreation and even in life partners. One must never stagnate or stay in one place. For millennials, the need to diversify will become a source of constant unrest and a type of mental subjugation.

Psychological thinking is an important tool for promoting democracy, which is so important to the Yuppie, among others because it cultivates exposure and preaches against denial and repression. People who know the truth about themselves and about others, are people with greater liberty, and liberty after all is the essence of democracy.

Blogs and social networks will in time take the psychological-confessional culture to a brand-new level. Generation Y is among others a creation of the psychological revolution and in many ways its radicalization and its victim.

If the nationalist-patriot stereotype focused on the male, the Yuppie stereotype includes a more equal component. This is because Yuppies have shaped the feminist revolution and were more affected by it than any group before them. Even in television shows that revolve around young Yuppies, gender equality played a central role. At one point, it even seemed like the scales were tipped in favour of women. For example, the sisterhood of powerful women, in the popular TV series *Sex and the City*, makes the men around them nearly obsolete.

The appearance of a new middle class (comprised mostly of immigrant and marginalized groups, which had undergone fast educational and economic mobility) also brought forth the appearance of nouveau-Yuppie cultural heroes that served as a bridge (in terms of their influence) between the old rich and new. Madonna, Michael Jackson and Michael Jordan are prominent examples of such cultural heroes (super-achievers) that reflected this phenomenon in their social background and media prominence. Along with their successors, they spread the Yuppie model to wider social circles.

Barack Obama's inauguration as the 44th President of the United States served as a refined symbolic expression of this process, which redefines social order in the twenty-first century. Obama, the son of a black immigrant and a white American, an attorney who graduated from ivy league universities Columbia and Harvard, represents the new Yuppie who has broken through the limitations of ethnicity, race and nationality. He is nearly the essence of the global man, and these traits make up a significant part of the secret of his charm.

A World Without Limits

As technology advanced, what was once a luxury reserved to a small group of well-off Yuppies has slowly been made available to millions of people. Humanity as a whole is closing the gap with the Yuppie lifestyle and assimilating it among the masses.

A shared culture is based on a collective memory, tradition and customs and a sense of camaraderie. All of these are conditioned to exposure to the same social stimuli. Just as the printing revolution in Europe was one of the main causes of the creation of national languages and national consciousness, so has the telecommunication revolution served as one of the main causes for the creation of the global cultural language. It has created a new fountain of shared stimuli across nations and peoples: popular (mostly American) television shows, commercials, news broadcasts, sport competitions, culture events and more.

Yuppies were the ones who launched the globalization process. Their millennial heirs/offspring came of age in the midst of this transformation and were actually the first global generation in the history of mankind. This is actually a transitional generation with one foot in the machine and nationalism age and the other in the computer and global village age. This liminality would also cause many problems and disruptions in the course of their lives.

The difference between young people in various countries across the world is still vast and deep. It will take many years to phase out the intercultural differences, but even now, we can see the growing similarities among young people across the globe and the blurring differences in lifestyle. Young people these days are exposed to the same (or similar) media stimuli of television and the internet, consume similar products (clothing, food, music etc.), use the same technologies (smartphones, tablets etc.) and are exposed more or less to the same global propaganda (in commercials, media etc.). Therefore, it's not just their lifestyle and language that are becoming similar (mostly in western countries) but also their worldviews and mentality. This is also why Israeli millennials are remarkably similar to their counterparts in other countries.

Srulik Goes Hi-Tech

Yuppie culture and lifestyle developed in Israel alongside the process of opening up to foreign influence and the growth of entrepreneurial economics and the free market, consumer culture and democratic sensitivity. Some consider the introduction of monthly magazine *Monitin* (1978) edited by Adam Baruch as the defining moment of the Israeli Yuppie. *Monitin* embraced the American model but added some local components that related to Israel's history, sensibility and mentality. Local (mainly *Ha'ir*) and national (mainly *Haaretz*) press embraced this model and expedited its distribution.

The Israeli advertising industry, which was quickly developed by Israeli Yuppies, also played an important role in shaping and spreading Yuppie culture in Israel, as did the launch of Channel 2. Alongside the printed press, the channel created cultural heroes in gastronomy, psychology, counselling, fashion, theatre (mostly stand-up comedy), cinema, music and more fields, and spread the word of ecology, the good healthy life and permissiveness. Channel 10, founded a decade later, followed the same path with a stronger emphasis on Yuppie culture.

TV dramas aired starting in the mid-1990s such as *Ramat Aviv Gimel* (which portrayed the rich Yuppie), *Florentine* (which portrayed the 'bobo' – the broke Yuppie) and *The Bourgeoisie* spread the Yuppie word to wider groups that connected to the electronic campfire, as did late-night talk shows like Gidi Gov's *Laila Gov* and Dana Modan's *Yachasim Mesukanim*. *Globes* (founded in 1983) was the first daily business newspaper made for Israeli businesspeople, which was followed by *The Marker* and *Calcalist* (both founded in 2008). They changed the economic discourse in Israel and helped spread the Yuppie's lifestyle and worldview.

The development of hi-tech industry in Israel boosted Yuppie culture and brought western and Israeli Yuppies together. 'Silicon Valley' in Herzliya Pituah, with its restaurants and cafés, became one of the phenomenon's symbols, followed by similar business and economic spaces in Haifa, Jerusalem, Ramat HaHayal, Rehovot, Ra'anana and more.

Yuppie culture in Israel couldn't have developed without the aviation revolution, which turned Israel from a closed off, provincial country into an open one where getting in and out of the country becomes routine for the leading business echelon.

Shenkin St. is definitely the geographic and cultural foundation for the growth of Yuppie culture in Tel Aviv. In time, the heart of Tel Aviv became a typical Yuppie space like Soho boroughs in major metropolitan areas.

By the 2000s, Israelis were completely surrounded by endless Yuppie messages: commercials, TV programmes and series, newspapers, books, websites, digital apps, stores and consumer products, restaurants and cafés, live shows, study programmes and more.

It should be noted: the dominant culture in Israel is still very different from other countries, and there are still quite a few nationalistic qualities that paint the typical Israeli portrait in the old patriotic colours. Furthermore, in a country that's far away from Europe, in an underdeveloped, undemocratic and hostile Arab space, the 'global village' vision still seems like a pipe dream. In fact, even Europe is far from fulfilling the vision due to severe crises in the fields of birth rate, the economy, immigration and politics, the rise of Islamic terror, radicalization on the right and on the left and the instability in Russia and its neighbouring countries. Nonetheless, 'the national colours' are fading in popular culture, and the lifestyle in Israel and in other western countries is becoming more and more similar.

Revenge of the Nerds

The nationality revolution centred around the brave, determined, authoritative warrior who works with his hands. Therefore, it is only natural that its stereotypical negative will be the anti-macho or post-macho. It is possible that this is the starting ground for the cartoonish image of the Nerd – the sensitive Yuppie's descendent and successor.

Undoubtedly, the computer revolution made post-macho man an important social phenomenon that later evolved into a leading cultural hero. It's no coincidence that Bill Gates and Steve Jobs, the two people most identified with this revolution, serve – in their biography and image – as the embodiment of this new cultural hero. They will later be joined by other 'nerdy revolutionists' like Google founders Larry Page and Sergey Brin and Facebook founder Mark Zuckerberg.

The growing legitimization of LGBT culture also indirectly contributes to the nerd's acceptance. Both because this is a general expansion of the boundaries of tolerance towards the other, the different and the exceptional, as well as because the strict gender division of 'tough man' versus 'soft woman' is increasingly fading.

National-Zionist culture in the late nineteenth century and early twentieth century as well as during the nation's early days glorified the Hebrew patriot, as reflected in the pioneer and Sabra stereotypes. They were described in Israeli propaganda outlets as strong, brave, skillful and independent. Their counterparts in popular folklore were naïve religious youths who did as they were told, and the diasporic new immigrants – outsiders whose stereotype was similar to the image of a nerd, i.e.: rejected, submissive, pale and soft.

Scholarly diligence was considered in secular Israel to be a diasporic attribute, both due to the religious context and because it involved staying behind closed doors instead of being outdoors – in the homeland. That's why for many years, honour students were looked down upon as 'squares'. A famous Israeli joke describes the Technion as a geometric place where all the squares meet. Even expressions such as 'bookworm' are remnants of that perception.

There's no denying that the turnover in nerd phenomenon's image, distribution and influence in Israel is linked to the meteoric rise of Israeli hi-tech industry. Instead of sturdy, handsome warriors, spectacled computer nerds like Yossi Vardi and Gil Shwed have taken centre stage in Israeli culture. In short, cleverness, boldness, initiative and positive Israeli Hutzpah moved from Yizra'el Valley to Silicon Valley. Successful nerds were gradually revealed to the general public in other fields: media, advertising, science, law, fashion and more.

In 2011, the great success of the Israeli version of *Beauty and the Geek* sparked debate in the media about the new nerds and their influence on our lives. For example, news site Mako published an article called 'Revenge of the Nerds: how nerds have taken over our lives', which discussed the revolution after which nerds became the new 'cool'.

The most iconic character of this revolution is, of course, media personality Erez Tal. Tal is considered by many to be a nerd who became the most powerful man in media and perhaps in all of Israeli popular culture. His personal career can serve as a mirror image for the milestones of nerd culture's journey from the outskirts to the social centre in Israel. From the playful and sarcastic *Ma Yesh* on *Galei Tzahal,* through popular comedy and satire programmes on radio and television to the position of manager, producer and all-powerful presenter on Channel 10 and Channel 2.

One can assume that Erez Tal's popularity is based on more than his strong presentation skills and intelligence, but also on his personal biography and the image he projects to his viewers: a media personality that's part cynic, part winner. Tal is a media startup master (he invented television formats and even exported them abroad) – the new Israeli hero, with a smug smile of satisfaction and nihilism on his face, a serial ratings magnet who shows the people that financial profit justifies almost any means.

In a way, Israeli millennials are a replica of Erez Tal's media persona – in their look, language and way of thinking. Although age-wise Tal could be their father, he manages to serve as a role model and an idol for young people. He is the epitome of the new zeitgeist and one of its primary creators.

A Generation of Wimps

The nerd who had a rough time growing up has taken centre stage in the western world and has been granted a positive image in part due to the childhood revolution that democratic civilization has undergone for about three decades. Gradually, the notion that we are all 'special snowflakes' is taking root, followed by the legitimization of childlike behaviour.

The nerd model came to power not just because it serves fresh, contemporary western values. But also because it became demographically common. It has become more widespread because it grew in Yuppie families with a similar nature of upbringing – paedocentric education (the child at the centre).

The nerd's pluralistic, protective upbringing included unlimited understanding and tolerance for anxieties, distresses and weakness, without the demonstrating authority or imposing punishment. This upbringing lacks an explicit demand for dealing with the world's difficulties and challenges. The nerd has no option but to channel his or her spiritual resources towards challenges where their competitiveness can be nurtured without endangering them.

The computer only reinforces the non-authoritative parenting syndrome. It may set a series of technological, educational and experienced challenges, but it does not require the nerd to deal with the emotional complexity of the grownup world. It also has no explicit demand to take responsibility or deal with the real world.

The nerd, therefore, is one of the outcomes of the collapse of authoritative culture and the fading dichotomy between the grownup world and the world of children. This collapse, next to the development of computer culture, is probably what boosted the nerd not only to the centre of the symbolic stage, but also to the cultural and demographic stages. Surprisingly enough, nerd culture has been absorbed by an entire generation without our noticing.

Millennials, born and raised by Yuppies or Yuppie-imitators, are actually a generation with distinct nerdy characteristics: emotional helplessness, seclusion, self-centredness, blurred gender roles, delayed adulthood, dependence and addiction to games, media and computer technology – these are no longer marginal characteristics, but rather generational ones.

In fact, an in-depth review of millennials' overall characteristics (on which we will elaborate in the next chapters) provides a complex picture: in some aspects, millennials have taken their parents' Yuppie culture to the extreme and turned it into a wide-scale social phenomenon. But in other aspects they rebelled against Yuppie culture, though it's a passive rebellion. For example, they refuse to be as industrious and as ambitious as their parents or devote themselves to their work. They don't aspire as much to lead or initiate and prefer to tread on peaceful, familiar ground. And mostly, this generation has made entertainment and leisure culture more important than work culture. This passive revolution has been paid for by their Yuppie parents.

Since today's social reality is very dynamic and fast some nerdy, post-Yuppie characteristics have undergone a metamorphosis among millennials. For example, this generation has lost its intellectual curiosity on one hand, but unlike the prototypical nerd, became more social.

Will millennials' Yuppie characteristics become stronger than their anti-Yuppie characteristics? It's hard to tell. Our study may help provide an answer to this question.

2

30-Year-Old Child –
Delayed Adulthood

Rite of Passage in the Age of Freedom

The weight human society attributes to young peoples' induction into the world of adults is expressed in the universal nature of graduation ceremonies, also known as initiations or rites of passage in anthropology literature.

Rites of passage in pre-modern societies provided the individual with a ticket to equal rights in the adult world as well as recognition as a fully-fledged member of the community, which included, among others, social permission to start a family and have children. Rites of passage are also common in modern societies. Occasionally this involves the preservation of ancient rituals, handed down from generation to generation (like the Jewish Bar Mitzvah), and often in ceremonies drafted according to the new spirit.

When examining Israeli millennials' trajectory towards adulthood, an interesting point comes to mind: formal and informal changes have occurred in almost every component that had defined maturity in Israeli society in the past, affecting the boundaries between childhood and adulthood. These are some of the most outstanding changes:

The Feminization of Rites of Passage

In the old world, rites of passage were usually intended for the males of the tribe, who were dominant in that society. Nowadays, following the spread of feminism and the equal rights ethos, there is a growing trend of modern rites of passages intended for females as well. Gender equally penetrated the heart of dominant culture in the 1980s and 90s, and came into expression, for example, in 'male' names given to the millennial girls (Daniel, Gal, Lior etc.), and in Brita ceremonies (a birth of a girl) and large Bat Mitzvah festivities (adolescence of a girl).

Even enlisting to IDF – which is considered an important and unique rite of passage in Israel – has undergone feminization processes in the past years, and nowadays even female recruits celebrate the occasion with family and friends. The same goes for bachelor parties, held nowadays by young men and women alike.

My First Passport

The ID card, issued to all residents of the country when they come of age (sixteen in most countries), represents their admission as full citizens with equal rights and duties in modern society. In previous generations, the ID card represented the young person's admission into the world of adults, while among millennials, the ID card has been replaced by the passport. More and more families nowadays go on vacations and trips abroad and therefore most children apply for a passport (which is essentially an international ID card) at an early age, even before getting their ID card. This reflects millennials' global nature and the high standard of living most of them have been born into.

Taking the Car to School

The driver's license has always been a symbolic as well as practical expression of maturity and independence. In Israel today you can get a driver's licence for a private and commercial vehicle at the age of sixteen and nine months. The reduced age limit for getting a license for a car and motorcycle (for many years the age limit was eighteen), next to the appearance of interim motorized options such as electric bicycles and scooters, mopeds and all-terrain vehicles, have in recent years blurred out historic rites of passage that separated the adults from the young.

Cigarettes, Hookahs and Alcohol for Children

With the rise of 24/7 convenience stores, and despite the minimum age for cigarettes sales, cigarettes have become more available to millennial youths than any previous generation. Cigarettes have not been a sign of masculinity for many years, and a large portion of millennial women smoke. Hookahs, which have become very popular in this generation, have also served as a gateway to cigarettes and are consumed as early as junior high. This trend has become an integral part of social gatherings, school trips, parties and other hangouts among young people.

The change in alcohol is even more dramatic. Whereas in the past, young people in Israel only started to consume alcohol after their army service, young millennials have been doing it since their teens, despite the law prohibiting the sale of alcohol to minors.

Growing Up with Pornography

Generation Y was raised in the post-puritan age, and when it comes to the average age for intercourse, the frequency of relations and of changing partners, they are more permissive than their parents and grandparents.

Does this mean they grow up too fast? Not necessarily. Although intercourse does require responsibility, self-awareness and emotional and physical confidence, there are those who claim that in some ways, having sex at an early age has had the opposite effect and has created a generation of 'sexual imbeciles'.

Access to internet has exposed millennial children to frequent pornography and explicit and harmful content at an earlier age compared with previous generations. This definitely affected their development and their views on sexuality, gender and more.

Gambling Children

The right to have your own money, and moreover to invest it or gamble with it, has long been perceived as an expression of independence. For many years, gambling was conducted on the outskirts of Israeli society, in private homes, and only few people did it. This all changed in the 1980s – when Generation Y were coming of age. Less expensive plane tickets (many Israelis fly to casinos around the world to gamble) and mostly the appearance of the internet, created a new reality. Not only has the number of gamblers in Israel grown significantly, the gambling age has steadily decreased and activities that were not open to youngsters in the past have become a common, normative pattern.

Gambling has become common among millennial youths even in the informal recreational setting. For example, groups of friends bet on sports, mainly major soccer and basketball tournaments. They come up with the rules together, and every participant adds a predetermined sum to the pool, which will eventually be given to the winner.

Army of Children

Israel is one of the few countries in the world where military service for men and women is mandatory (excluding the ultra-Orthodox, religious Jewish women, Druze women and Arabs). IDF plays a crucial role in the socialization of Israeli youths, shaping core experiences and creating a wide cultural common ground.

Recruitment rates have consistently dropped in past years and the number of soldiers who drop out during the service has increased. IDF is still an important body that leaves a major impression on the average Jewish Israeli youth, but its influence as a mechanism for growing up is diminishing. Whereas in the past, one of the first questions one would ask upon meeting someone for the first time was 'where did you serve in the army?', for millennials this question has become less relevant.

Between Biological Maturity and Mental Immaturity

A Boy Stuck in a Man's Body

A surprising thing has happened in the past years: while people live longer, their biological development actually comes earlier. This can be seen in the gradually dropping average age in which girls start developing breasts and get their first period.

Some ascribe the phenomenon to the standard of living: improved living conditions and sanitation, a healthier and more accessible diet, more sleep and less manual labour performed by children. The consumption of processed food products that contain estrogens might also affect precocious sexual maturity.

Some link precocious biological maturity to the collapse of the family as an institution in western society. They argue that stress in the family can disrupt the beginning of sexual development. Exposure to media at a young age has also been suggested as a reason for the phenomenon.

Precocious puberty among children of the western world has meant that physical adolescence is put on the fast track at the expense of childhood. The problem is that physical adolescence precedes mental maturity and emotional maturity, which are being pushed further back.

Waking Up as an Adult

The biological process of transitioning from childhood to adulthood ends around sixteen to eighteen, but in practice, people continue to gain experiences, develop and mature emotionally and intellectually throughout most of their lives. However, a person could be physically mature but stop developing emotionally.

The period between adolescence and adulthood (also known as 'moratorium' in psychology) started to extend in the western world in the early twentieth century and reflected the new generation gap that shaped a new cultural structure and stratification. What used to be a short interim period, however, has gradually turned into a long period (sometimes lasting over a decade), while in many cases there's actually no growth leading to an independent life. Turns out that the age of thirty, considered just half a century ago to be the midlife point, today marks the beginning of adulthood. This means that today's twenty-year-olds are actually 'teenagers'.

One would assume that a generation raised in an open democratic culture, exposed to the flow of free information and treated with respect from an early age, would mentally develop faster than the generations that came before. In reality, the exact opposite has happened.

In the late 1990s, a young psychologist named Jeffrey Arnett noticed that his students at the university think and behave childishly. Sixty per cent of respondents to his survey admitted that they feel 'grown up and not grown up at the same time'. Therefore, whereas in previous generations becoming an adult was perceived as an achievement, i.e. something to aspire to, young people nowadays see it as a type of prison – in other words, the stage where they settle down and lose their freedom and ability to have fun – a boring stage you want to put off as much as possible. This is a dramatic change, since the third decade of life, which was once dedicated to the process of settling down (marriage, having your first child and the beginning of a proper career), has been postponed. Arnett fittingly named this new stage Emerging Adulthood.

Updating Terms of Adulthood

According to the U.S. Census Bureau, in 1960, 77 per cent of women and 65 per cent of men passed all five milestones of adulthood by the age of thirty (graduation, getting your own place, gaining financial independence, marriage and childbirth). In 2000, slightly less than 50 per cent of women and about a third of men had done so by the same age.

Of course, one could argue that the whole concept of the five milestones of adulthood is less relevant to today's dynamic reality. Some young people nowadays choose not to get married or have children, others would rather spend many years building a career before committing to a spouse, and some have children first and get married later (if at all), go back to school later in life, etc. All of this is probably true, but it still doesn't explain why young people in their twenties and thirties today look and act like teenagers.

Evolution theorists argue that brain development among young people in the western world is delayed because they don't engage in work that requires practical training, but rather mostly study and absorb information. Therefore, the brain systems responsible for independent, practical functions develop more slowly, creating new interim stages.

Furthermore, neuroscientists once believed that the brain stopped growing at about the age of sixteen, when physical growth ended. However, recent studies have found that the brain continues to 'mature' well into people's twenties and doesn't reach full maturity until the age of twenty-five.

But beyond the empirical biological argument, it's possible that in a world with increasing longer life expectancy, the concepts of adulthood do need to be updated. Arnett did not see 'grown-up kids' as a sort of 'social malfunction' or as a sign of deterioration, but rather as a natural development process of a postmodern society that requires people to undergo a longer maturation process. According to him and the people who followed his work in research and psychological counselling, just like a hundred years ago, when changes such as these led to the definition of adolescence, the 'change in adolescence's timetable' is taking place today. Among the cultural changes that create the shift in adolescence's timetable, Arnett noted the need for longer studies (BA and MA) in order to get jobs that in the past you could get even without an academic degree; the change in society's view on premarital sex, which decreases the need to rush to get married; social openness to cohabitation and women's ability to give birth at a later age due to medical developments.

In fact, when you look slightly deeper, you can see that Generation Y's late adulthood is more complicated and complex than it seemed at first look. Why? Because in certain psychological areas this generation actually matures earlier compared to previous generations. These young people grew up during the age of information flow and things that were hidden from children and teens thirty years ago are now open to all.

If lack of maturity means innocence and lack of information, there's no doubt that millennials are the most grown up generation in the history of the human race. Even if we wanted to keep things from them, that's nearly impossible. It isn't by chance that they developed a kind of skepticism and realistic cynicism, which is very different from their parents' innocence (when they were their age).

Furthermore, in a world where grownups are no longer the ultimate authority of knowledge and in many cases, young people are more knowledgeable than the adults – the social resources that defined 'maturity' and separated children from adults are growing thin.

Perhaps we should look at human maturation in less linear and schematic terms? It's possible that the entire binary perception of childhood on one hand and adulthood on the other needs to be revised.

Sociological and psychological literature is riddled with examples and interpretations of the process of blurring the defined boundaries of the youth stage and the spread of 'youthful patterns' in other stages of life (adults who wish to be teens and children who wish to be adults). Whereas in the past, mature, considerate behaviour could be identified according to clear conventions of clothing, leisure, language and many other fields – today's expectations for age behaviour have become flexible and diffusible. In this manner, millennials' ongoing childishness is not only the choice of children who were raised in an overprotective environment, but rather an expression of deep social and cultural change.

And yet, despite all of these caveats, there are some serious questions hovering above. Since Arnett's first study was published, delayed adulthood has become a distinct generational symbol, and for the first time ever we've had the opportunity of observing millennial youths who underwent the decade of indecision. It turns out that after passing the age of thirty, most of them aren't doing great. Many are living under severe instability and financial pressure and a high number suffer from loneliness, anxiety and chronic insecurity. Is this really a necessary stage of social evolution? If millennial youths come out of the oven of socialization 'half-baked', it might reflect a cultural decadence rather than an evolutional stage.

What's clear is that even if adolescence is dragged well into their late 20s and even beyond, new adjustments will have to be made in all social systems. So far this hasn't really happened, and this has caused severe functioning problems.

30-Old Boy with High Fever

In the past, the 'in-between' or 'interim' period in Israel was mostly comprised of the military service and academic or professional studies. Nowadays, this is a long period of 'messing around' or 'debt relief' that lasts well into their 20s, and occasionally even exceeding that. It is characterized by frequent changes: apartments, jobs, partners and moods.

Israeli millennials struggle with old western institutionalized codes because they clash with two of their most basic habits: staying close to their parents and partying, a lot.

In fact, there's an entire generation of young people in Israel who refuse to settle down. Many of our interviewees candidly admitted that entering the grownup world scares and deters them, and that they wish to remain commitment-free at least for the time being. In their words: 'I want to do what I like, without any grownup commitments.'

One of the first public expressions of delayed adulthood is a popular song by Ehud Banai called *Maharai Na* ('please hurry'), which opens with the lines: 'the boy is thirty years old, he has a high fever / lying on the sofa at his parent's home / yes, he's thirty years old, he has a high fever / he's returning to the bedroom of his youth.' When this song debuted, many listeners smiled and nodded at the authentic lyrics and didn't really pay attention to the social problem they reflected.

Real echoes of this sociological phenomenon only started to appear in Israeli media in the past five years. Among Israel social scientists, only a few wrote about Israeli millennials and their delayed adulthood. The silence among Israeli scientists seems peculiar when considering that one of the Israeli Sabra's main features used to be growing up and toughening up at an early age. Thus, it appears that one of the most fundamental qualities of the Israeli code is being 'mutated', and this has deep social repercussions.

Millennials' childishness and their 'refusal' to grow up is expressed in a wide variety of behaviours: they laugh at the same kind of jokes they heard in school and in the army well into their 20s and 30s, they preserve childish speech patterns, tend to develop dependency, find it hard to make decisions, take responsibility or commit to stable relationships, are inclined to extreme mood swings and anxiety, have a hard time dealing with emotional overload and stress, make rash decisions, are unable to delay gratification, and live in the 'here and now' without making any plans for the future.

New Parent-Child Symbiosis

Mommy and Daddy

The fact that society expects young boys and girls to turn into responsible adults is hard for both teenagers and their parents, leading to conflicting emotions. The parents want their children to grow up normally, but have a hard time letting them go, and sympathize with their son or daughter's own troubles. Adolescents aspire to gain independence, freedom and recognition as equals, but are anxious about responsibility and the unknown. Generally speaking, adolescence is considered a rocky period, packed with emotional problems, mood swings, insecurity and many uncertainties.

All of this was true for all generations, but it seems that both millennials and their parents are more traumatized by the mutual separation process than ever before. Multiple factors and historic circumstances have created a situation in which both the children and the parents are unable to help each other and make it through this period of crisis, eventually getting stuck in a vicious circle of co-dependency. A symbolic, amusing or even sad expression (depending on your point of view) of this can be found in the way millennials talk.

The nasally, self-indulgent child-like speech is common among teens, but for millennials, it lasts well into their 20s, creating a general atmosphere of affection, allowing them to cuddle with the people closest to them.

Linguistic evasion from seriousness and formality can also be seen in millennials' tendency to embrace a shallow, over-the-top dialect, with no finesse or restraint, intended to attract attention. Just like children.

Not only do the parents embrace these speech patterns, they actually support them and even talk to their 20 and 30-year-old sons and daughters the way one would to a small child.

No Reason to Rebel

The generations raised in Israel during the twentieth century were distinctively rebellious. They dared to defy deeply rooted conventions and offered fresh alternatives in nearly every social field. The Palmach Generation and Early-Israel Generation developed Kibbutz and youth movements culture, which served as an alternative to the traditional, closed-off family and raised a modern, secular alternative to the diasporic, religious world.

The War of Attrition and Yom Kippur Generation rebelled against the old military and political establishment, tore down Israeli puritanism and brought the gospel of rock 'n' roll and feminism from abroad. They also implemented the humanist, anti-authoritarian approach in schools and in families and developed the critical, unapologizing media.

The generation of First Lebanon War alumni broke economic and technological norms, developed the international entrepreneurship industry and expanded the culture of protest and criticism, mostly on the psychological channel.

All of these rebellions took risks and personal tolls, but back then the feeling was that there's someone and something to rebel for. Millennials came into a world where the establishment was no longer conservative or strict. They were raised in a supportive, friendly and pluralist environment at home and in school. Most parents and teachers nowadays aim to please the children and therefore there's nothing to protest or fight anymore. Furthermore, millennials were raised in a very egocentric atmosphere, in which everyone cares more about themselves and less about society or the next generations. This is reflected in young millennials' passivity and sycophancy.

There two more important causes for their adaptability: first, the global world of capitalism offers great flexibility, both within the organization and between organizations, therefore there's less internal tension for changing the current construct. Second, rebelling against conventions requires courage and independence, but millennials' lack of maturity does not allow them to take charge and lead.

Childishness as a Lifestyle

Seinfeld's Overgrown Children

Some claim that millennials' childish behaviour is tied to the increasing influence of American culture on youths around the world (mostly via television and the internet), since childishness is embedded in this culture. American society is a frontier society, born with an ethos of liberty – the liberty of people who broke free of the chains and dreamt of going to the moon. Furthermore, the Americans led the modern psychology revolution, which among others led to the liberation of children.

The American childhood industry (amusement parks, gadgets, animation and adventure films and more) has become one of the most prominent American brands, while Hollywood has turned children and teenagers into culture heroes. However, it seems that what started off as a commercial endeavour, has become a deeper cultural phenomenon in the past half-century. America became 'childish', but it didn't stop in Disneyland or Hollywood.

The 'overgrown children' or 'childish adults' phenomenon did not start with millennials, but rather with previous generations, particularly the Yuppie culture of Generation X. The first signs of this phenomenon, which serves as part of an overall lifestyle and postmodern worldview, appeared in American television shows aired back in the 1980s – mostly in shows that dealt with groups of young people. The series that reflected this phenomenon the most and in many ways perfected the model and spread it all around the world was undeniably the sitcom *Seinfeld*.

The series' protagonists are young, selfish nihilists, who make it through the day using manipulations and humour. Some of them don't even have steady jobs and live their lives from one day to the next, without stability or any clear purpose. Overall, it's hard to tell whether the characters of *Seinfeld* are overgrown children or childish adults. What we can say for certain is that these characters are immature and that they treat the world like it's a giant amusement park. So why not have fun, and the hell with tomorrow? Thomas Hibbs, a philosophy professor in Boston College, claimed that the characters in *Seinfeld* are in a state of perpetual adolescence, and that their goal is to get all the advantages of being a grownup while performing the minimal duties of a child. The funny (or sad) thing is that this description is gradually becoming the definition of an entire generation that grew up watching *Seinfeld*.

In other words, 'the virtual prophecy' has fulfilled itself and a lifestyle that was previously seen on screen has become a reality of life. For example, millennials' tendency to live carelessly, do things on the spur of the moment ('here and now'), often without seriously considering any fundamental consequences for the future (for themselves or their environment). For example, leaving a steady job (because I need to unwind), renting an expensive apartment in the big city (even though I can't afford it), or having unprotected sex (I'm careful enough).

Wisdom of the Pretzel

A number of millennial heroes have appeared in recent Israeli literature, demonstrating their struggle with the notion of settling down. One book that undeniably reflects delayed adulthood in Israeli society in the deepest and most authentic manner is Ilan Heitner's bestseller *Wisdom of the Pretzel*.

Golan, the book's protagonist, is a childish guy in his late 20s who has trouble finding and keeping a serious job. He tends to have superficial personal bonds and futile relationships with women. He's attracted to childishness because it allows him to avoid commitment, but for a heavy price: confusion, financial troubles and immense loneliness.

The book was self-published in 1998, after Heitner failed to find a publisher that would agree to publish it. It seems that in *Wisdom of the Pretzel*'s case, the difficulty of finding a publisher also had something to do with the generational gap. One could assume that what seemed like a childish and frivolous novel to the old, frowny-eyebrowed editors, was perceived by young readers as a document that faithfully represented their personal biography. This is the reason why most of the book's readers were millennials.

Stand By Me

Israeli cinema has not produced many adolescence and youth movies in recent years. This could be related to the fact that millennials are generally more interested in television and the internet than cinema. Commercial television channels, on the other hand, are packed with shows that focus on groups of young people in Tel Aviv, with childishness as their main theme.

One of the most popular shows in this genre is *Ramzor* (*Traffic Light*). The difficulty and fear of settling down is a prominent motif in this show and is expressed in its theme song *Don't Want to Grow Up* (lyrics by Itzhak Cohen and Muki): 'I don't want to make decisions / take responsibility or think about the circumstances / don't want to know what they said on the news yesterday / small people with big problems / I don't want to grow up / cope and adapt / accept it and give up / I don't want to grow up.'

Women in Little Girls' Clothing

You would expect a generation that was raised in a visually-saturated environment to develop sensibilities in this field. In reality, the opposite has happened. Although millennials love clothes and devote a lot of money and attention to them, their visual language is superficial and often vulgar. They typically dress in loud colours with combinations more appropriate for children and young girls who have yet to develop subtlety and sophistication; flashy, excessive use of clashing colours and clothes that don't match their figures. What often seems like extroverted eroticism or even a kind of irony (clothes that are too short and too tight, doll-like dresses and skirts, baby overalls, shirts with Bambi and Sponge Bob on them etc.), is actually a childish clothing style they are obviously too old to pull off. Accessories and ornaments that used to be intended for teenagers are now sold en masse to people in their 20s and 30s – from hair bows and cutesy ponytail holders, through shirts and bags with sparkling sequins and figures from cartoons to kitschy iPhone covers.

This phenomenon has become so popular in this generation that fashion experts have labelled it with the 'paedophilic' title of *Toddlercore* – a conflation of the words Toddler and Hardcore. Famous trend forecaster Lee Edelkoort has referred to this phenomenon as 'infantilism' in her book *Fetishism in Fashion*. According to her, 'the use of children's clothes, diapers and hugging fabrics expresses the need to be pampered and the wish to never grow up. This generation has decided to stay babies for the rest of their lives.'

If a popular show like *Sex and the City* presented young women (from Generation X) who are addicted to clothing brands and designer shoes, *Girls* presents today's young women (from Generation Y), who exhibit a terribly cheap and childish taste, and not just due to lack of funds. A *New*

York Times article by Karen Schwartz provided several examples to demonstrate this phenomenon, such as the time when the show's main protagonist Hannah wore a tomato printed cardigan on her first day working in a law firm. Her best friend Jessa wore a sheer long dress over hot pink underwear for a babysitting job. 'The show turns the viewers' attention to the protagonists "fashion crimes", representing a generational pattern', Schwartz wrote.

One fashion that particularly represents this generation's visual illiteracy is the trend of piercings and tattoos. Piercings represent a convention that encourages maiming the human body in the name of (relative) outer beauty. Tattoos are basically a collection of recycled clichés that look like drawings from children's books or comic books (dolphins, butterflies, monsters, Chinese characters etc.) Young people pick them out of standard menus, like choosing toppings for a pizza or dressing for a hamburger. They are addicted to 'mass-produced fashion' as they are addicted to 'mass-produced food'. It seems that the whole idea of drawing a picture on your body that never fades away is fundamentally childish.

Decide For Me

Young Jewish people in Israel usually experience three stages of culture shock: the shock of enlisting to the army after high school, the shock of academic studies and the shock of entering the employment world.

Whereas in the past, when such shocks included a brief period of frictional transition until one got used to the new position and onto the path of a steady life, there are increasing reports nowadays – both by young people and by 'the adults in charge' – about a long period of 'spacing out' followed by an ongoing inability to fit in.

Most of the experts we've interviewed for this study presented shocking examples of new and unfamiliar problems and difficulties in young people's integration in institutionalized organizations. They are passive in nature, tend to get stressed out (and every now and then start crying) and get depressed and paralyzed (helplessness) when the burden of work is too much for them. They particularly have a hard time making decisions and finding solutions for professional and personal problems. Most of them have found a 'sneaky' way of bypassing the problem: they manipulate those around them (mostly their parents, but not exclusively) to get them to make the decisions for them. The request is sometimes made explicitly and directly while at other times it's done using indirect questions or statements such as 'what would you do if you were me', 'what do you think is the best option' etc. They also don't take criticism well, have a hard time meeting deadlines or coping with long-term mental and physical effort and commitments. They also tend to postpone difficult tasks to an undetermined future and quit on impulse. Usually they have a hard time delaying gratifications and are stuck in the 'here and now', like children. Of course, this is a very broad generalization, which obviously leaves out some exceptions.

What are the causes of this phenomenon? Here are some possible answers:

Frustrating Variety. The options open to young people in the modern society of abundance are wider and more confusing than ever. The feeling nesting inside all of us, and even more strongly among young people, is that whenever you make a choice you also give something up, and might even miss out on something. This paralyzes us, and in most cases, requires others to make a decision for us.

Mom and Dad will Get it all Sorted. Millennials were raised by independent parents with an entrepreneurial spirit – people who've developed strong problem-solving skills and responsibility. These parents tend to solve their problems and their parents' problems as well as their adult children's problems. Their message is this: don't worry, come to us and we'll clean up your mess quickly and efficiently. Then, without noticing, the generous parents 'emasculated' their children and denied them important life lessons.

Born with a Cellphone. This is the first generation to have their own personal cellphone from birth. The always-present phone allows them to 'phone a friend' at any time and any place and significantly lowers the need, and therefore also the accumulated experience, to make independent decisions. The temptation to consult with available people (mostly the parents) is so high, that in many cases it completely releases them from solving problems on their own. This mainly prevents millennials from making decisions that involve risk and personal sacrifice.

Due to cellular access, even the most significant Israeli frameworks for attaining independence (the army service and 'the big trip') lose their effectiveness. Since at every crisis point, every crossroad, every moment of indecision, they're no longer alone and there's always someone who can save them from trouble and indirectly spare them from taking responsibility. Meanwhile, the parents don't just answer their children's calls at all hours, they also frequently call them themselves to catch up ('what's up, where are you, when are you coming back') and stay in control. Thus, they reinforce their children's cellular conditioning and increase their insecurity about their ability to make decisions.

Anxious Parents. Since the children are available to the parents and the level of their anxiety about their fate has increased, in many cases it's the parents who initiate the intense involvement in their children's decisions. They often guide them every step of the way and reinforce their co-dependency. One mother was embarrassed to admit that she instructed her ten-year-old daughter once to prepare a serving of instant food. And not only that, she called her a minute later to remind her that the heated dish was ready to eat.

Quiet, Let Us Think. Millennials didn't get to spend much time alone with their thoughts during childhood. Even when they were alone, they were surrounded by digital stimulation. Since thoughts, ideas and plans come up and develop usually through a process of introspection and observation and mostly by concentrating for long periods of time, young people are left deprived. People who suffer from 'attention deficit disorder' and are unable to perform convergent thinking in order to analyze reality, will also find it hard to solve problems in a rational and independent manner.

Millennials' lack of independence has far-reaching repercussions on all social systems, particularly ones based on the recruitment of young manpower: the army, universities and colleges and workplaces as well, of course. Whereas once these systems assumed they were bringing in young people with a certain level of maturity, they are gradually discovering that the new recruits include many young people with lower mental readiness than before. If 'forty is the new twenty', as they say in the United States, we need to rethink the identity and abilities of the young recruit as well as the implications for the traditional requirements from IDF recruits, first year college students and new hires in an organization.

'You Promised Me'

Ahead of the new academic year of 2014, *Ynet* published a series of articles dealing with the disappointment many young people get from their academic degrees, which supposedly don't reward them with a high-paying job or even steady employment, contrary to their expectations.

The complaints voiced by young people do indeed echo the deepening financial crisis and perhaps even constitute a justified protest against a manipulative, exploitive market, which hurls them into a vague future. But this protest, and especially the way it's phrased ('you promised me and didn't keep your promises, so now I'm stuck'), also reflects a narcissistic expectation, and mainly a naïve view that life is supposed to go according to a tailor-made plan. After all, at this age adults are supposed to make rational decisions to fulfill their own aspirations independently, even if they're not always easy to achieve and even if the market isn't always welcoming and puts obstacles in their way.

It is possible that there's another childish component hiding here: innocence and the lack of criticism towards myths of success. A generation raised on misleading commercials and primarily on instant culture expects to achieve immediate success without a great deal of effort.

Generational Gloom

In our interviews with older people who come into contact with contemporary youngsters (parents, teachers, employers, counsellors, therapists and more), it was repeatedly argued that they only seem happy and jolly. Many described them as prone to mood swings and often experience feelings of despair and pointlessness.

Indeed, clinical studies show that depression has been more common among younger people in recent generations and even experienced in early childhood. In 2006 *Time Magazine* published a story about teen depression. The story presented a government poll, which asked high schoolers whether they 'felt sad and hopeless almost every day for two or more consecutive weeks, to the point of avoiding some of their everyday activities' in the past year (the common criteria for depression). A whopping 29 per cent of teens in general and 36 per cent of girls in particular said yes to this question. There may have not been comparative data, but it is likely that such a high rate is a new phenomenon.

On the surface, it seems odd that millennials suffer so much nowadays. After all, they have so many advantages that didn't exist in previous generations: sophisticated media (smartphones, multi-channel television, the internet), endless sources of entertainment, greater democratic openness and more personal liberties than ever, high standard of living (despite all difficulties), supportive parents and a global world that opens up borders and horizons. But perhaps this is exactly the root of the problem.

We believe there are several factors that increase the potential for this generation's depression and gloom:

Mood Swings. This is a more childish generation and as such it is more prone to being 'moody'. It is not uncommon to see them having a good time in pubs and parties on one hand, and delving into depression under the burden of existence on the other.

A Life Spent Sitting. This generation is less physically active. Movement and sports are critical for both physical and mental health. Exercising doesn't just diminish the damage caused by stress, it also has a specific effect on stress by releasing endorphins, which have soothing effect and give peace of mind.

On My Own. The high rate of single men and women in their 20s and 30s in this generation adds to depression.

Doing Everything and Nothing. Psychologists point at the 'multi-tasking' phenomenon (the need to perform several tasks simultaneously) and lack of concentration as factors that can have a negative effect on happiness and increase the potential for depression. It is only natural then that the world's most digital generation is also the gloomiest.

Financial Instability. Unlike their parents, who came of age in a time of growth, millennials faced a global financial crisis upon entering the labour market.

Life as a Horror Film. Israeli millennials were exposed to traumatic events (usually through the media) during childhood, and this has implanted feelings of helplessness, pessimism, anxiety and depression among them.

Low Breaking Threshold. Members of this generation are under immense pressure to succeed and fulfill themselves on one hand (as part of an achievement-based individualistic society) but lack independence and have a low mental strength on the other hand (among other things because of their overprotective parents). Generally speaking, reverse correlation has been found between the level of personal and communal strength and depression rates.

Depression as a Self-Fulfilling Prophecy. The childish fear of growing up and the desire to be protected by their surrounding (particularly their parents) create a sort of artificial depression, which is in many cases manipulative (either consciously or unconsciously) – i.e. it increases the parents' need to protect their children.

It's All About Me. It's hard to ignore the sense that there's a somewhat narcissistic and childish element in depression, i.e. constantly dealing with and picking at the self. A self-centred person becomes a prisoner of his own pain. Dealing with the self rather than with other people also distorts their perspective about life.

Emptiness in Abundance. This generation was raised in the culture of abundance and has never been deprived of anything material, which is why their drive to change the world is lower, weakening their joy of life as well.

Nothing New Under the Sun. Millennials' parents started the computer revolution, which changed the world beyond recognition. The following generation doesn't have the thrill of conquering new heights – of entrepreneurship of historic proportions. There's nothing left for them to do except improve on the existing reality. Furthermore, in a world of fast, giant industries, even if you do come up with something new, someone else has most likely already beat you to it and raised the necessary funds. This despairing feeling dries up their desire to initiate.

The Grass of the Friend is Always Greener. Social media highlights successes and pleasures over difficulties and failures. This creates a false, disturbing feeling that 'everyone is living well except for me'.

You Can (Not) Do Everything. When millennials were younger, their parents promised them they were special and that they 'could be anything they wanted to be'. Since reality usually works differently than promises, this leads to frustration.

Trendy Depression. Some of our interviewees claimed that depression has become something of a trend for this generation – in fashion and in music. The first culture hero to use it was singer Aviv Geffen. The motif of suffering and depression was prominent in the songs he wrote and in his interviews to the media, which helped him create an image that appealed to millennials.

Furthermore, millennials were raised in a time where it's easier to admit depression. The stigma around anti-depressants has also weakened and they've become more accessible.

On one hand, these drugs have made many people's lives better, releasing them from the heavy burden of depression. On the other hand, in an age where anti-depressants are viewed as vitamins, being young and depressed is almost 'normal' and even sexy.

Some consider anti-depressant therapy to be an expression of western instant culture – which spreads the illusion that you can relieve mental suffering with minimal time and effort. The American 'happiness industry' is also behind this phenomenon. Unfortunately, the first to fall for temptation are young people. Their hope to make the suffering disappear and catch a glimpse of happiness is also the catalyst of their collapse.

Refusing to Leave the Nest

Boomerang Generation

The phenomenon of young people who do not move out of their parents' home has been known in Italy for many years as *bamboccioni*, which roughly translates to 'overgrown children'. Though it was mostly limited to Italy in the past, it is now spreading increasingly to many other countries. A comparison conducted in the U.S. between Generation X and Generation Y about living with their parents found that 37 per cent of millennials live with their parents compared to only 12 per cent of Generation Xers who lived with their parents at the time (Gen X data is from 1989).

The millions of grown people from around the world who do not move out of their parents' homes have received unique, and mostly judgemental labels in different countries: in the U.S., they are called 'Kangaroo Children' (because they are carried in their parents' pouches) and 'Boomerang Generation' (middle-class youngsters who after college move back in with mommy and daddy). Upon their return, they seem to create a 'crowded nest' or an 'accordion family' (the family expands to take in the returning children).

In the UK, they are known as KIPPERS – Kids in Parents' Pockets Eroding Retirement Savings. The phenomenon in the UK is so widespread that even the government has a formal definition for it: NEET – Not in Education, Employment or Training.

The Japanese divide this population into two groups: 'Parasaito Shinguru'('parasite single') are the ones who refuse to move out of their parents' homes, don't work and live at their parents' expense; and 'Hikikomori', which are the 'recluses' – young, mostly male, who won't leave their rooms, turn night into day, their lives revolving solely around computers and mobile phones.

The problem has escalated so much that in recent years there have been quite a few articles directed at desperate parents, with tips and instructions for how to prevent 'Boomerang Children' from moving back home.

The situation in Israel isn't all that different. According to Taub Center's 2012 State of The Nation Report, in 2009-2010, 19 per cent of 25-34-year olds lived with their parents, compared to 14 per cent in 1995-1999. In Hebrew, this phenomenon has been described as the 'never-empty nest syndrome'.

Our study indicates that even when young Israelis leave the nest for a short time, mom and dad are still in the background. In many cases the children keep in touch on a daily basis and get all or most of the old 'services': laundry, food, ironing and an expanded 'allowance'.

They even maintain a close relationship with their parents during the big trip to the Far East or South America. Nearly all backpackers carry a smartphone and update their parents frequently. Thus, they sort of turn their parents into active participants in the trip and stay virtually connected to the family nest even when abroad. In recent years, many parents have even joined their children during some part of the trip or the entire run. The consequence is that the tradition of becoming independent loses its function and leads to further dependency.

The phenomenon of young couples living with or near their parents has also become more commonplace in recent years. Therefore, if any generational rebellion takes place nowadays, it's a rebellion in the form of role reversal: more and more parents are getting fed up with their children 'leeching off them' and show them the way out (usually in a subtle, implied manner, but occasionally more explicitly and firmly). We've heard quite a few parents say things like: 'I don't want them to live off me'; 'I don't want to see my pension disappear'; 'I want them out of the house already'; 'I've paid my dues'; and 'I'm also allowed to live and have fun!'

Why won't they move out?

Regrouping after Military Service. Unlike the U.S., where it's customary for children to move out for college, in Israel the return at the end of the military service seems natural for all parties involved: the parents are happy that their 'child' has survived the gruelling and dangerous service, and feel the need to pamper them, feed them and return their feeling of stability and security, and the 'child' (discharged soldier) is happy to come back to a warm, pampering home.

Period of Higher Education. According to the experts we've talked to, the period of higher education is when the child's chronic dependency on the home-base starts. Many parents see their children's academic studies as the ultimate goal in life and an important measure for their educational success. Therefore, in many cases they pay their tuition and allow their children to live in the family's apartment without participating in the daily expenses. They are not eager to see their 'little baby' lose the standard of living he/she is used to, living in a small, crumbling apartment on a shoestring budget. They just forget that that's how they themselves lived in their early days and how it made them more resilient.

Even getting their bachelor's degree doesn't necessarily make the chicks leave the nest. In many cases the first paychecks are sufficient for a very minimal independent standard of living and certainly don't allow them to rent an apartment in the centre of Israel and party properly. These factors keep the children at home a little longer, and sometimes, 'a little longer' turns into a year and then another year. When the 'child' reaches his or her late-twenties, the parents start to worry, but ironically, at this stage leaving home becomes harder, because they've become used to living in a great apartment with no roommates.

Postponing the Inevitable. The prolonged journey of self-discovery creates a situation where it's less and less clear for young people and their parents when exactly adolescence ends and when they need to start taking care of themselves. Most young people simply postpone answering this question, assuming that things will work out on their own, and therefore stay in their parents' nest for a long time.

Life is Hard. Many young people nowadays are diagnosed with learning disabilities, concentration difficulties and adaptability problems. This causes many parents to become anxious about their children's practical capabilities for living independently. That's why many parents start off by offering their children a long interim period of 'partial release of the rope', which includes getting a job or studying while still getting emotional and financial support. Obviously, this creates a self-fulfilling prophecy, as the parent assumes the child won't be able to cope because of his or her limitations and unconsciously communicates this notion, while the child gets the message and realizes this expectation.

Life is Expensive. The high cost of living and long periods of unemployment force young people to stay home or move back home after a short time outside. Everyday life has become too expensive due to rising current expenses (cellphones, internet charges, rent, food and more) as well as the fact that young people don't perceive leisure culture as a luxury, but rather as a basic need.

Safe Harbour in a Stormy Sea. The fact people marry later in life naturally makes their 'home farewell' delayed. Meanwhile, the rising divorce rate sends many millennials back into the arms of their supporting family. The parents' home provides young people with more than just a physical space that is willing to take them in no matter what. Many people nowadays suffer financial blows and devastating transitional periods: layoffs, relocations, break-ups and more. In order to make it through these periods they need a safe harbour where they can dock, refuel and go back out to the stormy ocean. The parents' home meets this need.

When the Prince and Princess Leave their Palace and Servants. Israel, like Italy and Spain, is a familial society in which the parents are somewhat 'chained' by their children. In fact, many millennial youths were raised by parents who treated them like royalty and never asked them to do anything: clear the table, wash dishes, do the laundry, change their sheets or even tidy up their bedroom. Many young people have a hard time giving up this pampering service and therefore are in no hurry to find their own place.

The sharp decline in standard of living (when leaving home) also burdens many young people, which is why they experience a shock when they first go out there, which in many cases leads them to run back home.

Mother Knows Best. In several interviews we conducted, male respondents (usually from a traditional background) stated that today's women aren't willing to do what their mothers did for their fathers in the past, i.e. serve the husband. These men admit that they find themselves helpless, which is why they 'have no choice' but to go to a woman who is willing to cook for them, wash and iron their clothes for them, i.e. their mother (and sometimes grandmother), who is both a sort of a girlfriend and in many cases something of a 'voluntary slave'.

There's Room for Everyone. In the past, moving to a place of their own reflected young people's strong desire to get away from their parents, mostly due to the generational gaps in lifestyle and worldview and the desire to become independent and get some privacy. But today's parents and children have similar worldviews and lifestyles – which diminishes the need to disengage.

The need is also weaker due to the fact that many apartments are spacious and include a separate bedroom (and often a separate bathroom as well) for each of the tenants. In this sense, living with one's parents is similar to living in a hotel or renting an apartment with roommates. And while we're on the subject of renting, better to save on rent and property tax and have 'considerate' roommates, who also occasionally take you out for dinner, buy you new clothes etc.

Furthermore, the younger generation is less concerned about privacy than their parents. This is because they don't hide things anyway and tend to share intimate details with them, and because western society is consistently lowering the need for discretion and raising the threshold of shame. Many young people have no problem cuddling in front of their parents and in many cases, it doesn't even embarrass them to have intercourse in their room while everyone at home is well-aware of this activity and often can't even avoid listening to it.

Parents Can't Let Go. Since millennials and their parents have somewhat of a friendly bond that's beyond the parent-child relationship of previous generations, many parents have a hard time letting go of their children and tell them, either consciously or unconsciously, that they better postpone the separation to a later date. This phenomenon becomes stronger in light of three reasons: first, the increasing tensions between parents within the family. In these cases, the positive relationships with the children counter the tense, unhinged relationship with the spouse. Second, more children nowadays live with a single mom (mostly divorcees). This has a double effect. On one hand, the children want to protect their mom, who in many cases is left alone, hurt and bearing a heavy financial and emotional burden, and are concerned about leaving her in an empty home. On the other hand, the mom unconsciously communicates that 'it would be nice if you stayed with me for a little longer'. Third, many families have grown accustomed to living in apartments and houses with big spaces so when all of the children leave the nest, home seems particularly empty.

Indifference to Other People's Distress. Millennials were raised in an ultra-capitalistic, ultra-individualistic and cynical society, and for this reason many of them have embraced a selfish and narcissistic worldview and lifestyle, like most people around them. It's easier for them to take advantage of other people – whether it's their boss, spouse or family member. Many of them aren't even aware of the one-sided relationship that the never-empty nest syndrome reflects, i.e. more taking than giving. Many of them are also not particularly interested in the price their parents pay, like losing their intimacy and their right to be independent after many intense years of raising children, not to mention the financial burden.

The lack of independence and 'impotence' among many young people expands the 'never-empty nest syndrome' even after marriage. Many couples depend on their parents even after getting married. Online forums for newlyweds are chockfull of discussions about cost versus benefit. Few of them discuss the ethical problem of the phenomenon (invading the parents' privacy) and the immaturity and dependency it may reflect. Considering whether to stay or leave is reduced mostly to the utilitarian field.

Counter-Reaction to Capitalistic Alienation. There's a natural tendency in the west to perceive the never-empty nest phenomenon as a negative thing. But one could look at this phenomenon as a positive thing, to wit: a somewhat balancing trend, which responds to the alienation and loneliness of modern life. It brings the old familial and communal conventions, in an unconscious and undeclared manner to a great extent, through the back door. Parents encourage their children to stay with them so they'd be less alienated and neglected in their old age. Moreover, when the children are married, another mutual profit could come from living in the same apartment or in adjacent apartments: on one hand, grandparents can see their grandchildren on a daily basis and on the other hand they help their children, who work long hours. It is possible that we're seeing the expression of a post-capitalist trend here, which among others comes into play with a rapprochement between generations and a return to the extended family pattern, which is still common in traditional societies (such as in Arab society).

Army of Children

The drive to cushion your child is natural and universal, but its magnitude and how it's done changes from place to place and from time to time. Generation X's parents (millennials' grandparents) in Israel gave their children quite a bit of freedom and independence and only offered moderate protection. They trusted their children and intervened very little in their lives in school, youth movements and definitely in the army. This is what allowed their children to gain their independence and resilience. Though it's true that Generation X also had its share of the 'polish mother' syndrome, who suffocates her offspring with love and care, but most of these worrying mothers' children fought for their independence. This was made possible among other things because a wide generation gap developed in many families between immigrant parents and their Israel-born children. Furthermore, Generation X's parents assumed that school teachers, youth movement counsellors and army commanders knew what they were doing, and in any case, they knew more than they did (most parents weren't even fluent in Hebrew). However, when Generation X became parents, they didn't necessarily feel like their children were in good hands (or rather 'good enough'). This strengthened their need to be involved, to protect and cuddle.

It turns out that parents' cuddling in the current age is growing more extreme, penetrating more fields and lasting even after 'the children' cross the 20 and 30 marks. This phenomenon has become so commonplace and prominent in the western world that it has earned the titles 'Overprotective Parenting' and 'Helicopter Parenting': parents who hover over their children like helicopters.

The public in Israel started to become familiar with this phenomenon mostly in two fields: the public education system and IDF. The parents' involvement in the education system comes into play in many aspects – from the selection of kindergarten and school teachers, through the firing of principals that the parents' committee doesn't like, to parents complaining about grades. Teachers describe countless arguments, 'negotiations' and even threats by parents in an attempt to change their children's grades. This phenomenon has become very strong, and the Ministry of Education has dedicated many meetings to the subject, and still hasn't decided exactly how this should be handled.

Whereas parents' intervention in school could still seem 'natural', in light of the poor state the education system is in, their growing involvement in 'the child's' military affairs and service is a completely unpredictable phenomenon. It makes sense for parents to worry about their children serving in the army and try as they might to make their demanding lives easier. It is even more understandable in a country like Israel, where many of the soldiers are at real physical and emotional risk. But it seems that in the age of anxiety and cuddling parenting, this involvement has been taken up a notch or two.

Many parents feel it's their job to protect their children even during the service, and they do it with the same level of assertiveness and sometimes aggressiveness they had when addressing teachers and principals. Many allow themselves to have patronizing negotiations with commanding officers over sleeping hours, time off and even safety conducts – things that were once considered taboo. They don't hesitate to talk to senior officers, file complaints to the IDF Ombudsman and apply pressure on the army by using the media.

Following the cellular revolution, parents now receive regular updates from their children in the army and even commanding officers have become more accessible than ever. In some places in the army (mainly in boot camps) contact with the parents is regulated through formal and informal procedures. For example, parents get the unit headquarters' phone number so they could leave a message for the company commander. Some commanders give their personal phone numbers to parents, and allow them to call them at any time. Some commanders even turn to the parents for help. For example, when a soldier behaves in an unusual manner and they need to consult someone who knows him well. But good intentions aside, many commanders are still having a hard time dealing with the new situation, particularly with hysterical, badgering parents. Parents today call commanders regularly for a variety of reasons, some of which appear somewhat bizarre: they ask them to give their children time off to go to a family event, beg them to undo sentences, or ask to send out birthday greetings. Even complaints about not being accepted to courses are submitted to IDF nearly every week.

The intense involvement/intervention of millennials' parents in their children's fate in IDF can be pinned on several factors:

The People's Army. IDF has always been the people's army, and the line between army life and citizen life had been ambiguous. However, with the growth of democratic culture and the decline in the army's status in the mid-1990s, IDF strengthened its relationship with parents and used them to mediate between soldiers and commanders. Many commanders are thankful for parents' involvement in the soldiers' lives, assuming that it helps soldiers and increases their sense of belonging to IDF.

Cellphones removed the soldier's separation from his or her family and they keep in touch on a daily basis. When parents are given real-time updates about what's happening to their son or daughter, they also respond quickly and strongly when they are in distress.

Financial Support. IDF has been in a budgetary crisis for years, and soldiers' basic needs are not met. In many cases, the parents pick up the slack out of their own pocket. Many even initiate outside donations and organize parties and treats for the soldier's unit. This involvement grants parents the right to intervene and get access to the base.

Tarnished Reputation. IDF has suffered increasing criticism over the years and no longer enjoys the unlimited credit it once had. Multiple disasters (like the Helicopter Disaster) have raised fears and doubts among parents. Nowadays, they demand explanations, investigations, and are not willing to fall in line with the 'Divine Judgment' ethos.

The Army Isn't Sacred. Many of Generation X's parents were immigrants who did not know IDF and its culture (and many were also not fluent in Hebrew). They worshipped leadership and military leadership in particular, and took its word as the word of a living god. Their children were born in Israel. They are much more critical and aren't afraid to assertively voice their opinion on any institution, 'sacred' as it may be. Furthermore, a great portion of millennials' parents were themselves soldiers and officers and have served in reserve duty, so they feel like they have the knowledge and authority to pass judgment 'from within'. The media encourages parents to make their voices heard because it delivers the message that the public keeping quiet preserves failures and shortcomings and the key to an efficient corporate culture is transparency and criticism.

The Army's 'Customers'. It's possible that the capitalistic notion of 'the customer' also affects parent involvement. Parents negotiate with the army authorities the same way they would negotiate with a cellular operator, contractor or school. They say: 'we provide the army with a product or resource in the form of our son or daughter, and as providers we reserve the right to negotiate the terms of supply with the establishment'.

Judicial and Media Dread. IDF's concern of the long arm of the law and the media creates overt and covert pressure on the Israeli security establishment to cooperate with the parents. Commanders make every effort possible to tone down the rage and prevent public condemnation and legal predicaments.

Left Right Left. Political positions also play a role. In other words, there are quite a few parents who no longer consider IDF to be a moral or just organization (mainly ones who identify as left-leaning) and therefore it's easier for them to criticize it and in fact encourage their children not to obey or agree to every command.

Commanders with no Authority. Generally speaking, Israeli society has become less authoritative and hierarchic. Officers see themselves more as friends of their subordinates and consequently also as indirect friends of their soldiers' parents. This opens the door to a relationship that legitimizes blurred boundaries and intervention.

IDF's 'Children'. Perhaps the most important reason for the parents' growing involvement in the military service of their sons and daughters is the common perception (of parents and heads of the army alike) that the soldier continues to be a 'child'. The children, meanwhile, accept their non-independent image and continue to have fundamentally the same relationship they had with their parents back when they were in high school.

The phenomenon of overly-involved parents has many aspects – military, ethical, organizational and more. One of the most important aspect is IDF's weakening role as an institution that turns adolescents into adults. Today's soldiers have become more dependent, and IDF is having difficulties adapting to that while paradoxically also making the problem worse. One of the results is the increasing number of exemptions from military service due to 'cultural incompatibility' with the army, like the inability to deal with institutions. Professionals have already noted that the 'mental exemption' has become a gray and black market in recent years. Many parents approve and even help young recruits get exemptions by commissioning medical and psychological opinions, some of which are false.

In the past decade, as millennials enter the world of employment and marriage, the phenomenon of over-protecting parenting has expanded beyond the children's regular service: from job-searching for them, to managing their bank accounts and renting an apartment for them.

The phenomenon of chronic dependency comes into play nowadays not just in the increasing incidence and its penetrating to many fields, but also in its velocity and style. Therefore, experts in the field have reported recently that not only do young people nowadays need advice, help and guidance for every step of the way, but in many cases, they categorically demand it from their parents, as if it were a basic democratic right. This phenomenon is known in psychological literature as 'Entitled Dependence'.

Blame the Parents

In late 2012, the London *Daily Telegraph* published a letter that made waves and became viral. Entitled *'I am bitterly, bitterly disappointed': retired naval officer's email to children in full,* it was written by sixty-seven-year-old Nick Crews. Crews wrote to his three adult children (two daughters and a son) painful things from the heart, which expressed his and his wife's disappointment and frustration with the choices they made in their lives. He criticized them for their failed marriages, their lack of maturity and their inability to make a living on their own. He angrily wrote that 'we're tired of the children's incessant whining, and we're waiting to hear good news, for once'.

The letter attracted over two thousand comments by both supporters and opponents, as one would expect. The echoes surrounding the letter were obviously caused not just because a father dared to criticize his children in public (let alone in the newspaper), but also because his letter expressed the feelings of many parents, and mainly the opinion of Crews' contemporaries. The debate over the controversial letter was expanded to other media outlets, including social networks in England and beyond, and has in fact become a debate on the problems and questions raised by millennials.

It's interesting, and perhaps not coincidental, that the retired officer's letter to his children was not reported in Israel. Nor was a similar letter by an Israeli father or mother published. This might be derived from the fact that criticizing 'our children', and especially doing it publicly, is still essentially taboo in Israel. However, lately it seems that Israeli parents are 'starting to wake up' and we can see articles and comments to articles here and there that reflect a critical attitude.

This begs the question, who really holds the 'blame' here? Our interviews show that millennials don't actually avoid responsibility, and admit their flaws.

Most young people we interviewed for the study admitted they are partly to blame, but also claimed that the main blame lies with their parents. Even the parents and teachers we interviewed admitted that educational mistakes were made that led to flaws and failures, mostly out of good intensions. The socio-historical reasons that created 'parenting noise' among millennials' parents and which contributed directly and indirectly to their children's immaturity and lack of independence are as follows:

Upbringing with no Authority or Boundaries. Many parents of millennials (Generation X) were raised by overbearing or neglectful parents. A great portion of parents were immigrants, who brought these perceptions from eastern and western Europe as well as from Muslim countries. Many children were required to blindly obey their parents, 'behave yourself' with no added explanations and adopt good manners and strict self-discipline. This was expressed in eating habits, talking, clothing and even standing and sitting ('stand upright', 'sit up straight'). This upbringing marked clear boundaries, albeit not always sensitive or considerate, and didn't avoid dishing out punishment for improper behaviour. Its effects were contradictive: on one hand it caused pain, intergenerational tensions and mental scars, and on the other hand it made them more resilient and respectful of authority and produced strong moral values.

Only in the 1980s, when Generation Xers became parents, did they start implementing the liberal approach towards upbringing in Israel which focused on 'going with the flow' of childrens' needs and wants. Compliments and hugs replaced reproaches and punishments, and the parent/teacher-centred education style was replaced by a child/learner-centred education style (paedocentric education). The new model would in time receive the hypercritical title 'education without boundaries'.

Research proves that setting boundaries excessively and with no guiding explanations could smother the child, instill anxieties and fears, shake his confidence and prevent the development of independent thinking and individualistic action. On the other hand, it's clear that children need boundaries as part of their normal development. Setting boundaries is essential, both for developing a sense of right and wrong, and for learning restraint, which are crucial tools for adults. Furthermore, boundaries are important because they give a sense of security. They make the child understand that there's someone in charge, who cares about him, who will protect and guide him.

By setting boundaries, children learn to accept that other people have needs and that they need to learn to compromise and control their urges. Children that have boundaries set appropriate to their age will eventually experience a feeling of success and believe in their capabilities.

There's no doubt that millennials' problems with growing up are among other things the result of education without boundaries. Since they didn't have to obey and show restraint throughout their teen years, they're having difficulties fitting into the adult world, which requires them to function within frameworks with laws and boundaries. Therefore, for many of them, the transition into the adult world is traumatic and can result in symptoms such as inability to cope, depression, job instability etc.

Parenting Guidebook Paradox. In the past, the firstborn baby was treated like the first encounter with the monthly period: people turned to friends, mothers, grandmothers and family health centre nurses for advice, and generally 'got along', which basically means 'made it up on the go'.

Paradoxically enough, as many guidebooks for treating babies and children hit Israeli bookshelves and as psychological-pedagogical knowledge became widespread and accessible to the general Israeli public, the lack of confidence among new parents only grew. Why? Because the new social expectations from parenting set a high bar of excellency. Furthermore, since developmental psychology has revealed to people that childhood is a critical stage for shaping one's personality and mistakes made at this stage, even in good faith, might cost the child dearly (developing personality disabilities), it planted fears in millennials' parents.

Therefore, to a large extent, millennials are the first victims of 'professional parenting', with one of its results being delayed adulthood and weakened independence. This is a generation raised not only under the mantle of paedocentric education, but also in an atmosphere of unbalanced parental confidence. There's good reason why strong criticism has been voiced against the self-help industry, which is part of the assault on pluralistic education. Unfortunately, it will be difficult to rehabilitate the victims of this method.

Child Worship in a Society of Abundance. In traditional tribal society, parents had to deal with everyday threats, and children were expected to help with the family's survival. Nowadays, parents no longer need their children for survival, turning them into 'pet children' who are given everything. This might sound cynical, but in many families the children's job amounts to 'spending their parents' money' to the delight of the latter. Furthermore, if in the past children were seen as a natural appendix of the extended family, nowadays they are perceived as the central component of the nuclear family (they are often more important than the parents' relationship) and everyone 'clucks' around them. The children, meanwhile, learned how to 'push their parents' buttons' and get what they want with no need to beg, struggle or confront anyone.

People who have been made to feel like they're special and always at the centre of things and never learned to listen to other people's opinions and criticism, tend to develop unrealistic self-esteem and become frustrated when reality doesn't meet their expectations. Child worship has led parents to create an impotent generation which has difficulty functioning.

Parents as Human Beings. One of the keys for developing confidence among adolescents is a revered, responsible adult, in their environment – someone close they can look up to, trust, identity with and try to emulate. These are usually the parents, who are seen as experienced authority figures. We all become disillusioned at some point by this myth of a perfect, all-powerful parent. It usually happens during adolescence and is part of the self-identity formation crisis and the launch of an independent life. Nowadays, though, in a world of demystification and cynicism, in a world with no authority, it's hard to create myths, particularly this parenting myth. Following the rise of awareness culture and personal exposure, many parents find it difficult to serve as authoritative role models, and many don't even try to be that for their children. Disillusion comes too young, shakes the most stable ground of life and creates a feeling of uncertainty and detachment among teens. This is reflected among others in their fear of growing up (and becoming 'imperfect' and vulnerable like their parents).

Forever Young. This generation of parents is terrified of old age, both due to the illusion of eternal youth shown in the media and due to the misery experienced by many elderly people in our time. It's no wonder that the beauty, fitness and health conservation industries are making billions of dollars every year.

One of their ways to stay young is by connecting to their children. Parents buy them stuff, compliment them, hang out with them, hold on to their world and wish to be part of the gang, in order to stay young. Many parents also adopt a similar physical appearance to their children (usually not very successfully). They buy the same clothes (it's not uncommon for mother and daughter to go shopping for clothes together), get tattoos and get their hair and make-up done accordingly. The parents' connection to their children sometimes comes to compensate for a deprived childhood.

Moreover, this generation of parents seeks to avoid a cultural gap with their children, like the one they experienced in their relationships with their parents. It's very important to them to have a good relationship with their children, because they too are often lonely and in need of support.

Do Unto Your Children As You Would Have Them Do Unto You. It seems as if all parents promise themselves at one point or another in their lives that they won't repeat the same mistakes their parents made. However, among Generation X parents, the basic desire to be a better parent has grown stronger for two reasons: first, the generation gap. Many of them were born in Israel to immigrants who came here with other (usually stricter) education codes. Second, paedocentric education invalidated authoritative-oppressive education. The result was that the new parents received social, ideological and scientific proof that their parents were wrong and the inner urge to create a 'corrective' parenting model grew stronger. The problem is that most of them tended to take this reaction to the extreme, taking the parenting dial from one end of the scale to the other. For instance, parents who were scolded and punished might be too easy on their children and completely avoid punishment even when a firm reprimand is needed.

This created a tragic paradox: the 'parental correction' millennials' parents created for themselves led to soft, liberal upbringing, intended to make up for the deficiencies and difficulties they experienced as children. In reality, without noticing, they emasculated their children by showering them with love. Hence, by trying to spare their children from past mistakes they made different mistakes, instilling them with a new kind of mental disability.

We Suffered For Them. Generation Xers have a particularly high work ethic. They have worked hard to provide for themselves and for their families and as well as save money for the future. But hard work has taken a heavy toll on them (exhaustion, tensions and even divorce), and many of them feel like it's best to spare this suffering from their children. In our interviews, many parents have said things such as: 'what did I work so hard for, if not to make their lives easier?'

Additionally, hard work and inheritances allowed many parents of millennials to find financial comfort, and the first priority for spending the family's savings is on the children. The message to their children was: you'll suffer less than us because we've already suffered for you. Is it hard out there? We will maintain the standard of living you've grown accustomed to. In this sense, it's easy for young people to remain 'supported children' rather than 'play in the big leagues'. Parents gladly give and children gladly receive. The problem with this unbalanced exchange is that it emasculates the children and perpetuates a hierarchy: the adults mostly give and the children mostly receive (even when they become adults themselves).

Price of Separation. Generation X's divorce rate is high and this has had a direct effect on the 'perfect parent' image. When the familial harmony falls apart, parents are no longer seen by themselves or by the people around them as 'perfect'. The divorce process brings emotional distress, anxieties and tensions, which are also projected onto their relationships with the children. This turmoil has made divorced parents weaker, guilt-ridden and emotionally dependent on their children.

On one side are divorced fathers, who usually don't live with their children. They face difficulties enforcing their authority, due to the limited time they spend with their children and often due to the negative manner in which they're portrayed by the divorced mother (who raises the children). On the other side are divorced mothers, who in many cases are left hurt and alone. They lack the emotional energy for dealing with the children and also wish to cuddle them following the family trauma. They equally need the children's support, which is why they tend not to confront them and give them an easy pass.

Compensating for Guilt. Parents have a hard time fully committing to the parenting role. They are forced to juggle work and home, between the dreary reality and society's expectations of them. This tension, which has been common among many parents in recent years, creates feelings of guilt. Many feel that the lack of time and their chronic exhaustion doesn't allow them to give their children what they deserve (according to social norms). This phenomenon is particularly notable among career women, who feel torn between two worlds. In order to compensate for that, they try to find favour with their children, shower them with materialistic pleasures and avoid reprimanding and punishing them.

There may be another aspect to this: perhaps the fact that young people continue to depend on their parents until such a late age is because they want to 'collect the debt' or make up for the emotional deficiencies from back when they were raised by nannies and daycare centres, while the parents dedicated themselves to their careers. Meanwhile, the guilt-ridden parents play along and allow this dependency. For this reason, they are unable (and sometimes unwilling) to put a stop to it and say, 'no more, go on your own way'.

Personal Trainers in a Competitive Jungle. Capitalist society is a competitive jungle in which only the strong survive. Israel, much like other western countries, has developed a culture that sends competitive messages from an early age.

As competition becomes tight and rough (mainly in the economic field), so does the fear of failure. In order to survive the competition, many parents start 'training their children' at a very young age and will do almost anything to make sure their children have an advantage. This comes into play in the acquisition of products, games and workshops at all ages, hiring private tutors and also coming with their children to sports classes and competitions as their 'personal trainers': they yell at the coach for not including their child in the roster and scold a child who dares to screw up a shot or miss a kick.

Sometimes, the urge to succeed compensates for the parents' feeling of failure in their own lives, which puts additional pressure on the children. Furthermore, the growth of a wide group of mobile population (social climbers), which has strong aspirations to go as fast and as far as possible, has raised the bar of expectations. Parents from this social class tend to see their children as a family proxy (whether they are aware of it or not) and treat their success as a personal and familial success. They give their children everything they never had when they were kids and even more, in order to help them in the race for achievements.

You might say that to a great extent millennials have been burdened with the most expectations (some of which are unrealistic), which is why many carry around a feeling of disappointment and inadequacy. Many have even developed a chronic fear of failure. In fact, this created a circle of anxiety that both sides are unable to break: the parents fear their children won't succeed, and the children are afraid of disappointing and upsetting their parents.

Looking for Meaning in an Alienated World. The joy of life greatly depends on the content and meaning that people pour into their existences. Beliefs, aspirations and ideals are powerful mechanisms for creating value in life. In past generations, the ideological challenge of founding a sanctuary country for Jews and defending its borders from vicious enemies, created a meaningful life experience and attached them to something powerful. Today, when ideology plays a secondary role (if at all) in the lives of Israel's secular citizens, the experience of existence is directed to alternative, more personal channels. The myth of invested parenting plays into this niche and has been undergoing processes of glorification in recent years. One of the results is extreme parenting, which is meant to create an artificial sense of meaning for the parent more than it does to promote the child.

Scary World. In the past, in the slow, communal and rural world, people were exposed to very few disasters and tragedies during their lifetimes. Today, in the age of frantic global media, we're all exposed to disasters and tragedies from all over the world on a daily basis. The flow of news and the lure of gossip have created an atmosphere of fear, terror and anxiety, which affect both parents and children.

Constant news about terror attacks, wars, motor accidents, rapes and robberies, natural disasters and other tragedies have created what sociologist Frank Furedi referred to as 'paranoid parenting'. This is also why parents tend to limit their children's freedom and instruct them to be careful wherever they go.

In Israel, this anxiety has been particularly reinforced during millennials' formative years, which were packed with traumatic events such as terrorist bombings and rocket attacks (Katyusha rockets in the north, Kassam rockets in the south and Scud missiles from Iraq), and the loud media that brought these disasters from the field into the viewers and listeners' homes in real time. The result is incremental pressure and paralysis. The First Gulf War was particularly traumatic for millennials and their parents since families were forced to sit helplessly in sealed rooms with small children wearing gas masks. This event, and other traumatic events, have definitely left their mark on millennials and reinforced their lack of security.

The media also undermines confidence in the government. The feeling we get from the news is that we're no longer in capable, reliable hands. This increases the fears and anxieties and creates a sense of chronic helplessness, which paralyzes them and makes them want to curl up into a ball, hindering the development of their resilience, which is one of the signs of maturity and independence.

Millennials' parents have also become anxious due to changes in young peoples' recreational habits. The developing club scene and consumption of alcohol (starting as early as junior high) have raised concerns. Parents allowed their children to party while projecting anxieties for what might happen to them if they do.

3

For the Sake of Ourselves – Selfishness as a Trend

Lost in the Big City

In May 2012, a new TV show called *Girls* arrived to Israeli satellite television. Lena Dunham wrote and directed most of the episodes of the series. An incredibly young writer (only twenty-five years old), Dunham is observant and extremely honest to the point of exposing herself both physically and mentally, which has made the series a fascinating study of a documentary nature. Critics have praised Dunham's in-depth dissection of millennials, and for good reason. They described her as someone who touches the generational nervous system, poignantly outlining the tragic reality of her peers.

The show's protagonist Hannah, portrayed by Dunham, lives in an urban commune-like environment with three other girls in their twenties. They live from one day to the next, mooch off their parents and friends, and divide their time between dead-end temp jobs and alcohol-riddled parties that mask their loneliness and hopelessness.

Critics tend to compare *Girls* with the popular *Sex and the City*, since both shows deal with a group of young, single women and their tales of debauchery in the lively city of New York. But *Girls* and *Sex and the City* are actually quite different, echoing the differences between Generation Y and X. Carrie Bradshaw and her friends had their share of hardships and problems typical of single Yuppies, but they also had high-paying careers, roomy apartments and *joie de vivre*. Hannah and her friends live in a terrifying reality, which reflects the dead-end their generation is in. The characters of *Girls* – both men and women – are young, self-centred people who are unable to grow up and are constantly struggling to survive with no future in sight and relate to each other in a cold and alienated way (at least from the point of view of the X generation).

Girls is a reflection of a generation that chose a major in college they knew beforehand wouldn't lead to a high-paying job, or any job for that matter. They compromise on a salary that doesn't cover their expenses, and on mediocre partners, because the media and personal experience have taught them that romance is mostly heartache. These are young men and women raised in a culture of selfishness and cynicism, which has turned them emotionally cold and sterile. They don't actually feel any guilt for the pain they cause to others or to themselves. They yawn, laugh and cry as life passes them by. They're living on the edge, seizing the moment, like someone on the verge of oblivion. You could say that this is a show about the suicide of an entire generation, which has become dead inside before even reaching old age. This generation has lost its ability to feel empathy, even towards their own relatives, and are unwilling to make a personal sacrifice for the luxury they consume.

Complaining about 'Young People These Days' Again?!

The phenomenon of the older generation freaking out over the younger generation is tied to the natural biological process of growing old, as well as rapid cultural changes, which create gaps and misunderstandings between different age groups. Add to this the growing concern of increasing liberty and individualism, which are mostly attributed to teenagers. They are perceived as threats to the social order and traditional tribal stability. For example, in the 1950s and 60s, when the flower children emerged and the age of pop and rock 'n' roll erupted, the long-haired hippies were accused of being rebellious, selfish, lacking in commitment to society and even of being anarchists – which today seems ridiculous, disproportionate and dated.

Even our tiny country has seen its share of periodic complaining directed at young people who dared to stray from the straight and narrow. An expression coined by mythological 'Shomer' Avraham Shapira in particular has been etched onto our collective memory: 'You call yourselves youth? You're crap!'

Over time, what was perceived as the loss of values turned out to be no more than the healthy follies of youth. In the current age, in which the adolescence process grows longer, it is natural for young people to behave as awkward teenagers. Perhaps it is pointless to freak out and label an entire generation as selfish.

But as we settle down and lower the flames, we cannot avoid the honest question: could this be another 'pulse' of traditional inter-generational tension, which isn't necessarily rooted in an actual increase in the level of egocentrism among the younger generation, but rather in cultural changes in an age of tectonic cultural shocks? These factors could be the basis for this resentment against the young. However, it appears that this time it's not just a recurring ritual but also a conscious understanding that moral equilibrium has been violated here, that which balances people's social duties with their own desires.

The staggering evidence in recent years shows that Generation Y is probably the first generation in human history to turn focusing on 'the self' into a positive, key value or at least much less negative than it was when their parents were their age.

A simple Google search paints a disturbing picture: people all over the world (mostly in the west) are growing more critical of today's youths. Many surfers describe this generation as self-involved. This criticism is almost always voiced by a 'responsible adult' – parents, teachers, employers, media personalities and the like. They're angry and concerned, and seemingly for good reason. This online picture matches what we heard from our interviews with people who have daily, close interactions with young Israelis. Millennials have been described as 'egotistic', 'self-absorbed' and 'selfish'.

Empiric Metrics for Egoism

Egoism is a normative, culture-dependent and hard to measure concept. Therefore, outlining the behaviour and lifestyle of an entire generation in such terms seems problematic from the get-go. Not only is it difficult to attach hard metrics to the egoism-altruism scale, we also don't have the tools to make historic and cultural comparisons in a manner that would allow us to empirically assess the change and determine whether this generation is more selfish than its predecessors.

However, due to our experience in behavioural science, we can draw a certain sequence of tendencies and orientations related to internal or external focus. In other words, we can present aggregated evidence for the increasing internal focus and weakening external focus in a variety of fields.

The first to do this methodically was a young psychology professor (born in 1971) from San Diego University called Jean Twenge. In 2006 she published her book, *Generation Me: Why Today's Young Americans Are More Confident, Assertive, Entitled and More Miserable Than Ever Before,* which presented a generational portrait that aroused enormous public interest. The book presents the results of twelve studies about intergenerational differences, based on databases cataloguing 1.3 million responses by young Americans (high school students and college freshmen) from the 1950s to the 2000s. Twenge also collected data from other sources, such as 'life stories'. Her study focused on young people born in the 1970s, 80s and 90s, to which she referred as Generation Me. Why call them that? She responds: 'because we've been taught to put ourselves before everything else. Movies, TV and educational programmes taught us we were special, and we believed them.'

Her study's data shows that young people today tend to have higher self-importance and develop narcissism and megalomaniac tendencies. Twenge claimed that U.S. pop culture encourages people to focus on their own satisfaction and achievements and 'feel good about yourself'. Generation Y has embraced the psychological language of 'self-reflection', 'personal growth', 'self-actualization' and the like, creating a 'theology of the self' in the post-collective age.

In 2009 Twenge published another book with Professor Keith Campbell of Georgia University, which stirred massive interest and expanded controversy around the sensitive subject. The provocative title announced its contents: *The Narcissism Epidemic: Living in the Age of Entitlement.* In the book, based on wide-scale empiric research, Twenge and her partner focused on the narcissism phenomenon. The respondents were asked to answer a standard questionnaire for identifying a narcissistic personality, and the result was surprising and troubling: 30 per cent of respondents matched the clinical definition of narcissism, compared to only 15 per cent in 1982. How symbolic that only a year later, in 2010, the American Psychiatric Association decided to update its definition of narcissism in the *Diagnostic and Statistical Manual of Mental Disorders* as no longer a 'personality disorder', but rather a 'personality trait'.

Maybe it's Time to Update our Concepts?

Age of Personal Vision

It's possible that labelling Generation Y as selfish is too schematic and doesn't do this generation justice, since they show more openness and tolerance in some fields than previous generations: in gender relations, treatment of LGBT people and their general approach to sexuality.

Some feel it inappropriate to label this generation as selfish for another reason: they simply lack an updated altruistic vision. You could claim that their parents and their parents' parents exhausted the experience of major social movements and proved that all the big collective myths and '-isms', which drove millions of people, have been eroded and become irrelevant. In short, this generation was raised in an age of ideological vacuum and right now they have nothing to connect to emotionally and no reason to make sacrifices.

The supposed altruistic ideology isn't dead. National idealism has been replaced in recent years with fresh global ideologies with an important message, for example environmental sensitivity (sustainability) or the war against poverty and ignorance. There is also the idealistic urge to restrain extreme capitalism and improve the level of equality in the world. But all of these ideological goals lack the tangible horizon that existed in nationalistic goals. When you're one social justice warrior out of a billion, you feel like a drop in the ocean of altruism.

Diversified Investment in Inter-personal Relations

Another argument in favour of Generation Y focuses on the deep change of the structures of human interactions. One of the signs of selfishness is less investment in the social environment. You could therefore argue that the small, immediate community (family, neighbours, friends etc.) is gradually being replaced by the expanded virtual community. Due to the scope of digital relationships made available by today's technology, people are forced to soften their everyday inter-personal relationships and diminish mutual commitment. One can settle for a polite 'like' and turn the volume of a relationship up or down. This is a more flexible and diffusible relationship, fitting of a dynamic, global world. According to this thesis, the old altruistic community was rather grounding, perhaps even smothering. There's no more need for a tight-knit framework in which people need each other.

In short, today's young people are breaking the traditional social framework, among others, by softening their previous relationships and commitments. Everything is more temporary and not as decisive. This is reminiscent of the state of marriage nowadays. In the past, people had to commit to being with one partner for the rest of their lives. Perhaps this is a requirements that today's public cannot meet.

Outsourcing Altruism

In regards to updated concepts, it could be argued that altruism has been 'outsourced' in a way. Generation Y has grown used to skilled professionals whose job is solving human problems and distress in a more organized and institutionalized manner than ever before. Paramedics, soldiers, police officers, doctors, firefighters, social workers, psychologists – they will all do what needs to be done when the time comes, while the citizens are off the hook. Their only duty is to keep paying taxes. The psychological mechanism of altruistic duty is becoming less vital to social function needs. Even small, day-to-day altruism, like raising children, helping elderly parents, cooking for friends, cleaning the public garden and washing the shared staircase are paid for nowadays, pushing people away from unconditional giving.

Admitting their own Selfishness

Most young people who took part in our study did not deny their selfish label, but rather provided examples for their selfishness as well as that of their friends. A repeating example is uncontrolled expenses, to the point of extravagance (particularly in the recreational field) and addiction to shopping (mostly clothing and beauty products). The tendency to abandon partners out of the blue with no explanation and the tendency to manipulate and avoid duties were also brought up.

Many of the young interviewees and online commenters blame today's selfishness on the spirit of the time (social codes), educators and mainly their parents. Statements like 'you spoiled us' were made repeatedly.

Coincidentally, this reaction in itself indirectly supports the selfish image, as it reflects a tendency to place the blame on others rather than take responsibility.

Ego Trip

Humility has never been a very popular trait in Israeli society. On the contrary, self-pride has been one of the fundamentals of the classic Sabra model, and is based on Jewish pride, Zionist pride (the new 'improved' Jew) and local pride (Israel as a successful society). However, while Israelis were taught to be proud of themselves at the time, this pride was usually associated with group affiliation. In the nation's first few decades, people who projected self-pride and displayed their noble qualities and personal achievements, were seen as conceited and were denounced.

This perception started to change in the 1970s. Taking pride in individual achievements became acceptable, and people were allowed and even encouraged to stand out, as part of the self-marketing culture inspired by US culture.

One of the expressions of the culture of self is the obsession with physical appearance. There's a reason why Generation Y has been labelled 'The Peacocks Generation'. They spent time and money (men and women alike) on clothing and accessories, tattoos and piercings, hair treatments, pedicure and manicure, various beauty treatments, going to the gym, dieting, plastic surgery and more. They also tend to look at themselves in the mirror a lot.

This behaviour develops at an early age and is influenced by the media. Young people are exposed to a cultural steamroller that glorifies appearance (with an emphasis on assertive sexuality), with the help of models who are viewed as superheroes.

This phenomenon has both negative and positive effects on millennials. On the one hand, the worship of appearance makes it feel like the 'cover' is more important than what's inside, thus encouraging narcissism, materialism and shallowness. It also creates insecurity and feelings of inferiority among young people who don't meet these strict standards.

On the other hand, today's young people are more well-groomed, cleaner and more aesthetic than previous generation (broadly speaking, of course). They tend to shower frequently, do laundry, wear perfume, cut and comb their hair. This aesthetic sensibility is also reflected in their working and living environments, which are usually tidy and well-organized. This orientation stands out particularly due to the casual, Spartan-like khaki appearance and culture of the pioneer and the Sabra.

The focus on appearance is represented in the great attention they dedicate to their Facebook profile picture. They often send pictures to their friends and ask for feedback. The majority of comments praise and admire these efforts. The Selfie – a self-portrait (often together with friends), which is shot using a smartphone at a compulsive frequency – is perhaps the most distinctive expression of the Me Culture that has taken our world by storm, and is usually practiced by the younger generation.

Positively Spoiled

The legitimacy for self-focus appears in the books and songs of Generation Y's childhood. For example, Yehuda Atlas's *This Child is Me* books and Yonatan Geffen's popular record *The 16th Sheep,* which includes the symbolic line 'but I love myself the most'.

Spot the Dog is a series of children's books centred on a small puppy. The series, published in the 1980s, was widely successful around the world and also became a must-have book for most parents in Israel as well. An entire generation of children were raised on *Spot the Dog.* In the original books (written by Erik Hill for his son Christopher), the dog is called Spot because he has spots on his tummy and tail. In Hebrew, he is called *Pinuki,* from the word *Pinuk,* meaning to spoil or pamper, probably because the publisher wanted a name that would appeal to both children and their parents. Supposedly, this book is intended for toddlers, focusing on the experience of discovering the world around us and on the affection parents have for their children, but on a deeper level, *Spot the Dog* expressed a trend in western society in general and in Israel in particular: becoming a society focused on making children happy – i.e. spoiled or more accurately, pampered. For the first time ever, Hedonism was considered an acceptable way of living in the west and the pursuit of gratifications and capsules of passing happiness became a watchword. This linguistic phenomenon also receives a sociological context as 'being spoiled' as a concept in Hebrew was perceived as negative for many years. Most young people today who grew up reading *Spot the Dog* are unaware of what this symbolic concept used to mean. Most of them truly believe that the goal in life is to spoil yourself, the more the better. The problem is that when your life's focus is to spoil and be spoiled, life becomes disappointing and discouraging when it turns out it's actually a gruelling journey and not a pleasure cruise.

The image of 'spoiled brats' was mentioned repeatedly in our interviews with parents, commanders and employers in different fields, as well as statements such as 'we spoiled them', 'they only think of themselves', 'they don't give a damn about us'. There were plenty of examples as well of their tendency to complain and avoid tasks, chores and responsibilities – at school, at home, in the army, in university and at work – to their agonized, angry look when someone adds to their burden. Many also noted that this generation knows how to get attention and get cradled by their parents and grandparents or anyone who's willing to embrace them.

This spoiling culture also increases the tendency to abandon frameworks and tasks: When 'I don't feel like it' or 'this doesn't work for me' – I just quit. Even if I made a commitment and even if walking away would have unpleasant repercussions on my surroundings, because 'I only do what's good for me.'

Limited Volunteer Work

Generation Y's self-focus supposedly doesn't align with the fact that, in recent years, volunteer organizations in Israel and around the world have been packed with young, eager, idealistic and well-meaning men and women. This contradiction fades away once you look into the most common motives for volunteer work. Our interviews (with young people and central activists in volunteer organizations in Israel) and other studies on this matter indicate that the main reason many of them volunteer is to add a notable line to the resumé, gain experience and get ahead in the employment market. In other words, they give back so they could check the box and then disappear after a short period of time, having achieved their goals and exhausted the experience. This has created a pattern called 'short-term self-serving volunteer work'. Young people often volunteer just for the sake of appearances which means they also make quite a fuss about it.

It should be noted that when young people leave after a short period of volunteering it's not only due to their code of values, but also because volunteer organizations have not adapted themselves to the needs, expectations and lifestyle of these young volunteers. For example, their need for flexible hours that don't clash with their private lives, their expectation for organizational efficiency, clear metrics of success, constant variety, short-term projects (they have no patience for long, gruelling processes), group work and constant feedbacks (particularly from the 'responsible adult').

Another external reason for the (statistical) reported increase in the scope of volunteer work is the fact that high schools and higher education institutes reward young people for what qualifies as 'volunteer work'. For example, 10th graders in the national education system are required to participate in an after-school volunteer programme or the national mentoring project in higher education institutes, which provides students with partial scholarships. In other words, volunteer work in this case is driven by utilitarian rather than altruistic motives.

Living in a Bubble

In 1993 a new animated comedy show called *Beavis and Butthead* was launched on MTV and shocked, captivated and infuriated many. The animated stars of the show were the exact opposite of Walt Disney's innocent and playful characters. Here were two teenagers with borderline intellectual functioning, gross behaviour and infantile jokes, which occasionally appeared to satirize MTV and its young viewers. A typical episode was comprised mostly of Beavis and Butthead watching music videos and making childish remarks. In between clips, the show presented the duo's escapades at home and in school and their frequent run-ins with the law.

Much like the witty, cynical script of *The Simpsons,* which provided an extreme reflection of American reality, *Beavis and Butthead's* writers also planted critical messages. The difference between the two shows was that *Beavis and Butthead* didn't just reflect reality, it also predicted it in a way. Since a decade later it turned out that the generation of youths who watched these two slackers – those 'neglected latchkey kids' who got addicted to junk music – have actually turned into a form of Beavis and Butthead.

Apathy may be common among all age groups nowadays, but it seems to have become a generational ID for millennials. Young people were often described in our interviews as self-involved, to the point that they're hardly ever bothered by questions such as: 'what did I do wrong?', 'could what I'm doing bother/harm/annoy someone?' or 'I wonder what the person next to me is going through'.

Apathy towards others can explain today's 'courtesy crisis'. The rules of etiquette were meant to refine and limit the way people communicate with one another through mutual respect and sensitivity. The modern western code dictates, for example, that we should greet friends and acquaintances heartily and respectfully, avoid insults or prying questions, be generous hosts, dress accordingly when attending social events, join conversations without taking them over, offer someone a seat or a helping hand, eat quietly, avoid disturbing our surroundings with loud music or other unnecessary noises, respect local rules of conduct, show up to meetings on time etc.

But despite the importance of etiquette, it seems to be losing its worth even in Anglo-Saxon countries – particularly among youths. In a 2011 poll, *The Chronicle* asked its readers whether Generation Y lacks the code of etiquette compared to previous generations. The results were not surprising – the vast majority (81 per cent) said yes.

Israel has never been a society that excelled in politeness or European tact. Israelis have preferred direct, informal and mask-free communication over courteous protocol. Some saw it as part of the Israeli charm, while others complained about bluntness and indiscretion. However, what used to appear as a gracefully direct and nuanced approach, has now turned into extreme impoliteness. Millennials have been saying 'I feel like having...' since childhood (the word 'please' doesn't exist in their vocabulary) and it's only natural that they'd continue with the same pattern. They're used to getting VIP service and bossing people around to perform 'small' everyday tasks for them (call for me, buy me, check for me etc.), without ever saying thank you.

The internet is both a reflection and a catalyst of blunt behaviour, because according to today's norms, you can say whatever you want whenever you want to, with no inhibitions or restraints, sometimes under the veil of anonymity and sometimes under your own name. Social media may encourage kindness and smiling empathy, but at the same time it also encourages bashing and disrespect.

Generation Y's lack of etiquette supposedly contradicts the code of niceness in their everyday language. American culture and Facebook have trained them to be courteous and kind to customers and to one another in order to create a calm atmosphere. They are sorry for your loss, wholeheartedly apologize, while insinuating that it's a shame you're not as calm as they are. They follow the script ('How may I help you?', 'Is everything good? How's the food?'), dish out many compliments ('looks good on you') and pleasantries ('have a nice day'). But it's mostly an American-style shell, empty gestures and not actual concern.

One pattern that potently expresses Generation Y's impoliteness and apathy is the all-too-common practice of sitting in public places, with their feet (and shoes) on the seat, on the sofa or the couch. This pose – as if they're in their own living room – demonstrated that they feel they can just stretch their legs in public places to achieve maximum personal comfort, completely oblivious to whether this may be uncomfortable for others.

Technological developments have had a crucial impact on the bubble, which has not spared any age group. But those who have been glued to the screen since childhood have developed a stronger habit of shutting themselves out to the environment and paying less attention to what goes on around them.

Millennials regularly sit in public places (buses, cafés etc.), hypnotized by their smartphones and immersed in digital stimulation, which is always preferable to the outside world. Their glazed eyes serve as a buffer between them and others – you may be physically near them, but your presence doesn't exist in their consciousness. This phenomenon is amazing because among others, it fundamentally contradicts the classic Israeli nature: bright eyes and the tendency to communicate and show a real interest in others. This gaze is more befitting the Anglo-Saxon culture which keeps its distance (mind your own business), and has apparently penetrated Israel, perhaps not just due to the influence of technology but also as part of the globalization process.

Many millennials are so occupied with their own wants, needs and pleasures that they can no longer hide or restrain spontaneous expressions of enthusiasm, enjoyment, passion and excitement. This is why they tend to eat loudly, chew with their mouths open while smacking their lips (like a child who just got a heavenly treat); chew gum loudly (including blowing and popping bubbles); shamelessly make out in public; yawn in other people's faces (without covering their mouths); talk very loudly (mostly on the mobile, usually on speaker) even when it's a very private intimate conversation; playing with their smartphones and surfing the internet in front of their teachers or lecturers; in short, if it doesn't bother them, they can't imagine that it may be bothering others.

They never offer help unless they're asked to specifically (and even then, they will often respond with a grimace that says 'oh well, if I have to'). Their lack of caring and thoughtlessness towards their surroundings are also expressed in clothing that isn't always appropriate for the location or event (for example, wearing casual clothes to formal events). An extreme example of this was shown in the media when a group of young girls arrived to meet President Obama while wearing flip-flops.

In restaurants, cafés, at home and in stores it's almost always 'I'll have this' or 'get me that' and not 'may I please have that'. They are demanding in nature and are quick to lose their temper when they don't get what they want immediately. It's not unheard of nowadays to see young people refusing to give up their seats to the elderly on public transportation. They seem to be blind to other people's suffering and problems – even in their immediate surroundings – and focus on their own needs.

Our interviews have shown that even after the standard age of adolescence (even after the army) they show no interest in relatives, or even in their own parents. For example, they are unaware that their mother or father may be physically or mentally unwell (even when they're living with them). Many didn't even know what exactly it is that their parents do for a living or how much they make.

Rolling the Blame

Moral reproach is an important social tool, designed to get sinners to admit their wrong-doings, understand their repercussions, offer compensation to those who were hurt, learn a lesson and improve themselves. In the past, parents and teachers would scold their children and students for immoral behaviour as part of the educational process. It was their mission. Although it's not always nice to hear and sometimes it's even painful, children understood that being reprimanded was a sign of their educators' morality and care for them.

Millennials, however, were raised in a different educational environment. They've barely been scolded, if at all, which is why they have a hard time dealing with justified criticism and are reluctant to scold others. In fact, for many of them reproach is somewhat blunt and violent, and when there's absolutely no other way, it should be moderate, implied and as short as possible. Whenever they are blamed for doing something inappropriate, most would come up with a typical series of arguments and excuses, designed to avoid responsibility and soften the mood:

'What did I do?' – the complaint surprises them. Since they are self-involved, they're unaware of doing anything wrong, unless somebody calls them out on it (usually older people).

'You don't understand the state I was in when it happened' – they frame the event as a miscommunication issue rather than a moral issue (I was misunderstood). Thus, they don't take responsibility and have nothing to regret.

'Everything I did for you so far doesn't count?' – at this point they present a checklist of everything they've done for the complaining party prior to the event. This is done in order to frame the event as something unusual rather than a sign of a personal problem. This reaction is also intended to vicariously roll the blame onto the ungrateful complainant, who tends to exaggerate and only focus on the bad things. Another technique of rolling the blame is the common phrase 'I'm sorry if you're offended', which means 'it's not my fault you're too sensitive'. The message is: 'if you stop over-reacting, everything will return to normal'.

'I'm only human', 'it was an honest mistake', 'haven't you ever...?' – this is intended to diminish the fault ('everybody makes mistakes'), produce misery and get empathy and forgiveness. In principle they tend to judge actions according to intent rather than results. What happened doesn't actually matter, it's the thought that counts. In other words, if you meant no harm, you're not to blame and should be spared any punishment.

'Okay, I'm sorry then' – this is the ultimate weapon. They assume that an apology will automatically settle the score and turn over a new leaf. The problem is that the apology isn't necessarily sincere, thus skipping the process of introspection (where did I go wrong), generalization and drawing conclusions and above all making a commitment for the future (the incident is perceived as a local error). They generally don't like to be reprimanded and avoid doing it to others. They perceive the admission of guilty ('Okay, I've made a mistake') and apologizing (usually half-heartedly) as sufficient for making amends and going back to normal. Anger, disappointment, punishment, promises? Not here. They don't take responsibility and express no regret.

So Why are they Selfish?

Victims of 'Love Bombing'

Intense, over-protective parenting leads to education without boundaries, without punishments, without learning restraint (children get used to instant gratification), without criticism and with lots of forgiveness and concessions. Parents who shower their children with unconditional love – 'my prince', 'my love', 'my life' – create a generation of narcissists.

The classic 'Jewish mother' may have worshipped her children, but in the past few decades this traditional worship has been upgraded with modern psychology brainwashing, removing the educational motto: 'He that spareth his rod hateth his son'. The new maxim is that people need a positive image so it's best to avoid criticizing them as much as possible. Children are supposed to feel special so they should be cradled with love and constantly complimented, even when they don't deserve compliments but rather are in need of some constructive criticism. Therefore, whenever they are scolded by teachers, counsellors, coaches or commanders, the parents are quick to back them up and scold the scolders. The message is almost always: you're not to blame, others are. If your grades are low, it's not your fault as it's the teacher's. This phenomenon builds an inflated ego and a sense of dominance.

This fear of hurting the child's feelings and the need to shower them with compliments are not only a product of psychological propaganda, but also of economic and demographic factors. In an ultra-competitive capitalist society, people believe that children should be nurtured to the point of giving them a completely false self-image of a genius in order to provide them with an advantage and the earlier the better.

In many cases, parents over-blow their children's ego in order to make up for their own personal failures and regrets. The children are expected to achieve everything their parents couldn't. This expectation is usually backed up by a very superficial and schematic view of what success in life actually is, and in most cases is cause for frustration for both parents and children, when anticipation and hope are crushed by reality.

The growing subjugation to money and career, alongside the rising divorce rate, have loaded parents with guilty feelings and made the 'love attack' model even worse. In fact, the past two decades has seen a combination of two destructive trends: the parents' subjugation to their jobs, which makes them less present in their children's lives, next to high expectations and guilt. This combination has led to a parenting model that helped create a generation of spoiled, egotistic and tyrannical children. This 'new parenting' style has helped spread the plague of selfishness among young people for another important reason: it prevented them from growing up.

'Follow Your Dreams'

Millennials were born into a society that tells them they should love themselves before they can love others. That self-realization is above all. Their parents promised: 'you could be anything you want to be', their teachers believed their most important mission is to help them feel good about themselves, and the media advised them to 'know yourself', 'be yourself', 'follow your dreams', because one day they'll conquer the world.

Technology has led them to believe that the world is at their feet with the click of a button. They determine the fate of reality show contestants, edit their own playlist on their smartphones and decide who lives and who dies on their PlayStations.

Millennials were also raised in an age of massive mobility. Jobs and roles that in the past were not available to wide groups within the population (due to education, status and financial barriers), have opened up quickly all over the world, giving the impression that everything is possible. The idea of aspiring higher in order to get more is true. But at the same time, people need to have the right amount of ambition, a realistic self-image and humility. These traits are not included in the 'educational bundle' given to millennials by their parents.

Free of Commitment

Millennials experience nearly unlimited freedom, which allows them to deal only with what they want right now, with no regard for tomorrow. They don't have to get involved or be committed to school, work, politics, relationships or even to a sex life with an emotional connection.

In fact, this unlimited freedom has weakened this generation's commitment to society and to general morals. It has also weakened restraints and fuelled the urge to try it all without a moment's thought, lest they miss any experiences or excitements (alternating partners, alternating workplaces, unlimited shopping etc.) because 'you only live once'. This freedom also doesn't require them to stop, ask questions or think about the person before them or about society.

Serenity Now

Generation Y is the first generation born into the psychological culture, which has many popular expressions (including 'self-help' books and workshops for 'the pursuit of happiness') and therefore they are very familiar with the language of psychology. On one hand, psychology has made them more open and able to admit weakness. On the other hand, it created new priorities such as the self above all.

This view is also expressed in the way millennials perceive the tension from time to time created between people. They see it as unwanted, regardless of the background, because it's negative and unpleasant. When your goal in life is to be happier, 'negative emotions' are a stain that must be cleansed. This is how this generation lost its 'holy outrage' – the moral anger required to right wrongs and heal the world. In other words, this generation's selfishness isn't just expressed in a high dose of self-concern, but also with low concern for society. They're simply a generation that doesn't fight for others as much.

Turned Off Emotions

When people are flooded by visual stimuli they get tired of watching which causes their vision to become blurry. One could also argue that generation Y has been flooded by emotional events, causing them to be more indifferent to wrongdoings. If you're exposed to disasters in Israel and around the world on a daily basis, you develop defence mechanisms, meaning you become indifferent to suffering over time. As a matter of fact, modern society trains its citizens to switch emotions with the click of a button. You sit on your sofa, watch some horrors, 'go to commercials' and then move on to the next stimulation. You cry a little, laugh a little, get a bit angry, you feel some sympathy. This turns emotions into 'snacks' where wiping your tears is the same as dipping a chip in salsa.

In the world of vast media, the lines between reality and fiction also start to blur. Staged violence mixes with real violence, and good mixes with bad. Everyone is the hero of a never-ending drama, while the ratings go up and down. When life is but a stage, people become passive audience members, mostly looking forward rather than sideways. Generation Y sees a lot but does not look. Their image of reality is flat and therefore also lacks moral depth.

Anti-socials on the Auspices of Reality TV

Although there are no metrics for television ratings among millennials, based on the general ratings we can assume that their favourite programmes over the years, and the ones most culturally identified with them, are reality TV shows – led by rating bonanzas *Survivor* and *Big Brother,* which were adapted for the Israeli audience. They particularly love this genre, not just because it has a beat, human drama, variety and surprises, but also because it turns them into active viewers.

One can assume that many millennials have co-opted the messages delivered by these programmes – some of which are positive. For example, equal opportunities to all, cooperation between contestants, sportsmanship, facing up to challenges, losing with dignity, majority rule and more.

On the other hand, this genre includes quite a few 'anti-social' messages that have penetrated their consciousness: life is nothing but a game and it's all pretence; being manipulative and hypocritical is necessary for survival; introversion and humility are not useful traits and in order to succeed in life you should be assertive, extrovert and even outrageous; you can achieve success and fame quickly, without putting in too much effort. All you have to do is get attention and be 'discovered'.

But above all, shows like *Survivor* send out a problematic message in which the most important thing in life is becoming a celebrity by any means necessary, including exposing yourself both mentally and physically as well as violent and bizarre behaviour. When *Big Brother* contestants enter or leave the house, the studio audience receives them with a round of applause. They're not being cheered for any kind of accomplishment other than becoming famous. In short, they reflect a new kind of celebrity that was born in the United States and has also made it here. In most cases these are people that haven't done anything, and don't stand for anything. They're famous because the media decided they are famous.

When in Sodom

Altruist instincts of human beings are connected to how much they trust the society around them. People tend to be good when they feel like the world is fair. When evil grows, they become more suspicious and their motivation to do good drops. Furthermore, evil absorbs more and more people, both due to desperation and the tendency to fall in line with the majority and due to the declining power of deterrence.

It's practically impossible to measure the level of morality of Israeli society over time. But the feeling among the general public – which is widely expressed in the media – is that the state is going down the drain. Many believe it has become a materialistic, greedy and corrupt society, where politicians, businesspeople and ordinary citizens lie, cheat and trick at every turn in order to get ahead or benefit their niche group.

With this in mind, it's no wonder many young people have developed a cynical and solipsistic world view. In their minds, 'if everyone is screwing everyone over, there's no reason I should be any different'.

The fact that inequality in Israel is particularly noticeable when it comes to social duties, makes young people feel like they're living in an unfair society, which lowers their motivation to contribute.

The development of the judicial approach to injustice also erodes their trust in justice and reinforces their indifference. They live in a world where everyone sues everyone and there's no more good and evil but rather just 'parties in a legal dispute'.

Perhaps we're Judging them According to Outdated Terms?

Maybe the younger generation isn't selfish at all? Perhaps millennials have managed to break free of the hypersensitivities of previous generations and live more naturally and freely according to updated conventions. They simply have a different culture with different sensibilities. For example, when a young man sits in a public space and his feet are on the seat or on the table, his behaviour mostly disturbs the older generation. As far as his friends are concerned, there's nothing wrong with this behaviour, and it doesn't evoke discomfort or anger.

This argument is problematic, because it ignores the backdrop of these behaviours (i.e. where they come from and what they represent) and mainly their social repercussions. The western code of polite (considerate) sitting wasn't created by hypersensitivity. It is designed, among other things, to maintain hygiene, prevent damage to furniture and upholstery and intrusive occupation of public spaces. As a matter of fact, a person who puts his legs on a public chair or table seizes a space that doesn't belong to him or her alone. That makes him/her selfish. In other words, it's not about a specific convention but rather what it represents.

4

Work Is Your Life – Not Ours

Separate Work and Ethics

The term 'work ethics' pretty much sums up the values of modern capitalism. The core of these values is the notion that your job should be more than just a job, it should be your passion. In the past, work ethics usually referred to several corresponding values: commitment to the organization, diligence, obedience, perseverance, responsibility, initiative and loyalty to the job. Dedication and loyalty to the workplace have been a fundamental criterion for achieving professional recognition and promotions within the organizations, and has given birth to an entire folklore of ceremonies, symbols and rewards, both spiritual and material.

The values and economic significance of 'work ethics' in western culture explain why it has become a central issue in public discourse in the past few years. It happened because for the first time since the dawn of the industrial revolution, a new generation has suddenly come forth to undermine this value, essentially threatening the current economic and social order.

The general criticism of millennials has grown increasingly in recent years as more and more youngsters have entered the labour market. Countless articles, comments and posts in different languages describe millennials as lacking basic motivation and skills, indifferent, childish, demanding, easily broken, disloyal and ungrateful.

Over time, a statistical aspect has also been added to this criticism. Surveys posted from time to time in various countries ratify the feeling of generational gaps in the labour market and point to a general unease among veteran employers over the performances of their young employees.

There are some who flatly reject this criticism, viewing it as nothing more than bitter panic over the transition of generations and the difference of perception in an ever-changing world. Some of the employers we interviewed were quick to dismiss the debate over the younger generation's work ethics as a product of conservatism perpetuated by the 'elders'. Though this might be true, one could also argue that elders have always been conservative and critical towards youngsters, and yet we have never seen such an extensive, aggressive and emotional wave of accusations, especially in the labour market.

By refusing to commit, youngsters are making a statement, whether conscious or not, that they refuse to be slaves to their careers like their parents and grandparents before them. If their parents' motto was 'work is our life', you could say that their motto is 'work is your life, not ours'.

A recent argument states that it's actually the previous generations (the parents and grandparents of today's youths) who are the selfish ones in this story. This is because they secured lucrative pensions for themselves and basically doomed their offspring to a lifetime of enslavement. Furthermore, as a result of the increasing lifespan and generous pension plans, many financial organizations nowadays refrain from offering new employees even the most basic social benefits.

Indeed, the statistics paint a picture of deepening economic gaps between generations, regardless of ethnicity, gender or education. Studies show that previous generations benefitted from a period of unprecedented economic growth and financial opportunities that the younger generation doesn't. For example, low housing prices, low interest rates on mortgages, lower taxes and a sharp rise in pay. A considerable portion of the older generations own apartments and houses that have tripled in value and produce high revenues from rental payments.

The recent financial crisis has also caused a feeling of paralysis and despair, which projects on the younger generation's motivation for working hard and climbing the ladder, like their parents before them. In other words, they're not necessarily saying 'I don't want to work', but rather 'I don't want to work for you under the conditions you've created for me'.

Whether you agree with the 'prosecution' or with the 'defence', one important thing is hard to ignore: the rage against this younger generation is authentic and it points to a problem. It's also difficult to ignore the fact that Generation Y perceives the individual's social duty, their future and the meaning of their existence very differently than previous generations. Our findings show that youngsters are indeed 'removing their feet' from the work and production pedal.

The younger generation's work ethics, or more accurately their perception of work, is without a doubt a product of structural changes in the labour market as well as worldviews and values tied to Generation Y's habitat and educational background. So why do they tend to make less of an effort and why is work not as sacred and valuable to them compared to their parents? There are several causes:

Cynical Labour Market. Many millennials have learned even as early as in their teens that the world of work is far from its innocent, altruistic image. Disillusionment with the myth of mission and fairness causes them to feel that employment isn't necessarily a source of pride and also doesn't fill an emotional void. This is also why they tend to be suspicious of their employers more than their predecessors, making sure their rights at the workplace are protected and tend to complain more whenever they feel they are being mistreated.

Contract Workers. Traditional employment systems have been known for their steady wages, workplace tenure and social benefits based on collective agreements. Most employers nowadays are switching to individual and independent contracts, where the employee has no social security, and usually no structured path for promotion either. Without fair and stable employment conditions, it's hard to develop empathy, involvement and loyalty, or the feeling that your workplace is like a second home. When it's clear that you will part ways sooner or later, the motivation for making an effort and excelling at your job decreases.

The End of Obedience to Authority. The old employees were naturally obedient, both due to being raised to be grateful for the opportunity to provide for themselves and for their family and because in the past people were generally more inclined to obey authority figures and social conventions. Generation Y was raised in an anti-authoritative, anti-obedience atmosphere.

Working Hard or Hardly Working. Some claim that youngsters are simply not accustomed to working. From a young age, their parents and teachers did not require them to work hard, or even work at all, and the tendency to take it easy on them and let things slide at every turn has made them unprepared for the employment world.

Is This the Right Place for Me?

Just as the enormous variety of products in the supermarkets replaced the basic products in the grocery store, the endless supply of opportunities in the employment market is also both a blessing and a curse. This problem is less known to older workers, who have been 'stuck' in the same job on the way to retirement, but for the younger generation it's an entirely different story. 'The variety is very confusing,' one youngster says, 'whenever you choose something you get the sense like you've missed other opportunities.' The problem is that these 'opportunities' usually don't make us happier, quite the opposite.

The rapid changes in the employment world add to the difficulty of honing in on the right profession and the most suitable workplace – the 'inflation' of general academic degrees, waves of migrant workers (from Africa, Asia, South America etc.) and the enormous change caused by the digital revolution – make it so that many youngsters arrive at the market and are surprised to discover that their professional training doesn't offer them any real advantage in the labour market – which reinforces the uncertainty over planning their professional paths.

It should be noted that the period of confusion and indecisiveness has always been part of young people's journey. However, in recent years this uncertainty seems to go on for much longer, is more tormenting and also doesn't fade even after the choice has been made and the youngsters have entered a successful career route.

Some argue that the younger generation's eternal indecision is also the result of immaturity, which makes it hard for them to make complex decisions and look at reality objectively. Most of them have high self-esteem, a result of constantly receiving praise for their many virtues, which creates an inherent dissonance between their personal aspirations and the disappointing reality.

The parents reinforce the syndrome of eternal undecidedness both directly and indirectly. Since many of them experienced personal frustration and fatigue in their work, they encourage their children to only do what's right for them – perpetuating the illusion that life is all about fulfilling each and every one of your dreams.

This is often due to the parents' need to make up for their own regrets. The overt and covert message that many parents have for their children is 'don't work hard like we did. Enjoy life while you can before it is too late'. The problem is that this approach is out of touch with reality in most cases, which only makes the youngsters miserable.

Operating Instructions

The difficulty in making decisions in life also comes into play when working in an organization. Since millennials are not inherently independent, and tend to be anxious and concerned with fulfilling their own personal desires, and since they've been accustomed to always seeking out guidance and assistance, they have a hard time acting independently in the workplace, fail to set goals, need constant management and guidance, preferably orally rather than in writing (after all, growing up they were 'micro-managed' by their parents, teachers and counsellors) and tend to act openly helpless when something goes wrong. In this aspect, they are fundamentally different from their parents' generation, which was raised on the ethos of initiative and self-reliance and the notion that you can make it on your own, against all odds.

Next to immature dependency, two other factors stand behind their expectation for elaborate instructions: their need to 'be okay' (in order to maintain the harmonious atmosphere that they require to function properly) and the urge to put in only the most minimal effort possible. That's why they also tend to shed responsibility and pass it on to others. They were taught that the key to completing tasks is asking nicely, and someone else will eventually come along and do it for them. They are not inclined to develop an active, innovative approach – a drive of 'let's expand our horizons, take things up a notch, change the rules, leave our mark' – an approach that was very typical among Generation Xers. That's why they prefer short-term projects with specific objectives.

Keeping up with Appearances

Another typical pattern for Generation Y is their need to get immediate, consistent and preferably positive feedback – especially when they start out in an organization. This shows them whether they are on the right path, how they function compared to their colleagues and to the expectations and goals set for them. They appreciate an employer that compliments them and strive to get encouragement and ratification for their contribution.

They will accept the boss's authority if he or she is open, flexible and fair, like their parents and teachers were when they were growing up, who understand their difficulties and 'meet them half way' as much as possible and mostly 'help them grow'.

When something goes wrong (for example, a customer complaint), youngsters may ask their superior for help, but they'd just rather repress what happened and move on. They're not prone to take responsibility, apologize, analyze what happened or try to figure out how it can be amended and prevent the problem from reoccurring in the future. Furthermore, they tend to please all sides: customers, bosses, colleagues and their own conscience.

Half-assed Job

The tendency to cut them some slack at home and at school has created another obstacle in the employment field that serves as a constant source of tension between them and their employers – the lack of perfectionism (they submit a final product that isn't 100 per cent finished). They tend to produce careless, imperfect work that's patched together. They simply don't see sloppiness as a problem, because they've grown accustomed to a world without scrutiny. This means that they don't correct errors, root out mistakes or proofread ahead of the final presentation. Not only does this less than thorough and lax attitude towards themselves create problems, it also generates a superficial way of thinking, which prevents them from progressing and developing.

'Long-term'? Not on my Watch

Millennials tend to live in the 'here and now', from job to job, with no long-term career planning and often no planning at all. They are unwilling to 'suffer now' for some ambiguous future. Some claim that the mere concept of a 'career' is gradually becoming anachronistic. Either way it needs to be updated from a linear career with promotions, full time jobs and the journey up the corporate ladder into a modular career, in which people change jobs and occupations while adapting their employment to the varying needs of the market and of their personal lives.

This pattern has taken its toll on employers, who have yet to accept this change and adapt to the new reality. Entire industries in the United States are unable to recruit professional workers, mostly for specialized manual labour: mechanics, electricians, carpenters etc. Young Americans fresh out of college often refuse to work with machinery. They would rather sit in an air-conditioned room in front of a computer screen for nine hours. But the main reason is their fear of being 'caged' in a 'closed' job with one path and no freedom. They would rather not commit.

The situation in Israel is similar and perhaps even graver. Israeli industrialists have been complaining for years about the worsening lack of skilled, professional workers.

Parents usually support their children's inclination to keep all options open, among others because they fear their children will get 'stuck' in the same workplace like they were. This also explains young people's preference to study professions that supposedly provide them with a wider leeway in the work market – such as law, business management and communications.

Fishing on the Web

The internet is rapidly changing job demand patterns and search practices. In the past, people looked for jobs usually through friends and relatives, who recommended and introduced potential workers to potential employers, or through want ads in newspapers. The supply of jobs was limited and many landed a job purely by chance. Many also stayed in one workplace for years due to force of habit and comfort. Others stayed simply because it wasn't proper to leave a stable job.

Searching for jobs online comes naturally to millennials and over the years has become an integral stage in their coming of age. They tend to use search engines and apps not just as a means for finding an available job that suits their needs, but also as a means for comparing alternatives, guidance and collecting essential information on the employer and the terms of employment.

Slaves to the Resumé

Writing a resumé was once considered an American tradition and was also common in Israel, mostly among academics and senior businesspeople. Nowadays, youngsters may type up their resumés as early as high school. This phenomenon is tied to the computer and internet revolution, the development of shortcut culture, branding and marketing, the general increase in education, the strong competition in the labour market and the rise of employment agencies, which also sells illusions to youngsters.

The change is noticeable not only in the prevalence of resumés and the declining age of the people who write them, but also in the content, which has also been affected by American culture. Youngsters have embraced the idea of hyping every single thing they've ever done into a resounding line in their resumés.

Paradoxically, the more common the process of writing a resumé becomes, the more it loses its importance in the employment world. As recruiters get stacks upon stacks of resumés, it becomes quite difficult to address every single one. When all of these resumés look more or less the same, their value drops – a phenomenon paralleled by the declining value of degrees.

Meanwhile, an interesting new employment pattern is developing. When people start working at a company, they don't do it so they could develop a long-term career there, but rather so they could 'add another line' to the resumé, in order to increase their chances of getting a better job in the future. In other words, the workplace is carefully selected as a step on the way to better things, which is why many youngsters agree to work as interns or apprentices, for miniscule pay and occasionally for no pay at all.

Many employers have identified this trend among youngsters and are cynically abusing it to their advantage, i.e. offering unfair employment conditions, fully knowing that these youngsters are planning to move on to the next stop anyway.

What Can You Offer Me?

Young candidates used to show reverence and awe when arriving at a job interview, determined to impress the interviewer in order to get the job. Nowadays, they're more proactive and selective during interviews. This pattern is common not only in interviews for complex and demanding fields (such as hi-tech), where it's particularly necessary to manage expectations, but also in simple, supposedly trivial jobs, such as waiting tables or deliveries. Millennials also want to get down to brass tacks in order to understand exactly what's expected of them and what they're getting into (among other reasons to see how the job could integrate with their other occupations).

In Israel, the 'interviewee turned interviewer' has probably become more common and prominent compared to Europe and the United States, both because Israelis are inherently more assertive and because unemployment is relatively low, so candidates are less anxious to get just any job.

Life is a Movie

Many youngsters are driven by altruistic motives. Many still serve in the security and rescue forces, give to the needy and occasionally even go out to protest for a worthy cause. But the heart usually follows other paths, both personally and globally.

Recent surveys have shown that youngsters definitely give a lot of weight to the salary. However, as much as they care about getting paid, they care more about variety thrills. Most are unable to define what a thrill is, as it is usually a fleeting thing. Many speak of 'personal growth'. This seems like a cliché and in many ways it is, but it does express their desire to work in something that's more than 'just a job'.

The ultra media and digital world is packed with images. We're not only being sold products nowadays, we're being sold dreams, most of which are unrealistic. Every profession is wrapped in a seductive package, which emphasizes the advantages and hides the disadvantages. Handymen become 'maintenance contractors' and guards become 'security officers'. These overblown images have created high expectations for a challenging, independent, flexible professional world, with fast-track promotions and high salaries.

The gap between the glamorous image and the grim, monotonous and demanding reality often cause frustration, disappointment and even depression.

Many young people fall for the image trap, both because commercials have become cleverer than ever and because they're used to living in a world with simplistic images that prey on their emotions.

One could argue this also relates to the naivety of the new middle class. Many youngsters today come from mobile families who have not instilled a developed sense of criticism in their children. They fall for the image trap, particularly when it comes to professions and positions that were once glamorous and respectable (which were not accessible to the lower status from which they sprung), such as law, media etc.

The tension between expectations and reality in the employment world, including salary expectations, are obviously also linked to young people's tendency to overestimate themselves, but the main reason for the gap is the low salaries in today's market, which are the result of the employers' greedy, exploitative culture. Youngsters are forced to work more hours for less money, which in many cases isn't enough to make ends meet. The basic conditions that their parents were generously given, including pension plans, convalescence pay, recognition of degrees, overtime and car expenses, have been cancelled or diminished in recent years. Many public and private workers are employed under modern slavery, which not only includes low wages, but also unlimited hours that even require them to work from home. Since they are not inherently rebellious, they accept these conditions unopposed and abandon ship quietly, once they've had their fill.

Not Unemployed, Between Jobs

In the past, the image of an unemployed person in western society was that of a poor, old and uneducated new immigrant. Apparently we need to update this image, because unemployment in western countries has expanded in recent years to educated citizens as well.

Furthermore, if in the past a great portion of job seekers were temporarily unemployed, nowadays this problem has developed a chronic nature. Young people are at the epicentre of the global unemployment crisis. Many sociologists see youth unemployment as one of the identifying features of Generation Y and refer to it as 'the lost generation'.

And what of Israel? The unemployment rate is about two-thirds of the OECD average (6.9 per cent compared to 10 per cent), meaning that at least as far as dry data is concerned, we're better off than most western countries. In fact, in the past decade (2000-2011), there's been a gradual increase in labour force participation rate in Israel and unemployment rates are consistently dropping. Even those who don't work find work rather quickly due to the growing market.

But beneath the statistics, things aren't that bright. Actually, many youngsters don't even register at the Employment Service Bureau because the interim periods between jobs are too short for them to be considered 'unemployed'. This creates a strange situation where the periods of unemployment are short, but the total time out of the work cycle is significant.

The reason for youth unemployment isn't just economic, but also and perhaps mostly cultural and psychological (two intertwined factors). In fact, many millennials treat themselves to a long break between jobs, thus creating a 'fragmented career'. These breaks aren't perceived by them or by government institutions as periods of unemployment, thus they slip under the surveys' radar. In other words, unemployed youngsters cannot be seen only as helpless victims of the times, for the following reasons:

Forever Young. Young people struggle with entering the labour market because they are afraid of growing up and growing old. They're not too keen on leaving the nest and taking responsibility in a threatening, unstable world. In this respect, holding off commitment to a career is a form of denial.

Anti-bourgeoisie. Millennials hold freedom and flexibility in the highest regard and aren't too keen on taking on responsibilities and a closed off, cyclical schedule (bourgeois). Since they are discouraged by a strict, binding workplace, many of them (at a much higher rate than any previous generation) choose artistic professions and occupations (acting, music etc.). This phenomenon isn't just the result of aspirations and fantasies propagated by the media (mainly celebrity culture), but is also due to the fact that western society has generated a great deal of tolerance towards people who dedicate their lives to the arts. The notion is that they should be supported because they're doing something spiritual, and allow them to be 'discovered' (i.e. realize their potential). The fantasy of 'I'll become a star soon' (without analyzing opportunities in the market or taking note of the fact that even successful artists in Israel struggle to make ends meet), is often supported by the parents, and is one of the reasons that many youngsters don't look for a steady job with decent pay for years upon years.

Unemployed, No Longer a Dirty Word. Some claim that voluntary unemployment among many youngsters is also a result of the stigma not being as strong as it used to be, in regards to both serial quitters and the 'unemployed' status in general. If chronic unemployment was once considered the hardship of people on the fringe, nowadays many youngsters see unemployment as something temporary or as a type of paid vacation (even if it's on their parents' dime) for the purpose of regrouping. In other words, going on welfare has become legitimate rather than a source for embarrassment and shame.

Millennials' work pattern can be described as a type of 'job eclecticism' or 'occupational nomadism': they arrive, do some work, and quit for either a short or long break. The fact that many of their contemporaries are in a similar position makes it easier for them to view reality this way, and this actually escalates a problem, which only increases as they become older. Some claim that an entire generation is living in a state of financial denial.

It's Okay to Break Down

Beyond all the aforementioned factors, there appears to be a cultural factor at the base of young people's expanding unemployment: the fact that they are more vulnerable than their parents. Reports of young people with low thresholds have multiplied in recent years. They give up easily, fear failure and tend to avoid dealing with difficulties, rely on others and abandon demanding jobs and tasks more than their parents. Why, then, do they lack resilience?

Wrapped Up in Cotton Wool. Some claim that this phenomenon is rooted in the fact that this generation was largely raised in a stable society of abundance. Unlike their parents and grandparents, they didn't experience humiliation and persecution nor did they suffer from lack of food or severe shortage, which is why they haven't become mentally strong.

Furthermore, Generation Y's parents demanded less from their offspring and spared them from hard labour and often even any labour at all. Many children learned that they can get what they want through smiles and flattery. Parents also avoided meting out formative punishments and setting boundaries, frequently let mistakes slide, didn't force their children to grind their teeth and show restraint, and tried as hard as they could to cushion the children's path to adulthood. The youngsters simply didn't practice standing up to pressure and crises. Many parents told themselves: 'I worked hard and had to suffer under pressure, but I'll spare my children from this' – paradoxically and tragically acting against their children's best interests.

Easily Offended by Criticism. There's an established educational-psychological convention among parents and teachers that criticism is unwarranted aggression and it's best to focus only on positive feedbacks, preferably very frequently (from employers, colleagues and clients). The result is that this generation is unable to handle criticism of any kind, let alone constructive criticism, which shapes a strong, durable personality. Many of the employers we've talked with indeed told us that when they offer their young employees professional criticism, many of them regard it as an annoyance, take it personally, get offended, become withdrawn, pout, and in many cases cry, stand up and walk away.

In many cases, the youngsters don't actually understand what all the fuss is about. They are usually baffled by it whenever they deviate 'slightly' (in their eyes) from what's expected, such as when they come in late for work or take a long lunch break. Israeli society tends to be lenient on rules, regulations and laws, but for millennials, leniency has become the rule.

Lower Ideals. People used to make a personal sacrifice, among other reasons because they were raised from a young age to think not only about themselves but also about wider implications of their actions. But today's materialistic, egocentric world is not as open to high ideals. When the choice of profession and workplace boils down mostly to materialistic terms rather than values or moral purpose, going the extra mile is deemed less feasible and lowers the threshold.

Social Legitimacy for Weakness. The patriarchal society glorified the strong – those who come under pressure but never break. Humanistic psychology and feminism, developed in the twentieth century, generated awareness to human weaknesses and offered scientific and moral legitimacy for breaking down and giving up. But one could argue it went too far. Today's mass media glorifies misery and has turned weakness into a kind of mock heroism, which gets high ratings.

It's All Good. It seems the main reason for young people's tendency to crack under pressure is the changing values in Israeli society. In recent years, it's become legitimate to avoid making an effort and only do what's right for you. Sisyphus is no longer an attraction, and people only ever climb the tallest mountain for sport. Traits that were once considered to be the highest qualities of mankind have lost their value, and today's youth have fostered a new approach: 'if it ain't fun, I don't have to do it'.

Economic Price of Dropping out of the Race

The tendency to crack under pressure has taken its toll also on demanding fields such as engineering and medicine in the recent years. This crisis is only growing stronger since in these fields it's difficult to import workers from third world countries or fill up the ranks through retraining. The Israeli hi-tech industry has been the focus of much praise, gaining titles such as Silicon Valley 2 or Startup Nation. But all of the encouraging data here refers to previous years, before most millennials were incorporated in the work market. Will the next generation of this industry's founders be able to keep the ball rolling?

One would assume that a generation born into the digital world, with educated, computer-savvy parents, would become worthy heirs to the pioneers of the hi-tech industry. In reality, this is probably not happening. Apparently, it has become increasingly difficult to recruit competent workers for the industry, and many of its leaders are concerned for the future.

When the basic hi-tech traits – independence, maturity, depth, diligence, perseverance and mental strength – are weakened, the change even leaves its mark on this competitive industry. All the big exits we've seen in recent years paint a misleading picture of optimism, since this is usually the fruit of labour of previous years, and most of the entrepreneurs behind them do not belong to Generation Y.

Yet there is one thing about millennials that leaves room for optimism in the field of entrepreneurship. Since they are very fast, quick-thinking, skilled in the digital world, highly social, avidly adventurous and love entertainment, they might turn out to be an important brain pool for developing the app industry. They love talking about ideas for cool games and diverse services that can save time and energy, and generally turn life into a fun game. In short, they are 'copywriters' who need experienced leadership and coaching.

Butterflies in the Field of Employment

Up until a few years ago, job-hopping was a negligible phenomenon in the employment world and was mostly typical of older people going through a midlife crisis or who were fired or highly sought-after workers in the hi-tech and finance fields. Nowadays, this phenomenon is rapidly increasing.

The data streaming from polls are staggering: for example, a 2012 poll in Israel found that 45 per cent of job seekers change jobs every two years, and 75 per cent didn't stay in one workplace for more than five years. Many of those who quit also turn down a promotion, which not only means walking away from a position offering power and prestige, but also the significant raises that come with rank and seniority. Although this is a general public trend, studies show that the phenomenon is more common among younger people.

Studies from around the world as well as our own study show that this phenomenon is much deeper than commonly thought, and it is gradually changing the old employment model. In fact, most youngsters enter a workplace with no intention of staying for too long, even if they don't always have a potential alternative or even know where to look.

The job-hopping trend has recently spread also to professional specialties. Many youngsters change profession right after graduation, i.e. before they even get to work in the field they studied. This phenomenon has even reached prestigious professions such as medicine, engineering and law.

Instability in the employment world is a problem for many managers. Companies don't like high employee turnover, because recruiting and training new employees is a complex and expensive process. When employees leave, beyond the loss of knowledge and experience, it also undermines the organization's internal social and communal structure. What are the reasons for this trend? Let's examine a few:

Not at any Cost. Millennials are the first generation who are unwilling to 'sell themselves' at any cost. Young people nowadays have a developed sense of criticism and high (some might say unrealistic) expectations from life. When they feel a gap being formed between their expectations and reality, they have no problem cutting loose.

The goal – change. Today's youngsters were born and raised in a frenetic era, where everything is temporary and disposable. The name of the game is never stay in one place, renew yourself and replace constantly. The need for change is also tied to the illusion propagated by advertising firms, as if you could reinvent yourself time and time again – i.e. getting a makeover or restart by buying new clothes, a new apartment or maybe getting a new job.

Different Priorities. If the goal of employment is mainly to get money to pay for your hobbies and entertainment, where and how you do it is not as important.

Taste Everything. Job-hopping patterns also have a clear component of egocentricity and the desire to experience whatever life throws at you, juggling between one thrill and another.

No Guilt. Generally speaking, today's youth have less empathy for others, including the organizations and companies that employ and train them. When there's no guilty conscience, it's easier to 'betray' an organization that has invested and believed in you. Many don't just abandon their place of work while violating a contract or a promise, they do it at short notice, or even no notice at all.

Exploitative Tycoons. Some consider high job turnover to be a hidden manifestation of how tycoons have taken over society as well as the expanding gaps. If the rich used to exploit the lower classes for the most part, now they're also exploiting the middle class. In fact, the employment market has produced a negative ecology, which is destroying the traditional fabric. Many employers assume that young employees will betray them and therefore have no qualms about mistreating them. Meanwhile, the employees assume that the employer doesn't have their best interest at heart, and this assumption pushes many to 'cut corners', 'take advantage' of situations at work and eventually makes it easier for them to bail.

Pit Stops. Job-hopping is part of a general way of life of putting off decisions, typical among millennials. This is due to their struggle with decision-making and their tendency to shop around before making a final decision.

Work with no Tenure. Stability in life (due to the need for diversity), and consequently occupational tenure is not as important for millennials. This perception might require the State to establish an alternative employment structure that will combine a financial safety net (through socialist legislation) and occupational mobility (similar to the change from 'budgetary' to 'accrued' pension). Either way, even youngsters who want occupational tenure have a harder time finding such jobs nowadays.

Boring Routine. Millennials were raised in an environment riddled with stimuli and therefore tend to grow bored quicker and feel like everything in life is temporary. Many employers we've talked to spoke of apathetic, joyless, gloomy and frustrated young employees, who only perform the bare minimum in order to 'pass the time'. Once they start a new job, it is only a matter of time until they walk away.

Working with No Sense of Purpose. Without creativity, without the urge to develop, improve and expand, with no sense of purpose or responsibility, then work becomes pointless and eroding. Millennials weren't taught to make an effort, change the rules or contribute to society – which is why they struggle with staying in one place. They walk away from one job after the other, out of hope that the next one would be more interesting than the last, unaware of the insight that emotional and intellectual satisfaction comes from within rather than obtained externally.

No Point in Long-term Planning. In a reality where you never know what tomorrow might bring – economically, politically, technologically and socially – people lose the urge to make long term plans even when it comes to their jobs, and focus on the 'here and now'. If they're not happy, they move on.

The Pursuit of Happiness. The American psychological shrine to the individual has reached the workplace. Everyone is in constant search for happiness, which supposedly is right around the corner. The prevailing assumption is that if you search hard enough you'll eventually get what you seek. Therefore, when reality in the workplace knocks on young people's doors, they move on to another job to look for their own happiness.

Endless Work Hours. Another important reason for high job turnover is the increase in work hours, particularly in demanding professions, leading to more erosion. The short work week was supposed to produce more free time. In reality, the exact opposite has happened. Add to that the high digital availability to bosses and customers beyond work hours, and you get significant erosion.

Evolutionary Process. Some see the phenomenon of job-hopping and even profession-hopping as a healthy natural process that exposes the distorted ways of the old world and takes the world of employment on an advanced stage of a functional evolutionary process. Resigning is no longer a 'failure' (similar to divorce, which is no longer considered a 'failure' of marriage). People have always been unhappy with the existing arrangement and felt exploited, today they're just less willing to take it and have enough independence to unshackle themselves.

It should be noted that while there are good arguments in favour of sacrificing stability for the sake of flexibility and constant mobility, in practice, today's labour world is still not ready for this change.

The Working Tribe

Millennials were raised in a more open, warm and equal atmosphere than previous generations – within the family, at school and to some extent even in the army – so they naturally expect a similar code of conduct in the employment world. They are surprised when they encounter hierarchic organizations that appear to them as too demanding and alienating.

Most youngsters prefer to have informal relationships with their employers and tend to see their (mostly older) managers as parents, older brothers or even friends. Since they have not been accustomed to authority, they don't follow their employers blindly and have no qualms with disagreeing with them and suggesting a different way of doing things, i.e. 'their way'. They expect to be appreciated for their character and personality no less than be judged according to their professional achievements. And they mostly want to 'fulfil themselves' (a term that has been repeated in interviews). What exactly does that mean? They can't always explain.

Their lack of formality is noticeable in their clothing, manner of speaking and writing (they avoid using titles or following proper etiquette) and their tendency to be 'chummy' even in places where the rules dictate a certain distance. The whole concept of distance seems wrong to most of them, certainly in the context of the job.

Many youngsters prefer to work in groups and intimate teams with a good, close relationship among friends. They function well in a group and seek out partners for everything from brainstorming to actual execution.

When they are given authority within the organization, they refuse to act 'like a boss'. Since they don't like to be punished or scolded, they also tend to avoid scolding and punishing their subordinates. They would rather have an open discussion or alternately say nothing at all. When they do get scolded (usually by a generation X boss) they withdraw into themselves, delve into depression and self-pity.

A workplace for them is first of all a social and friendly framework, and as such it should be welcoming and present a young, smiling and vibrant atmosphere, similar to the café and bar.

The Search for Balance

The working week as reported by employers may have become an hour and a half shorter than in the 1980s, but in practice most of us continue to work from home, while these hours are not reported, essentially counting as volunteer work.

Furthermore, the age of computers and smartphones allows employees to be available at all times, even unwillingly, and many managers take advantage of this in order to drop assignments on them beyond the formal requirements. This sometimes comes from the clients as well. Many feel like they have no free time and that they are 'slaves' to the workplace.

Millennials are, to a great extent, victims of the modern bondage of employment, which has reached its boiling point. They see what this has done to their parents and as they enter the labour market they also begin to understand what it's doing to them. The phrase 'I also have a life' has become a generational symbol of sorts, and it expresses young people's discontent with the overload of overtime as well as their urge to rebel against the old priorities.

The new social values, which try to reach the proper balance between work and other facets of life, is reflected in some of Generation Y's typical patterns in the employment world:

Custom-tailored Jobs. More and more youngsters demand a job that fits them perfectly. Human resource experts and recruiters told us that more candidates present demands that were once unheard of. For example, 'I want to go on a month-long trip in a year' or 'I have to take my kids to kindergarten in the morning'. Not only do they expect the organization to meet their needs, they also have no qualms with presenting their necessities as fact.

Make Our Own Vacation Time. Many youngsters create sabbaticals of sorts or long breaks, by changing jobs and even professions. The time between jobs serves as a sort of vicarious balance they bring into their lives.

Promotion? No Thanks. Many millennials are deterred by promotions, even when they offer a significant improvement to their salaries and benefits. There are four main explanations for this phenomenon: 1. They fear losing their place in the social fabric of the workplace and would rather continue being part of the gang; 2. They're under-achievers compared to previous generations and struggle to cope with difficult challenges – mainly the men; 3. A promotion creates a bigger obligation to stay in one workplace for long periods, and this usually turns them off; 4. A promotion usually comes with more work hours, responsibility, higher expectations and risks and generally more hassle. Unlike employees from previous generations, they carefully weigh the pros and cons (overt and covert) and in many cases pass, to the surprise of their employers. The meaning for organizations is a chronic shortage of managers, mostly in middle management.

Flexible Hours. Young people hate to 'punch the clock', stay at the office for no reason, and the idea of overtime – particularly when sprung on them – enrages them.

Materialistic Incentives. It's very important for today's youngsters to get bonuses for effort and success. The bonus is an important incentive for them because it adds a challenge and interest and serves as public proof that they met expectations. This generation also likes surprises and parties and getting a bonus is always cause for celebration.

Part-time Job. One popular solution for creating a balance in recent years is the part-time job. This practice was mostly common among women in the past but recently men have started to embrace the model. So far it's more common in the United States and Europe, but polls show that it's also starting to catch on in Israel, particularly among young people.

Taking it One Day at a Time. An increasing number of youngsters who have no kids and live in the Tel Aviv area would rather take it one day at a time, work in small doses and just pass the time 'chilling'. They work, but only occasionally. When they feel like it, when they run out of money, when there's an opportunity to do something that sparks their curiosity, they buckle up, but on their terms. The concept of a career is losing its familiar meaning and work becomes a means that allows them to achieve more important goals.

Are the employers adjusting to meet Generation Y's employment expectations? So far, most companies continue to operate under the old patterns, leading to high friction between employers and young employees. Furthermore, flexible employment is still perceived as an organizational tool more intended for women than men. Although more and more organizations offer young men the conditions of a 'working parent'- i.e. less hours and less pay – they are still a minority.

Our study shows that working from home, which supposedly enables flexibility, isn't popular among youngsters. One of the main reasons is Generation Y's tendency to live in packs and their need for human contact. Cafés serve as an alternative that allows them to be in touch with people and work outside the office – as they can use laptops, tablets and smartphones to keep up with their work.

5

Overdrawn – Consumption at any Cost

Buy Buy Buy

Millennials tend to spend their time shopping in stores, malls and online, carefully following new brands and products that hit the market (mainly in fashion and electronics), and consider shopping to be a form of a shared, recreational experience. They were raised during the age of malls and became avid shoppers. The massive abundance found in stores, the urge and temptation to constantly upgrade their devices and the increasing threshold of excitement encourage a sort of bulimic consumption. If eating out, staying at hotels, vacationing abroad and playing video games used to be enough to make them happy, nowadays a generation that has been consuming these activities from a young age requires more exciting and more expensive things. Furthermore, people who got used to these luxuries from a young age, see their recreational expenses as an inseparable part of their budget. For these young people, going out at least twice a week to a bar, restaurant or café isn't considered a luxury, but rather a basic need.

Since young people are naturally less restrained than older people and due to the influence young people have had over their parents in recent years, millennials are now considered the world's most sought-after demographic and those that set the tone for manufacturers. Many advertising firms have special departments dedicated to young people. Studies have shown that the DNA of ads from around the world is comprised mostly of content that interests young people, such as fashion, sports, music, relationships and sexuality. Mass gatherings used to be organized by political parties and youth movements: dance festivals, popular marches etc. Today it's mostly events by advertising and marketing firms, such as Coca-Cola Summer Love Camp, Goldstar Festival or Guinness Nights.

One of their trademarks as consumers is buying products that used to be considered for teens only (mostly in the fields of fashion, food and entertainment). They usually prefer products from their childhood in the 1980s and 90s and are nostalgic for stuff that's no longer on the market. It's easy to sell childhood products because they love to play and they are not ashamed or embarrassed to stay forever children.

Millennials' main advantage as shoppers is their fluency and speed when it comes to online shopping. They are actually the first generation that isn't deterred by digital shopping and use the internet wisely: they do their research and compare prices through dedicated websites, Facebook recommendations, videos, blogs etc. and get regular updates on special sales and offers. In many cases, online shopping is actually cheaper because it allows open competition and cuts out the middleman. They generally have a developed consumer consciousness, in the sense of what and where to shop, and they regularly discuss the issue and offer advice – shops, new products, prices, discounts, support services and so on.

Although millennials have a developed consumer consciousness and despite the fact they know how to shop around and get their money's worth, many of them still make irresponsible purchases. Many of our interviews with parents of millennials as well as financial consultants from various fields have shown that young people nowadays consume far beyond their means and tend to run into financial difficulties (singles and young couples alike). In many cases the parents have to cover debts caused by over-spending and spur-of-the-moment purchases. They often don't consider the cost and its implications for the future. In our focus groups as well as in personal interviews, millennials admitted having a chronic problem with balancing a budget and put the blame on internal and external causes (see below). Many families hold serious discussions on this matter, but it seems that usually both sides just give up.

Why are Millennials Prone to Over-spending?

No Code of Restraint. Many millennials were raised by parents who had their share of poverty when they were growing up and have undergone a rapid financial shift in the past three decades. This overwhelming and often artificial wealth, alongside media manipulation and herd mentality, have thrown parents off their game. They now often swallow the world like children who can fulfil their every fantasy and spend money like there's no tomorrow. This model has had a broad impact on their children, who were raised without a code of restraint and have grown accustomed to consume whatever comes their way.

Making Up for Lost Time. Many young people also see their recreational expenses as a compensation of sorts for the pressure they were under when serving in the army and during their studies. Their worldview dictates that people who do hard, demanding work (usually for society's sake) should get some kind of reward. Shopping is a type of reward. Many feel that the effort they put into the army and their studies also fulfil their parents' dreams, therefore it entitles them to a treat.

Why Not Both? Many young people have trouble choosing one thing over the other because they've been used to getting it all since they were small children. Many interviewees repeated the phrase 'why not both?' – often with dead seriousness ('why should I choose something over the other? I want the best of both worlds'). Many young people have simply not developed into responsible adults who are aware of the fact that every purchase is actually a financial choice that involves sacrifice and calculated loss. They assume that they can buy one now and buy the other later.

YOLO (You Only Live Once). Millennials are the first generation raised in the society of abundance, with a hedonistic view that argues you only live once, so you might as well have some fun, and their fun comes mostly from shopping and outings. Therefore, it is natural that this generation hasn't developed the restraints seen in generations that were around when spending money on momentary pleasures was frowned upon as wasteful and frivolous. If, in the past, making do and avoiding extravagance and over-indulgence were central to education at home and at school, today's education system doesn't even deal with it. On the contrary, social activities in many schools nowadays are the pinnacle of showing off, specifically when it comes to graduation parties and proms.

Never Want for Anything. The fact that millennials have never experienced a real shortage makes it impossible for them to objectively grasp their actual financial situation and feel grateful for what they have and what their parents did not (many simply have no historical consciousness – such as life under austerity or raging inflation). When young people complain about how they 'can't get by' they also mean getting the latest iPhone, weekly outings to the pub and even nature retreats and the annual trip abroad. Are these the basic products of the times? Perhaps, but the question remains: who exactly pays for all of this? They clearly lack perspective: for the standard of living in the past as well as for the standard of living in most of the world (including the western world). They're probably not aware of how fortunate they are compared to most people their age around the world. Coincidentally, backpackers we interviewed confessed that only when visiting poor countries were they able to finally grasp the wealth they have in Israel and how lucky they are. 'I'm ashamed of all the times I opened the fridge at home and complained that there was nothing to eat' a backpacker in Nepal told us. But it seems like this insight doesn't last long after returning home.

Everlasting Allowance

Studies conducted across the western world in recent years have shown that the age of independence and financial stability increases over time. One of the expressions of this phenomenon is young people in their 20s and even 30s who depend on their parents financially, even when they work full-time jobs.

In Israeli society, it has always been common practice to support your children, but it seems that in recent years this trend has been taken up a notch. If in the past, parents used to help their children with major expenses such as paying for the wedding and becoming homeowners, this support has now been expanded to daily needs – rent or mortgage payments, electronics and even stocking up the fridge with homemade cooking. In many families it's common to wire a fixed monthly sum to the grown children's account, and many parents even help fund family vacations for their children and grandchildren. Even after the wedding, many young couples still depend on monthly support from their parents and in many cases even their grandparents lend a hand. A comprehensive study conducted in 2013 for one of the leading business newspapers in Israel found that no less than 87 per cent of parents report they provide monthly financial aid to their children, and/or help them with major one-off expenses. It should be stressed that this survey only checked support for adult children, who are parents themselves, i.e. ones who have already embarked on their own independent path. In other words, this isn't support given to soldiers, students or singles (whose percentage is high), nor support for children who live with their parents for financial reasons. If they had included this population, the support rate would have obviously leapt further upwards. Naturally, the more money the children make the less support they get from their parents, but the interesting thing this survey proves is that the support doesn't go away even when the children actually make a good living.

It should be noted that the regular financial support isn't exclusive to parents and grandparents with means and excess funds, but rather also happens in less affluent classes.

The survey also shows that this financial support evokes mixed feelings. Parents see the real financial distress that their children are in, and gladly offer their help, but in many cases this support comes with an unpleasant feeling that the children are spoilt, irresponsible and rely too much on their help.

The parents often have to deal with eroding wages or pensions and with the skyrocketing cost of living, and are required to make significant sacrifices in order to help their children.

Why, then, do millennials depend on their parents' support, and why are the parents so inclined to offer this support, even when it requires making considerable sacrifices?

Life is Expensive. The high cost of living makes it hard for young people, and particularly young families, to make ends meet. The fact that what they consider to be a reasonable standard of living is higher than it used to be also has an effect.

Tied to the Apron Strings. Some claim that young people who live with their parents well into their adult years suffer from chronic financial helplessness, since they don't experience 'real life' and aren't accustomed to dealing with everyday expenses. One respondent told us: 'you don't practice "income and expenses" when you live with your parents. Only when you get your own place do you discover property tax, the high electricity bill and also… that you eventually run out of dishes…'

The Single Life. It's possible that the fact people marry later in life causes young people to get used to balancing personal expenses rather than a shared account. People used to get married young and manage a family budget. Today, however, each spouse brings his or her own habits and income to the relationship and in many cases, this leads to an inefficient financial collaboration.

Rising Divorce Rate. The rate of divorce at a young age, which has soared in recent years, adds to this chronic financial dependency. Divorce is costly, especially for young couples with children. When this happens, the family steps up, and parents maintain and prolong the dependency also out of concern for their grandchildren.

Cash Flow. Higher life expectancy puts the inheritance 'on hold'. Parents start giving out chunks of it to their children and grandchildren while they're still alive, both directly and indirectly.

Investing in the Next Generation. The rate of mobile families (the new middle class) has grown significantly over the past decades. This group tends to invest heavily in the next generation, in order to enrich the entire family and make dreams come true.

The Need to Please. Millennials' parents have raised their children to receive more than to give from a young age. They never even asked them to clear a cup or a plate from the dinner table. Whenever the children said 'jump', the parents asked 'how high?' When you're used to getting everything you want as a child and giving nothing in return, it's hard to break that pattern when you're older.

The 'child in the centre' approach encourages parents to make their children's lives as easy as possible and please them at any cost, even after they've grown. Many see their adult offspring as children who still haven't grown up, creating a self-fulfilling prophecy. In many cases, parents also feel guilty for neglecting their children when they were young because they were working late or because of divorce, and therefore try to make it up to them or 'buy' their love with ongoing financial support when they're older.

Getting the Cheque. Many parents act like their adult children's pals, eating out and even taking family vacations together, and this relationship becomes awkward since the parents have more money to spend. In order to create an 'equal' atmosphere among 'friends', the parents pay for everything and even give their adult children some 'pocket money'.

Joy of Receiving Versus Joy of Giving. Many parents suppress the true meaning behind their children's dependency. Others acknowledge that they are 'poisoning' their children with infinite giving and are troubled by it, but at the same time admit that it's impossible for them to cut the cord, among other reasons because of the fear that their children are not independent enough.

In fact, it's possible that more than the calf wishes to suck, the cow yearns to suckle. In this cold, alienating world, children are the last anchor of love and giving serves a deep need for the parents in this aspect. This creates a co-dependency or vicious circle if you will, which meets the psychological needs for both sides.

Many millennials are blind to the price their parents pay or will pay in old age for their financial support. They also fail to see that their support often comes at the expense of their parents' financial security. Since they've been led to believe that their parents always have available funds for them, they assume this aid will not and should not ever stop. A great portion of interviewees believe that their support is a moral necessity because they've run into harder times than their parents experienced when they were younger.

This imbalance is also influenced by cultural differences. While previous generations in Israel were told that happiness is achieved through giving, millennials were taught that happiness is achieved by receiving. Therefore, in many cases both sides are supposedly pleased with the unbalanced deal. The problem is that the joy of giving is fundamentally different – both psychologically and morally – than the joy of receiving, and the latter collects a heavy toll on the personal and social level.

Family therapists we interviewed said that this creates a vicious circle: assistance of parents not only makes it harder for their children to become independent, but rather creates dependency. The children rely on the additional funds they receive from their parents beforehand and spend it as well. The motivation for putting money aside for a rainy day is also compromised.

Life is a Hustle

The heavy, everyday expenses compared to the modest earnings were supposed to lead many millennials to a life of poverty. In reality, this usually doesn't happen, and not just thanks to their parents' help but also because they learned how to manoeuvre and improvise and have developed different techniques for urban survival. For example, they 'spike' themselves with drinks before entering the dance club or bar (in order to avoid paying for overpriced drinks); they pool their resources, so if one person drives the other takes care of drinks; they sell anything they don't need at the moment on Yad2 (Israel's version of Craiglist); they redeem points, coupons and credits in restaurants and venues; they take advantage of 'happy hours' and discounts for bringing a friend.

Some of these survival techniques are on the gray area of the law. For example, sub-letting their apartment for a few weeks while on vacation without informing the landlord, or scouting the apartment they lease to the next tenant. This pattern is very reminiscent of the behaviour of backpackers or alternately of urban nomads and homeless people, who manage to get by with whatever they find and live on a tight budget.

No Longer Saving for the Future

The financial values taught to the parents of Generation Y included the following expectations and conventions: be financially independent and make an honest living; try to be financial stable so you won't fall into hard times and crises; don't spend like there's no tomorrow; try not to show off; focus on long-term investments (like education); try to improve your financial situation consistently and moderately; don't spend more than you make and avoid loans and big debts; both partners are supposed to provide for the family; put something away for a rainy day.

Young couples in Israel used to save money in order to become homeowners (in most cases with help from their parents and a mortgage) and later to support their own children after they move out.

In the 1980s, when the Israeli market switched to a more capitalistic model of an open entrepreneurial society, an increasing number of Israelis started to see their conservative savings plan as too slow and turned to more speculative investments. But most of the family's investments were routed mainly to savings plans with a modest interest rate and pension plans. Almost all middle-class couples and above devoted a portion of their monthly wages to future savings.

It should be stressed that it's very hard to quantitatively (statistically) define young people's current savings patterns for several reasons:

(a.) A comprehensive, systematic study on the savings habits of people in their 20s and 30s has yet to be conducted in Israel. Furthermore, the issue of savings was also not studied in Israel in the distant past so it's difficult to nearly impossible to statistically compare generations in this context. This kind of comparison gets even more tangled when we try to introduce other important (time-based and place-based) variables to the equation such as financial expectations, lifestyle, cost of living etc.

(b.) It's difficult to compare the data with other countries, since military service and academic studies at a late age (compared to western countries) postpone the age of financial independence. The 'big trip' tradition also affects the savings picture, since a great portion of funds saved during the military service (including grants given to soldiers upon release) and first post-army jobs, as well as money saved for the young person by his or her parents and grandparents, are dedicated to this trip, which has become an inseparable part of most secular youngsters' experience in Israel.

(c.) Savings plans change over the years and this affects motivations and preferences. For example, it's harder to save nowadays because the banking system offers no conservative savings channels. The public pension system has also become much less generous than in the past. The Israeli economy is basically pushing today's consumers to consume more in the present and save less for the future.

(d.) Savings are also affected by the expectation for profit. Some generations saved with no expectation of increasing their equity by simply stashing money away. Today, since it's customary to expect a significant profit from savings (particularly long term), people have no choice but to invest in speculative channels and basically gamble – such as investing in the stock market (there was no such inventory in the past). Coincidently, some believe that investing in stocks doesn't count as savings because in many cases this risks the money rather than saves it (an important part of the motivation for saving is to put money aside for a rainy day).

(e.) The definition of savings is problematic and fluid. Almost all of us (both young and old) have some money in our bank accounts (in checking accounts as well as various deposits). If the account's balance is positive rather than negative it's technically a savings account. However, some may argue (rightfully so, to a certain degree) that it's not a savings account because it only counts as savings if the money is set aside and cannot be used on a daily basis. It's also important to distinguish savings plans and funds that depend on the person (who opens them and commits to them) from those opened by the employer's organization.

(f.) When defining savings on a generational view, it's not enough to ask how much is being saved (nominally and relatively) but also for what purpose and for how long. It's also important to ask how 'sacred' this savings account is. Accordingly, many young people start short-term savings for goals that used to be considered a luxury and even wasteful like trips and vacations, electronic devices, fashion and leisure etc.

(g.) It's very difficult to get hard data on savings and savings accounts since the banks and funds tend to avoid sharing this data with the public. It's also noted that there's a large gray market in Israel and a great deal of the public's savings are hidden.

(h.) Some surveys published recently abroad (mostly in the U.S.) on the younger generation's savings are biased surveys conducted by interested parties.

Are millennials following their parents and grandparents' saving patterns? A look at their adherence to past expectations and norms paints a surprising, possibly disturbing picture. It seems millennials are less financially independent than their parents (when they were their age), tend to avoid long-term savings and spend more than they can afford without qualms. In many cases, the overdraft isn't the result of genuine financial troubles but rather the result of no restraint and wasteful spending.

The attitude towards savings is undoubtedly one of the most distinguishing differences between generations today. What used to go without saying in the savings field has increasingly become less common in the past few years. Not only do young people all over the world tend to save less nowadays, in many cases they even fail to meet the financial commitments they have made.

Even when millennials do save, they only manage to scrape together a limited amount. Their savings are usually short term. In our interviews, many young people told us they cashed in money put aside for them by their parents or grandparents in order to fulfill their immediate dreams like the big trip to the Far East or South America.

The interesting thing about Generation Y's financial conduct is how well they manage to deny the future and their inability to resist temptations. They tend to live in the here and now, with no regard for a rainy day. They tend to spend a lot of money on expensive housing, recreations, vacations, clothing, mobile phones etc. in a manner that doesn't match their income.

A tour of Tel Aviv can provide a visual demonstration of this phenomenon. The majority of people sitting in cafés, restaurants and bars are young people. Though many venues let you sit there for two hours and order nothing but a $4 cup of coffee, millennials usually order more than just coffee. When expenses are high, there's nothing left to save. At best, they're hanging on a thread. At worst, they're amassing an increasing debt.

In recent years, this wastefulness has been met with strong public criticism from economists, parents, educators and other ordinary citizens (in online comments and on Facebook). They describe the younger generation as spoilt, selfish and irresponsible children who are cutting a hole in their pockets. They're 'living large' because they are unable or unwilling to control their urges and look beyond the moment.

This wasteful tendency was acknowledged in our survey as well. When asked whether they agree with the wasteful image they've been labelled with, only about 5 per cent of millennials responded they didn't. Over 70 per cent agreed or strongly agreed with this label.

A demonstration of the materialism, wastefulness and selfishness of the younger generation's consumer culture and financial conduct can be found in the recent culture of grandiose weddings. Many young couples rely on the cheques their guests leave them, their parents' support and hard-earned savings, and 'pour' massive sums on a single night, instead of using this money as the foundation for their new lives together. Generally speaking, it's easier for young people to spend money on pleasures and fleeting experiences like fine wine, chef dinners, pampering massages etc.

Although the costs of bringing a child into this world are very high, many desperately cling to the standard of living they had before having kids. More than once, young interviewees have made statements such as: 'we'll deal with this problem when it comes. Why lose sleep over this now?'

High living expenses push their financial abilities to their limit and beyond and make it hard for them to set substantial sums aside, if at all. Many also don't keep track of their income and expenses, which would have allowed them to maintain a balanced budget and perhaps even find a way to save some money. They often spend money on the spur of the moment, with no consideration for their budgetary consequences and without planning ahead.

Perhaps the most concerning fact is that young people in their 30s and 40s don't pay attention to their pension savings, basically leaving their future to chance. Furthermore, due to mandatory employer pension plans, young people mistakenly assume that they're 'covered' until the age of retirement. They're usually unaware that employers only deposit the minimum amount required by law, which might not be enough for them to live comfortably when they retire.

What's behind this phenomenon of uninhibited consumption and financial denial? It seems that a combination of factors related to the nature of the Israeli economy as well as world economy in the age of globalization, next to factors related to the mentality of both the younger generation and their parents, could offer a multi-dimensional answer to this question.

Childish Inability to Resist Temptation. The ability to put money aside is linked to maturity and mental independence. Immature people put themselves in the centre, find it hard to resist immediate temptations and make temporary sacrifices, are oblivious to the future beyond the horizon (they lack perspective) and are less sensitive to the price their loved ones are forced to pay for their dependency. Furthermore, financial independence is the result of an individual's belief in his or her ability to shape his or her own fate. Therefore, young people who don't believe in themselves find it difficult to leverage themselves financially. They develop a state of 'learned helplessness'. This helplessness and lack of initiative is demonstrated in the lack of joint economic initiatives. There were a number of attempts by young people to create economic co-ops and even community banking, but so far no initiative has taken form or penetrated the mainstream. This generation hasn't produced any alternatives to the high cost of living in Tel Aviv or the cost of traditional academic studies. The 2011 protest may have increased social sensitivity to financial distress and distortions in the market (mainly the high cost of living and housing), but hasn't managed to create an economic alternative to take young people by storm. They mostly continue to complain and do 'more of the same', wallowing in their problems instead of solving them together. They mostly seek out empathy and solidarity for their pain and suffering and in many cases justify their financial irresponsibility and wastefulness by blaming the 'older generation' that supposedly 'screwed' them and their future. 'It's not our fault', they say, 'it's yours'. Therefore, 'you' need to change the rules for us. The idea that 'we've been duped' reinforces the common notion of economic determinism and egocentrism among many millennials – 'I'll do what suits me'.

Poor Financial Education. The Israeli education system doesn't really provide its students with financial tools. Children are not taught any financial basics, nor do they receive any essential training for managing a household (balancing accounts, keeping and sorting documents etc.). When schools fail to pay heed to structured thinking, correcting mistakes, meeting deadlines and delivery of assignments properly, they also make it hard for children to acquire habits of order and discipline in the financial field.

Since millennials aren't prone to deeper understanding of processes to begin with (they are the 'skim through generation'), they arrive at the capital market with limited financial skills. They often don't bother to check how much they're being charged or what the different risks are.

Banks and insurance firms, meanwhile, don't make it easy for their customers to understand what they're investing in and why, and make young people sign long, detailed forms with lots of 'fine print'. Many millennials sign contracts without properly reading the terms. Bills that arrive in the mail often go straight in the bin. Many young people prefer to have their parents run their financial affairs, and the parents gladly agree. This preserves the 'financial handicap'.

Hedonistic Temptation. Millennials grew up in a hedonistic society where businesses operate powerful mechanisms intended to make people consume whatever comes their way, enjoy themselves and live in the moment. Furthermore, people tend to share their enjoyment in real time, creating constant pressure to join the party. Many millennials simply can't stand the pressure and yearn to achieve the same high standard of living that surrounds them. This creates the impression that everyone is 'living large' – everybody's flying abroad, always trading up their phones, eating out, going to hotels and managing somehow. The banks add to this pressure when they advertise the following message: we'll lend you some spending money, and you can pay us back later...

Extended Single Life. Married people with kids tend to be more financially careful and calculated because they have more mouths to feed. Since millennials extend their bachelorhood they tend to develop less cautious consumption habits and find it hard to adapt when the time comes.

My Parents will Care for Me. Many parents have a hard time with their children's objective and subjective struggle with savings, so they do it for them. They often take it upon themselves to cover the debts their adult children have amassed. They give their children the impression that they will help them whenever they need bailing out. It's unclear how much longer this safety net can continue to carry entire generations on its shoulders, but the current young generation lives with the understanding that if something terrible should happen, they'll always have someone to lean on.

Low Wages. Gaining an academic degree later in life postpones the starting age for careers, which means you also start saving later in life. It's harder for young people today to put money aside for the future because academic degrees are more common in today's market and therefore less financially rewarding. Furthermore, since many millennials define themselves as temps in advance (as do most of their employers), their wages are low and barely sufficient to make do.

Since the average salary is lower compared to their needs – and in many cases also very unfair, compared to the effort and hours, and barely covers the expenses – many young people are led into a mental state of giving up and possibly even become spiteful towards their environment. They tell themselves (even subconsciously): if they treat me this way, I'll 'screw' everyone back.

Lack of Investment Channels. One of the main reasons for the drop in savings is the lack of profitable conservative investment channels. The policy led by the governments of Israel and the banks in recent years has made it the case that the public isn't offered any lucrative savings plans, and is essentially driven towards unnecessary expenses and financial risks. Those who can afford it invest in real estate. Most young people don't have that option. When there are no rewarding conservative investment channels (with reasonable interest), people are less prone to save. It's also a common belief in Israel that there's no point in saving if you can't increase your funds with some kind of interest. In other words, savings are perceived merely as an investment rather than a safety net. In practice, it makes sense to save even without interest – not just for a 'rainy day' but also in order to increase the asset, even if only a little.

Furthermore, without inflation, many people nowadays keep at least some portion of their funds in cash in the bank and at home, and aren't quick to invest in various channels.

Even those who are interested in pension savings, are concerned that by the time they retire the savings plan won't deliver what it promised. Pension funds are suffering heavy losses nowadays, and young people are rightfully not interested in working with and supporting inefficient financial bodies. Furthermore, the generous pension arrangements their parents got no longer exist for millennials due to the rise in life expectancy, the decline of professional unions and downsizing in public and government bodies following privatization.

With a Little Help from my Friends. One of Generation Y's advantages in the financial field is their tendency to consult one another (tight relationships with friends on many forums). On the surface, this appears to be a major financial advantage. In reality, this also creates a problem, since a private investment also eventually requires independence (the ability to make difficult choices), as one Israeli capital market executive once said: 'sometimes you need to isolate yourself and not let anyone affect your decision'.

Credit Card Curse – Never-ending Debts. Generation Y grew up into the American payment model, which has transformed shopping patterns in Israel. Nowadays, people believe you can buy anything with money you don't actually have. Just put it on the card and spread it out. This model encourages uncontrolled consumerism and doesn't encourage savings. Many people don't realize that paying in installments is a loan for all intents and purposes, and make purchases without calculating long-term costs and often without doing the math at all. The urge to buy in this instance, rather than resist temptation, causes many people – particularly young ones – to spend sums they cannot afford. Such as going abroad on holiday.

One of the phenomena that surprised us during our research is young people's tendency to use credit cards rather than cash for every expense – even when it's only a few bucks. Supposedly there's something natural about the switch to digital currency in the digital age, since cash is gradually losing its importance anyway. But this pattern actually has other reasons, related to this generation's nature: it's easier to spend with credit cards 'because you don't see the money' or 'because it's convenient, and I don't feel like looking for an ATM'. The problem is that depressing time of the month that always comes when you discover the hole in your account, as a result of your spending. And then either the overdraft grows, or mommy and daddy cover it.

I Deserve a 'Haircut' Too. Young people feel more comfortable going into debt because Israeli society has generally become more violent and antisocial. People have simply grown used to lying and cheating, and feel less guilty about it, if at all. Business owners and landlords talk about debt-holders who simply don't pay their debts and give checks with no cover. In this kind of atmosphere, it's hard to take the high road and keep your promises. Furthermore, young people see the 'haircuts for tycoons' pattern and tell themselves: if they can get off the hook, why can't I?

Everybody Gets a Loan. While most banks around the world don't allow their customers to exceed their overdraft limit for long, in Israel the credit framework is very generous and the banks are quite compassionate towards those who exceed it. Even the social stigma for overdraft doesn't actually exist in Israel.

The banks escalate the public's overspending problem because they also encourage their customers to take loans without thoroughly reviewing their ability to pay the money back. A massive percentage of Israelis living beyond their financial means are stuck in a cycle of loans that finance 80-100 per cent of the cost of their apartment, car, designer clothes and recreational activities in Israel and abroad.

The banks' seduction policy, alongside Israeli mentality, have created a culture in which many private accounts in Israel exceed their overdraft limit for long periods of time and even permanently. Since 2003 there has been an effort to diminish households' reliance on overdraft as a financing means, while gaining more control of the family expenses and other loan channels. The Bank of Israel ordered the banks to stop allowing people to exceed their credit limits and this has helped restrain Israelis to a certain degree, but even these directives can usually be bypassed by expanding your credit line or taking a loan 'to cover the overdraft'.

Young people from all socio-economic layers aren't particularly troubled by financial commitments. According to surveys, even single men and women find themselves in financial turmoil – up to their necks in debts, even prior to commitments like marriage, mortgage and kids.

One Day we'll Hit the Jackpot. Many young people believe they can 'hit the jackpot' one day (either through some enterprise or through rolling properties) and this perception manages to ease their conscience. There's definitely an American influence here, which inside the Tel Aviv bubble creates the notion that life is one big hustle. For instance, many young people perpetuate the illusion that one day they too will become landlords, meaning that one day they'll have a rental property and all will work out.

Eat, Drink, and be Merry, for Tomorrow we Die. Many young people feel that at this stage of their lives there's no real need to plan the future due to their fluid personal situation. They're not married yet, still haven't decided what to do with their professional lives and are contemplating what would be best for them in this world. When the future is so fickle and unstable, it's better to focus on the 'here and now' (including when it comes to spending) and roll with the flow of life from one point to the next.

Moreover, millennials are the first generation born into the communication and information revolution, and media exposure to countless traumatic events creates an aggregated emotional overload and a feeling that they should 'live for today because tomorrow we might be gone'. This global feeling is particularly magnified in Israel, both due to stressful security events and the familial nature of a society that experiences everything 'together'. The Israeli media also tends to feed the flames of anxiety and creates an alarming feeling of emergency. Imagine you were told you only have one year to live. You'd probably drop all your responsibilities and start partying. This is the prevailing opinion among young people nowadays. They tend to live the moment, because tomorrow may never come.

Beyond existential anxieties and a feeling of uncertainty towards the future, the flood of bad news, financial and otherwise, creates a kind of pessimism and bubble of indifference. When the news reports stock market collapses, bankruptcies and mass layoffs on an almost daily basis, the general feeling is that long-term savings are simply redundant.

Generally speaking, young people's confidence in the capital market decreases over time and this affects the motivation for long-term savings and investments. The lack of trust is also reflected in the banks' failing image. People used to stick to one bank branch in the same way as they would stick to their local health clinic. Nowadays, not only have people stopped being loyal to one place, the banks are portrayed in the media as a bunch of thieves and crooks (among other reasons due to high commissions). Scandals of major embezzlements and outrageous executive salaries have reinforced the financial system's negative image and further shaken people's confidence in it. Generally speaking, people have become more suspicious and cynical, with an increasing feeling that they're constantly being cheated and screwed over.

The distrust in political leadership also sways people away from investing in the future. Their view is why should I save when the stock market is one big casino, when tycoons get free 'haircuts', when the ultra-Orthodox pressure the government into increasing their budgets and when politicians use public funds as if they were their own?

No Apartment, No Pension

Many in Israel claim that today's young generation's financial distress is due to low salaries and the high costs of living. This argument was largely the focus of the public protest in the summer of 2011 and of the ripples that followed. Is that truly the case?

A closer look at economic data published from time to time reveals a more complex, confusing picture of the economic situation. For example, surveys don't distinguish between essential expenses and expenses that could count as luxury, therefore the information they provide for what people spend their money on is insufficient. Education, culture and leisure, for instance, fall under the same category (yet as we know, recreational expenses are nothing like education expenses). Communication and transportation expenses also appear under one category for some reason, further distorting the picture. One person can spend money on public transportation, which is naturally inexpensive, while another could spend it on luxury cars or taxi rides. Furthermore, there are different, often contradictory motives for purchases. For instance, when young people buy new smartphones and tablets, it isn't always due to an essential need, but rather because the device is trendy and they're afraid of being 'left behind'.

The definition of a 'basic product' (compared to a luxury product) is also not that simple and depends on your values system. Our interviews show that young people as well as parents perceive many products, which used to be thought of as luxury items, as basic products (like vacations). Naturally, this affects the definition of their financial situation.

Central Bureau of Statistics surveys also don't take into account that the negative gap between income and expenses in the household doesn't necessarily indicate the existence of shortage. For instance, a survey that shows household expenses and income per deciles indicates that also among the upper deciles (i.e. the rich), expenses are higher than income. In other words, even the rich in Israel are living with debts. In fact, for many Israelis, expenses expand to match their income and often to match the overdraft that their bank allows.

Whether today's young people's feeling of economic distress is based on actual shortage rather than a gap between expectations and reality can be concluded from standard of living surveys. Apparently, the standard of living in Israel since its establishment has been growing if not soaring. Products and services that just thirty years ago were seen as luxuries, such as eating out, travelling abroad and staying at hotels, have become available to many during millennials' lifetime. Even in other economic metrics, such as food energy intake, housing density and average wages, Israel has had a tremendous leap and has achieved a high global ranking. The rising standard of living is also expressed in the scope of sales and purchases in the market and in the variety of products available to Israeli consumers.

When compared to the world's leading economies (the sheer comparison is proof of the progress we've made), Israel still has a way to go to join the major league of global consumption. However, we're pretty high on the global scale and this is reflected well in surveys that examine the citizens' satisfaction with the Israeli economy. In short, millennials are far from living in a poor country and a poor lifestyle (generally speaking, of course).

However, not all is bright, as in some aspects the country is worse off today compared with the past and this situation affects young people the most. For example, the State used to subsidize basic expenses such as health, education, housing and mortgages but, nowadays, in the age of privatization and the decline of the 'welfare state', many are left to fend for themselves, and often find it difficult to bear the burden of expenses.

And what of this generation's purchasing power (products and services that can be purchased in local currency). Are they worse off than their parents in this case as well? The answer to this question is inconclusive, as some fields have seen an increase in purchasing power while others have seen a drop. This is the result of salary fluctuations and changes in the cost of various products and services. Either way, young people are struggling under this burden because the basic basket of goods in their time has grown. It includes, among other things, cable or satellite internet, smartphones, transportation and computer upgrades – all of which are considered essential consumer products.

The main financial challenge young people face is home ownership. There are three economic metrics for reviewing a family's ability to become homeowners: the ratio of housing cost over household income, ratio of mortgage payments over household income, and the initial capital raised for buying a house or apartment. These three metrics have seen a significant turn for the worse in recent years.

If in the past, many (if not most) young people in their 20s were able to afford a small apartment as newlyweds or as singles for a reasonable mortgage next to a steady income, nowadays home ownership for many is a luxury they simply cannot afford. Interestingly enough, the inability to save money to buy an apartment creates an extravagant lifestyle and vice versa: the extravagant lifestyle makes it hard to become homeowners. In 1961, a salaried employee in Israel needed some 40 paychecks to buy an average apartment, while in 2014 it requires 140 paychecks. For comparison, in France it takes 90 paychecks, in the United States 60, and in Sweden 30. Since there are significantly more single people in this generation, the problem with becoming a homeowner has grown and is causing a deepening socio-economic crisis.

6

Let's Have Fun – Entertainment as Purpose

Born into an Age of Leisure and Entertainment

During the pioneering period, leisure was considered by many to be a hedonistic activity – wasteful and lazy – in complete contrast with the values of diligence and hard work. Leisure didn't mean what it means today: relaxation, entertainment, fun, but rather was intended for recharging your batteries so you could get back to work.

Israel's formative years included mass immigration and economic development, which left very little time for pastimes. In any case, the new immigrants' salaries were barely enough to make ends meet, and there wasn't much money left to fund leisure and entertainment. Most families would get up early in the morning and go to bed early after a hard day's work. There were also very few sources of entertainment within the home so there was no reason for staying up late. Radio broadcasts ended early and Israeli television broadcasts didn't exist yet. The streets also emptied early. Restaurants and entertainment venues were prohibited from opening their businesses after midnight, and anyone who broke this law was fined. The lack of financial means also affected weekend outings. It usually entailed paying visits to friends and relatives (usually in the same neighbourhood or city) and trips to the beach or public pool.

The Israeli entertainment industry, which has evolved immensely since the dawn of Zionist settlement, initially focused on a number of fields: seminars and lectures, books, classical music, plays, movies, sing-alongs and folk dancing. Some of these were not available to large portions of the immigrant population.

Israeli entertainment became more popular and accessible to the general public with the development of 'light theatre' during the 1960s, 70s and 80s (musicals, comedy acts, musical comedies and singing and dancing shows).

Since the mid-90s – when millennials hit puberty – there has been a dramatic increase in the scope, variety and access to leisure and entertainment in Israeli society. Under this trend, time dedicated to watching TV had doubled; the variety of entertainment shows expanded; community and recreation centres developed to include local choirs and dancing ensembles, music lessons, community theatre etc.; recreational centres multiplied outside cities – in malls, kibbutzim, parks, museums and heritage sites; expansion of the tradition of annual festivals (theatre, cinema, dance, music etc.); cuisine culture, shopping and vacationing in hotels became more widespread.

The changes in Israeli pastime culture are the result of several factors: a significant increase in the standard of living under Israel's transformation into a western consumerist society; a general rise in the level of education (there is a positive correlation between the level of education and participation in leisure activities); the increased consumption of 'high culture' (partly due to the wave of immigration from the former Soviet Union, which is known for a higher percentage of consumers of 'canonical' art such as theatre, ballet and classical music); the development of Israeli commercial media; the shift to a shortened working week; the rise of workers' committees in various factories (as expressed in the development of worker benefits such as company retreats and other leisure activities); entertainment venues extending their working hours.

The changing values of the times were also a contributing factor, namely the focus on the present rather than the future, and the importance attributed to pleasures and leisure (at the expense of work) as well as the rising value of individualism.

In the early 2000s, Israel became a developed leisure society. Family outings became common partly due to the rising role of children in society and their increasing influence on popular culture.

Formative Entertainment Experiences

A generation's spirit is shaped, among other things, by the everyday experiences related to the world of consumption and services. Thus, it is only natural that a generation which grew up into the leisure revolution would also acquire different perceptions and habits than previous generations. In addition to their sophisticated pastime skills, millennials have also redefined the concept of leisure. Let's review some of the basic experiences that have shaped their leisure culture.

Active Vacation

A significant turn in the family outing culture and the juvenile entertainment industry experienced by millennials during their childhood took place in the early 1980s, with the development of amusement parks for children and adults, under the expansion of the global leisure and entertainment industry phenomenon (led by water parks in Shefayim and Golan Beach). Millennials were actually the first children to visit amusement parks (a completely alien experience for previous generations) with the whole family. This is also why they tend to like this type of entertainment as adults.

Another important pastime phenomenon that deeply influenced millennials as children and teens under a series of global trends is the development of 'extreme sports': all-terrain vehicles, paragliding, windsurfing etc. The ski vacation also gained popularity at the time, becoming part of the emerging active vacation tradition in Israel. Israelis started to flock in droves to Mount Hermon ski resort, which became one of the most popular attractions of the 90s.

Thus, it's very rare nowadays to see any Israelis, young and old alike, spend a Saturday or holiday reading newspapers or watching TV. Many take their cars to the mountain, beach, desert, forest, river, waterfall, fountain or cave, looking for thrills and experiences. Millennials were born into this reality, which deeply shaped their consciousness.

From Recovery to Family Vacation

In the mid-1950s, the surge in tourism in Israel and the newly signed Reparations Agreement with West Germany gave birth to new hotels, recovery houses (small hotels also known as 'rest homes') and modest guest houses owned by the Histadrut, Shekem and local entrepreneurs. The term 'recovery houses' represented a Zionist-socialist ideology, according to which vacations are intended for rest and recovery, i.e. replenishing one's energy in order to resume life's most important purpose: work. But at the time, only a small portion of Israel's population could afford the luxury of 'recovery'.

As the standard of living grew in the early 1980s, the hotel experience started to normalize. The public started opting for big, luxury hotels and gradually drifted away from HMO and Histadrut-run houses. More and more families from various social layers visited hotels for the first time in their whole lives, and what was once a luxury experienced only by a wealthy minority had become available to many. The demand for hotels grew rapidly and the supply of rooms was expanded accordingly.

In the 1990s there were already hundreds of luxury hotels operating in Israel, hosting hundreds of thousands of citizens. Israelis are particularly fond of hotels in Eilat, which over the years has become the Israeli resort capital – somewhat of a distant planet, where Israelis can escape only to return later to society.

Children and teens' influence on the destination and itinerary of the family vacation has increasingly become part of a global trend, but in Israel it is apparently even stronger. Hotels have learned that Israelis want to spend time with their children and offer a variety of attractions for all ages (18 months to 17 years), from kid cars, trampolines and carousels to bouncy castles, pool games, arts and crafts, dance parties and more.

Normalization of the hotel vacation and the new emphasis on family vacations (i.e. with the kids) have resulted in many millennials spending time with their parents in hotels since childhood, and this experience eventually became a basic necessity for them.

The late 1990s also saw the rise of rural tourism in Israel. Dozens of communities in the Galilee, northern valleys, the Negev and Arabah opened B&Bs that attract hundreds of thousands of guests per year. Many millennials spent their formative years at B&Bs with their parents and siblings, and this has become the ultimate treat in their eyes. For many, spending time 'out in the woods' serves as a break from their everyday urban lives. Even young parents leave small children with their grandparents and head out to 'work on their relationship' away from the erosion of everyday life. In many cases, the vacation is paid for by the grandparents.

The Short Unwinding Road

The change in Israeli pastime culture has helped change a time-old Zionist tradition and fundamental experience, which had shaped the minds of generations that came before millennials: the 'study the country' hike. What was once perceived as an ideological expression of patriotism, in recent years has become mostly a tourist-entertainment production, filled with picnics, games, gourmet meals and other treats.

Furthermore, if people used to hike in the past, by the turn of the millennium hundreds of miles of land had been fitted for bicycles, off-road and all-terrain vehicles. Away from asphalt roads, people can enjoy orchards, picnic spots, pools, famous burial sites and lookout points. Even the lunchbox, canteen and picnic cooler are no longer essential, since at the top of every mountain, at the bottom of every road, in every forest clearing and in every parking lot at the end of the woods there's an over-priced vendor waiting.

The lessons millennials draw from this is that you can reach remote locations in nature without breaking a sweat, and that the nature experience isn't all that different from regular urban experiences.

Even the traditional annual school trip has changed character, becoming more like a party than a journey. The old truck has been replaced with an air-conditioned bus, the long hike with 'sightseeing tours', backpacks with trolleys, sleeping under the stars in sleeping bags with lodging at a comfy inn, and camp cookouts have been replaced with restaurants. The trip has turned from a national consciousness-shaping journey into a group outing or a mere educational-professional seminar. In fact, the educational aspect has also faded, since students are completely immersed in their cellular screens, which are much more interesting to them than anything going on around them.

Children of the Festigal

In 1981, the first Festigal was held in Haifa in celebration of Hanukkah, and over the years the show has migrated to other cities as well and become a popular, inseparable part of Hanukkah vacation. Many children also watched the Festigal on television, and watched it time and time again on videotapes. The show's songs were played in kindergartens, cars and homes thanks to audio cassettes followed by CDs.

Over the years, the Festigal has spawned many challengers: festivals and shows starring contemporary childrens' stars next to veteran theatre actors. These shows are held mostly during the holidays, when parents take their children to all sorts of activities. Even shopping malls in cities started holding similar small-scale productions in order to attract parents and children. This has turned childrens' music in general and Festigal songs in particular into one of the most fundamental experiences for millennials.

Another focus of leisure culture in millennials' world was the community centre. The National Community Centre Company was established back in 1969, but only spread across Israel in the late 1970s and during the 80s and 90s, offering high quality facilities with an impressive variety of classes, leading to a significant increase in afternoon art and sports activities, particularly in small, remote communities. Meanwhile, public playgrounds also multiplied and improved in cities and shopping centres.

Millennials were the first children in Israel to have an unprecedented variety of public pastime activities and facilities right around the corner. This is also the first generation that was often accompanied by their parents on these activities, who used to join in with the fun.

Generation of Espresso, McDonald's and Sushi

Since the mid-1990s, new café chains have taken Israel by storm, transforming the Israeli coffee map. Polls published at the time revealed that the change in café culture came into play not just in the quality of the coffee and the food served next to it or the frequency of visits, but rather in the customers themselves: more women, more young people and more passersby, who pop up by themselves for a short coffee break in the middle of the day. The café has also become the perfect place for dating, thanks to the pleasant atmosphere and because it's relatively inexpensive.

In the early 2000s, cafés joined the internet revolution and started offering their customers wi-fi hotspots. This service reinforced the domestic image of cafés and attracted a younger population.

The café revolution was followed by the restaurant revolution. International fast food chains (McDonald's, Pizza Hut etc.) landed in Israel one by one, turning eating out into an everyday event. The first to get addicted to ketchup, mayonnaise, cream cheese and bread rolls were youngsters. The number of private restaurants and the variety of food types they serve also grew exponentially as did the products on food chain shelves. The luxury of the past became accessible and mundane for the majority of the public.

Millennials were born into a culinary revolution, and have even perfected it to a great extent. The hamburger, pizza and sushi are staple food for them, almost what falafel was for their parents. Cafés and restaurants across Israel – particularly in Tel Aviv and its environs – are packed with young people (many of the owners of these establishments are young) and their atmosphere reflect the lifestyle and values of Generation Y.

Generation of Screens

Out of the Street and into the Bedroom

Video rental libraries made their debut in Israel in the early 1980s. They offered an alternative to the single-channel television, which ended its broadcasts come midnight, and led children and teens to stay at home. Millennials, then, were the first generation that had the option of watching more movies for a low price during their childhood and teen years.

Video games also took millennials off the streets and into the home. Computer, office supply and bookstores started offering a variety of computer games (followed by the PlayStation and other gaming consoles), and this habit became addictive for many, even past their teen years.

The appearance of cable television companies in the early 90s, followed by the satellite TV company, next to the formation of Channel 2 and Channel 10, revolutionized Israeli culture and television watching habits. Israelis switched from a controlled drizzle of a buttoned-up state-run channel to a flood of dozens of local and international channels offering rich, dynamic television broadcasts 24/7.

Millennials experienced the development of commercial television in real time, and their consciousness has been shaped by its influence. While once there was a divide between children's watching hours and adult watching hours (specifically on school nights), over the course of Generation Y's childhood, this divide had nearly vanished. Furthermore, the scope of programmes produced and broadcast for children by commercial channels grow exponentially, as they were considered the most enthusiastic watchers in the family, and the ones dictating the tone at home.

Intense watching has affected many of the Israeli family's patterns. For instance, it pushed family dinners aside and created a pattern of 'snacking' in front of the television, which millennials are fond of to this day.

TV as a National Babysitter

Israeli Educational Television broadcasted in the morning and noon for over twenty years, and these broadcasts were aimed at Israeli school children. In the 1990s, Educational Television's broadcasts expanded to Channel 2 and cable TV.

Many programmes produced on the channel became very popular among millennials, serving as an inseparable part of their childhood memories. Alongside the children and youth programmes and educational programmes about road safety, history, Judaism, English, literature and maths, new light entertainment shows, culture magazines and comedies were added, as well as current affairs and talk shows.

But the real revolution in Israeli children and teens' watching culture was performed by the Children's Channel, which hit the airwaves in 1989. The channel's broadcasts were successful and gradually expanded, with the hosts gaining immense popularity.

The channel's studio and game shows were beloved by children, who started sitting in front of the TV set immediately upon returning home from kindergarten and school.

The addiction grew when, in 1994, the channel started broadcasting U.S. action shows for children and teens as well as popular series. One of the most influential series was *Beverly Hills, 90210*, which focused on a tight-knit group of high schoolers and their romantic relationships. This show taught young viewers that hanging out with friends and your appearance are really what matters.

Youngsters in Trance

Digital Ecstasy

Music and dance culture in Israel has greatly evolved from the Hora circle dance in socialist settlements and youth movements, through the ballroom dancing of urban society and the discotheques of the 60s to the Tel Aviv mega-clubs. The Dolphinarium, Colosseum, Penguin, Cinerama, Allenby 58 and the TLV are only a handful of clubs that were part of the local mythology known to people born in the 70s and 80s. Each of these venues added another layer to the development of youth pastime culture in Israel.

Indoor and outdoor rock concerts also had a role in this development, from the days of Nuweiba in Sinai, through Arad Festival to concerts in Caesarea and Yarkon Park.

The penetration of computer technology caused a massive shift in the music world. Computer programmes provided an entirely new method to make music, giving birth to a new type of artist-entertainer who is part musician, part technician, part producer and part disc jockey. These laid the foundation for the development of trance culture, which serves as an umbrella for different genres of electronic music. On the edge of the scale is techno–instrumental loops meant to hypnotize, much like a chemical drug.

Trance culture is more than just pastime culture, much like pop and Flower Children phenomenon in the 60s had more to offer than merely musical entertainment. It includes a number of typical components: loud computer music (with an emphasis on bass, drums and metallic sounds);

visual effects that create an ecstatic atmosphere (flashing lights, colourful fabrics, Indian style clothing, computer graphics and more); 'robotic' dancing comprised of intense, simple movements of the body, head and hands; frequent use of alcohol, 'soft drugs' (cannabis) and hallucinogens (acid, coke, ecstasy etc.), intended to amplify the sensation, lower inhibitions and give in to passions; the DJ is the party's leader, serving as a makeshift shaman; the parties are held in pastoral nature sites and last all through the night and until the sun comes up.

Trance music gained momentum in the late 1980s in London clubs, later spreading to other western capitals and backpack centres in the Far East, where youngsters from all over the world were gathering (particularly Goa, India and Ko Pha Ngan, Thailand).

Israelis soon caught the new bug, due to their curiosity and tendency to adopt foreign cultures, and mostly because they flock to the Far East in droves. Trance parties have become an integral part of the 'big trip', and the model was gradually imported to Israel as well.

Israeli 'trance community' was initially comprised of no more than several hundred 'India graduates', most of which knew each other and operated away from the spotlights. Over time, the nature parties grew from dozens of partygoers to hundreds, who gathered on weekends in parks and beaches across the country.

The parties were not advertised and mostly relied on word of mouth. At first there were run-ins with the police, but their attitude has softened since the mid-90s, focusing mainly on catching drug distributors rather than disrupting the parties themselves. Meanwhile, public pressure to allow the parties grew in the name of personal liberty and freedom of expression.

Towards the late 90s, the media also started to be more sympathetic to the trance phenomenon and its coverage became more positive. At this point, the Israeli 'trance tribe' included about 200,000 people. Some argue that at least a third of the 18-30 demographic regularly attended electronic music parties and clubs.

One of the reasons for the increasing popularity of trance culture was the deepening influence of New Age culture on the young generation in Israel. This came into play, among others, in the new tradition of 'spiritual festivals' in the wild, which actually imported and capitalized on recreational patterns that evolved among backpackers in the Far East and South America.

Meanwhile, trance music also arrived in the clubs, which enhanced the parties using audio-visual effects (multiple colour-painted walls, aluminium ceiling, massive sound speakers, balloons, confetti, fireworks and horns), computerized pyrotechnics (smoke machines, giant video screens, lightning systems and laser and flicker headlights) and spectacular designs (DJ stages, dance floors on different levels, scantily-clad dancers on stages, galleries or dance cages hanging from the ceiling etc.). The profit-making mechanism was also upgraded to include promoters, DJs, security guards (including bouncers) and bartenders. The big clubs organized one 'rave' every once in a while, as well as major productions in various locations around Israel, attracting thousands of partygoers. The party phenomenon grew and improved so much that by the turn of the new millennium Israel had become an international trance superpower.

Millennials Join the Party

If most clubs in the early 90s were located in the Tel Aviv area, at the turn of the new millennium the phenomenon had expanded to many other locations across the country. At this point, millennials joined the party in droves.

The 2001 terror attack at the Dolphinarium, in which 21 youngsters were murdered, and the wave of terror attacks over the course of the Second Intifada, held the phenomenon back, but in time normality was restored. The clubs ramped up security, creating an outlet for youngsters away from all the anxiety surrounding them.

Many clubs across Israel had specific 'lines' designated for youngsters, allowing teens (ages 14-18) to have their own parties. One of the trademarks of these clubs at the time was the long queues of young people, staggering on the sidewalk at the club entrance well into the night. They are greeted at the door by bouncers who decide who gets to go in and when.

Another emerging feature of these club parties is how late they start. A weekend's night out used to start in the evening and end shortly after midnight. For millennials, the party only starts late at night and often goes on until the next morning. Many clubs only open after midnight. Many youngsters – particularly during summer vacation – turned day into night and night into day. They party or hang out with friends at nights and sleep during the day.

On certain dates (usually around the holidays), the big clubs produce an 'afterparty' or 'after' for short, which starts before dawn and lasts all throughout the day (until the holiday's end).

The trance and club phenomenon is undoubtedly one of the most important symbols of the death of the Sabra lifestyle. The Zionist 'hora' may have created a social 'trance' that brought friends together, but the foundation for this dancing experience was fundamentally different. Almost every aspect of trance culture is foreign and even goes against the Zionist circle culture: from the use of universal codes (English, computers) to the focus on individualistic, hedonistic gratification. The flourishing of this culture, under Generation Y's wings, is perhaps another sign of the ongoing decline of Zionist culture and the end of an era.

The booze-filled, drug-ridden dance party became routine for millennials even before they enlisted to the army. However, this culture has lost some of its power in recent years, after losing its innovative charm and being absorbed by the mainstream but also because Tel Aviv has turned into one big endless party. Youngsters have found other alternatives to the nature party and mega-club experience in the city – vibrant bars, theme-specific clubs, street parties, roof parties and more.

Millennials, their older siblings and their parents essentially pulled trance music into the mainstream. Nowadays, this music is also played in hotels, Bar Mitzvah parties and weddings. Even full moon and half-moon parties in the Far East have become trivial: they come, dance and continue with their vacation.

No Booze, No Life

From Austerity to Plethora

Alcohol consumption in Israel was low for many years, due to Jewish tradition as well as to the culture of austerity and frugality. Grocery stores offered a very limited variety of low-quality alcoholic beverages. Most Israelis drank sparingly – mostly sweet wine for Kiddush, brandy (cognac) and local beer – usually on Friday nights, holiday dinners and family gatherings.

The end of austerity and the fast increase in standards of living brought some more awareness to alcohol consumption, mostly among the Tel Aviv bourgeoisie. At the time, only a handful of European-style bars and pubs had operated in Israel. The Israeli alcohol industry slowly developed with minor strokes of innovation, such as Sabra liqueur, Fantasia wine and Maccabee beer.

The scope and variety of alcoholic products grew steadily during the 1970s and 80s, but the real revolution in Israeli drinking culture started in the 90s. The change was caused by a number of developments:

Beer Brand Manufacturing and Import. Tempo and Israel Beer Breweries started manufacturing international beer brands in local factories, and local boutique brewers popped up all across Israel. Importing beer and other alcoholic drinks increased immeasurably, with the expansion of the Israeli free economy.

The Development of a Wine Industry in Israel. The development of Golan Heights Winery, which produced high quality local wine, propelled the entire industry. Sixteen wineries operated in Israel in the late 1990s, including some family-owned boutique wineries. They improved the quality of wine in Israel and promoted it by using in-country tourism, during which visitors can partake in wine-tasting and buy bottles on site.

Rise of Air Travel. Buying alcohol at the duty-free shop has become an essential part of vacation culture. Meanwhile, more and more Israelis have been exposed to western drinking culture and started adopting more modern tastes and habits.

Media Revolution. Public awareness to wine and everything about it (manufacturing, quality, tastes, etiquette etc.) also grew due to the media, which devoted more columns and articles to the issue while covering the developing pastime culture.

Soviet Union Immigration Wave. Hundreds of thousands of Russian-speaking immigrants brought new drinking habits to Israel. Liquor stores that sell beer, wine and mainly vodka opened one after the other to meet the immigrants' demands.

Convenience Stores. Retailers for small, everyday commodities that operate around the clock – in cities and gas stations – made alcohol more accessible.

Generation Y Coming of Age. The arrival of a new Israeli generation of alcohol consumers is both the cause and the result of the revolution in this field in Israel.

Normalization of Alcohol Consumption among Millennials

Millennials are unlike previous generations when it comes to alcohol consumption in several aspects: first, they were exposed to abundance since childhood (commercials, television shows, supermarkets etc.) Second, they started consuming alcohol during puberty (junior high) – mostly while partying at dance clubs. Third, they consume more alcohol more frequently. Fourth, gender gaps in regards to drinking greatly diminished in this generation.

The phenomenon of minors gathering on a Friday night for the purpose of drinking together (beer, vodka etc.), around dance clubs ('hangers'), in movie theatres, on the beach, in public gardens and other hangout places, became commonplace back in the last years of the previous millennium. Despite the law prohibiting the sale of alcohol to minors, they usually had no problem getting what they wanted. Because drinking was forbidden inside the clubs, many youngsters would 'juice up' before arriving at the dance floor, with drinks they bought in kiosks and drank in plastic cups on their way to the club.

Surveys conducted at the time by the Ministry of Education with other institutions showed that a troubling increase in the number of intoxicated children and teens began in the late 1990s. Many youngsters were driven into excessive drinking due to inexperience, childishness and neglect by their parents.

It should be noted that energy drinks entered the Israeli market in the late 90s, led by Red Bull, which gave an extra boost to alcohol consumption

– (mostly vodka with Red Bull, bought in kiosks) – and particularly among the young population (this phenomenon is common in all western countries).

The city of Eilat played a historic role in the development of youth drinking habits. Amusement rides, food and drink stands, fashion stores etc. started appearing on the beach near cheap hotels and night clubs, turning the city into an attraction for youths, particularly during the holidays and summer vacation.

Over the years, the volume of youth groups of younger ages flocking to the southern city has grown. They fill up the pools, the clubs and beaches and party all day and all night with booze – often ending in violent outbursts and vandalism.

As drinking became more common, so did violent incidents around clubs across the country. News of violent incidents and casualties started appearing in the media more frequently than what Israeli society has come to expect, and stirred much concern. Statistics published occasionally by different bodies (the police, Israel Anti-Drug Authority, Ministry of Education, local authorities, academic researchers, the Knesset and State Comptroller) also indicated that this trend has been expanding.

Tel Aviv Bar Culture

A Bar at every Corner. In the past decade, Tel Aviv has become a completely cosmopolitan city: architecture, performing arts, plastic arts, fashion, technology, transportation, restaurants, clubs, hotels and naturally bars and pubs as well.

The main streets have been completely transformed, and going out for a beer or a drink has become routine for thousands of the city's residents as well as visitors from outside. Millennials, who spent their teen years drinking, have become significant consumers, serving as the patrons of most bars (in Tel Aviv as well as other cities).

There are currently some 500 bars operating in Tel Aviv, usually displaying a high level of design due to elaborate planning and significant financial investments. The selection is very diverse, in almost every aspect, starting from 'classic neighbourhood bars' with few tables, through vibrant 'pick-up bars' to 'dance bars' where there's a large space designated exclusively for dancing. Over time, the lines that distinguish the different types have blurred, and currently you can find countless bars across the city that combine different genres and attract diverse clientele. In recent years, Tel Aviv municipality has permitted more bars to set up tables and chairs also on the sidewalk, which adds to Tel Aviv's lively 'non-stop city' vibe.

However, the lifespan of most bars is relatively short, and many don't survive more than a few months or a couple of years. There's only a handful of bars that have survived in Israel for many years, and those that have are located mainly in Tel Aviv.

We don't have data on the demographic profile of bar owners, but our general impression is that this group's age has dropped over time. Most bar employees are young millennials, who know the needs and passions of their contemporaries all too well. It's difficult to get an exact number, but in our estimation bars in the Tel Aviv area provide a living for thousands of a post-army youth, most of which are students looking for a part-time job. The young employees know how to 'treat' the clientele – be it a chaser or a snack – which they usually offer their friends and associates.

Partygoers and their Needs. Millennials live in packs, making social gatherings an important part of their everyday lives. They meet and hang out as much as possible, whenever they can and with whomever is available. Their preferred weekday activity is something spontaneous, light, available and inexpensive. They send a WhatsApp or Facebook message and meet at someone's apartment or at the nearest bar. The bar is the perfect setting, because they can 'drop by' for an hour or two with some friends or just one friend and sometimes even by themselves. They can also randomly drop in and stop for a quick chat or join friends sitting at the open bar on the sidewalks. They go drinking when they're happy, sad, or simply when they feel the need to unwind, meet new people and feel like part of a community.

The weekend activity is more selective and planned. People usually go on dates over a bottle of wine or a cocktail, or go to bigger bars and clubs like dance clubs, meeting a bigger group of friends.

Some say youngsters prefer to drink when they meet not just because they're naturally social and in need of intimacy, but also because they get bored quickly and their emotional and verbal handicap makes it hard for them to communicate without 'props'. What do they usually talk about? Work, relationships, friends, studies, television, shopping, sports, hangouts, trips, their parents, routine complaints about the government and the high cost of living.

Weekday outings usually entail everyday clothing, and usually they only up their game on weekends. Girls usually tend more to their appearance than boys, because it's in their nature and also because it's become the norm.

Choosing a Spot. Choosing one bar over another is a matter of location (people from Tel Aviv prefer to stay close to home), general atmosphere, food, variety of drinks and price range. Tasty nachos or a specialty beer could be an attraction for the girls. Boys might prefer a bar known to attract female customers (pick-up bars) or one that screens live soccer matches. Discounts and special sales on drinks and snacks are common in bars and serve as an important criterion for choosing the time and place for the evening (particularly if they have 'happy hour'). Trendy bars attract big groups, and crowded places attract even more people. Youngsters hop from bar to bar but every group usually has its own base of operations.

Drinks, Snacks, Music and Sports Broadcasts. Drinking is an inseparable part of millennials' lives. They drink when meeting in their apartments, in bars and at parties. As a matter of fact, most of their social gatherings (usually with a close group of friends) involve drinking. One might say that beer and wine for them are like what coffee is for their parents.

They go to the bar 2-3 times a week: at the beginning of the week, on the 'holy day of Thursday' and on the weekend. Naturally, on weekdays they don't stay out as late as on the weekend.

Most youngsters stick to one kind of beer or vodka, but taste in alcohol gets finer over time, and curiosity pushes them to try out new flavours. More youngsters have been switching to wine in recent years, particularly women. This reflects a process that's also taking place in Europe and the United States. There are quite a few wine bars that offer a variety of global wines next to local brands. Many young people, mostly women, enjoy a cocktail every now and then.

Bar food tends to change depending on the type of venue. Most places offer small dishes to 'snack' as you drink. The menu is usually basic, but quality has improved in recent years.

Music is also an important component of the venue's atmosphere and branding. In some bars the volume is so painfully high that people stare at their phones instead of talking.

Nowadays, every self-respecting bar has at least one giant television screen with matching sound system and speakers. The screen usually shows music videos, sports, fashion shows and news. Dozens of fans cram into the bars whenever there's an important match or tournament.

Most bars offer the basic variety (Goldstar, Maccabee, Heineken, Tuborg etc.), though in recent years more and more places also offer new local and imported brands.

A typical night for millennials ends with 0.5-1 litre of beer plus a chaser, or 2-3 shots of vodka. Men usually drink more than women, although as we noted earlier, the differences between men and women when it comes to drinking patterns are fading. It should be noted that drinking in Israel is still moderate compared to Europe, Australia and the United States (where they chug one glass after the other). However, the statistics clearly show that the younger population in Israel – and around the world – is drinking more than the older generations.

Global studies show that the young people's official purpose for drinking is not just to cut loose and lower inhibitions but rather to get properly drunk. Many expressions have been created around this custom: 'I'm going to get wasted today', 'let's get nuts', 'tonight's gonna be sick' etc. Our impression is that teenagers and soldiers are more prone to 'get wasted'. Twenty and thirty-year olds drink more conservatively, mostly so they could get 'high' and cut loose among friends. For example, at weddings, which are perceived by youngsters as booze parties, or as they phrase it: 'at weddings you drink yourself senseless, it's free so you take advantage of it. You drink mostly because of the dancing, so you can cut loose'.

Various studies published by the World Health Organization and Israel Anti-Drug Authority have shown that the drinking age in Israel has dropped over the years, and the number of minors who become intoxicated is steadily rising. Intoxication is now one of the threats to public safety in Israel, since it leads to violence, delinquency and car accidents. Many youngsters ignore the dangers of drink driving, but it appears awareness has spread lately, and many groups appoint a designated driver. Others solve the problem by taking a taxi to and from the bar.

Kosherizing the Cannabis

Smoking Weed in Secret

Under the British mandate and the first years of the State of Israel, drug use in general and cannabis in particular was a marginal issue. Most of the public did not experience or was even aware of the phenomenon, which took place in slums (drugs were sold in falafel stands, cafés, hair salons, small shops and private apartments). Even smoking cigarettes was seen as immoral by many.

In 1961, the State of Israel signed an international treaty that prohibited the production and supply of narcotic drugs. The term 'junkie' appeared in newspapers for the first time, broadly attributed to all drug users. Eilat was only a developing tourist city, and became well-known as a sanctuary for people who want to avoid the long hand of the law. Naturally, it attracted cannabis enthusiasts from Israel and abroad.

The higher standard of living also made its mark on cannabis culture. Every other week newspapers would report the arrest of cannabis dealers (they were sentenced to short prison terms – usually up to a year), while a growing number of people were caught smoking 'red-handed' – some of which were tourists ('beatniks') from western Europe, the United States, Canada and Australia.

After the Six-Day War, Israel was flooded by hashish from the West Bank, East Jerusalem, Gaza and Khan Yunis and also from Europe and the US. The golden beaches of Eilat, Taba, Nuweiba, Dahab and Sharm el Sheikh were flooded by youngsters, and drugs became an inseparable part of the hippy atmosphere.

Israel became an attractive destination for foreign backpackers at the time, thanks to the positive image associated with the country, lower flight prices, and mostly the Kibbutzim's image as a place where you can volunteer and have some free-spirited fun.

Over the years, as the number of soft drug users grew, the Knesset passed stricter laws while the police increased the scope of raids for catching such offenders. Paradoxically, though, society's attitude towards soft drugs became slightly more lenient, partly due to the effects of western rock 'n' roll culture.

The media has brought up the public dilemma of whether to arrest young people, minors in particular, caught smoking. The older generation saw cannabis use as a symptom of the loss of purpose and values. The younger generation, in contrast, started to perceive smoking as a small niche of rebellion within the web of responsibilities teenagers were faced with.

In the 1970s, Flower Power culture's influence grew and cannabis smoking became more legitimate, especially among the Tel Aviv bohemians. Some well-known artists were arrested for drug use and possession (mostly with tiny doses for self-use), and the arrests resonated in the media. Meanwhile, op-eds that dared to ask defiant questions started appearing in the media, questioning the laws and the police's actions against the phenomenon.

The status quo, under which the police mainly go after serious dealers and ignores most users, has been maintained to this day. The courts have maintained a general trend of convicting offenders who were arrested according to the letter of the law while giving out lenient sentencing. The media also upheld its course of action, publishing articles about the alarming scope of the phenomenon while criticizing the police and questioning the law prohibiting soft drug use.

Cannabis and Generation Y

The early 2010s seem to have brought change to the status quo. This is reflected in the scope of cannabis use as well as in social conventions about the drug. The main reason for the change is Generation Y's attitude towards cannabis. Below are some generation characteristics (perceptions and behaviours) in this context:

Extensive Use. A high percentage of millennials (it's difficult to determine an exact number) uses cannabis regularly or occasionally (usually during outings), and an even higher percentage consider cannabis to be similar to alcohol, for several reasons:

Cannabis is produced in mass quantities nowadays – both privately and commercially – and in the age of globalization and information, it is more accessible than ever. Not only does the internet make soft drugs more accessible, it also helps normalize their use by distributing massive (and often positive) information about the phenomenon. Millennials were raised on the importance of personal liberties and the concept of live and let live; this generation has been getting high from a young age, at parties and trips to South America and the Far East; this is a generation that considers entertainment to be a supreme purpose, therefore any means that can lighten the atmosphere are perceived as positive; this is a bored generation that has difficulties achieving gratification and excitement, which is why they need external means; the millennials are full of anxieties and distress, therefore they search for ways to escape and relax; they're fundamentally open to adventures and experimenting; this is a socially developed generation that lives in packs, and cannabis is an inertly social drug; they're less critical and more self-absorbed; this is an ADHD generation that isn't afraid to take chemicals (like Ritalin) and needs focus (cannabis helps you to concentrate). This is also the reason for the dramatic increase in party drugs sold at kiosks in recent years; this generation has no long-term plans and tends to live in 'the here and now', which is why they're also not concerned about possible long-term effects of intensive cannabis use.

Stoned Backpackers. Smoking drugs was part of the 'big trip' experience in previous generations as well. However, while in the past this was a relatively negligible phenomenon, it has grown to a completely different scale with Generation Y. Not only has it become acceptable and common to smoke cannabis with friends while in the Far East or South America, there are also colonies of smokers (mostly in the Far East) where many millennials come to stay for a long period of time. It has also become legitimate to take hallucinogenic drugs, thanks to trance culture (it is also not uncommon to combine drug use and sex with local prostitutes). The list of popular countries for drug use includes India, Thailand, Laos, Colombia, Ecuador, Mexico and Amsterdam in the Netherlands.

Many backpackers ignore or are unaware of the risks and damage caused by drug use abroad, particularly the risk of run-ins with local law enforcement, leading to arrests and serious penalties (as serious as life imprisonment and even the death penalty).

Many backpackers fall victim to the devastating effects of hallucinogenic drugs. Approximately some 2,000 backpackers suffer harm as a result of using these drugs every year, 600-800 of which suffer severe damage, often requiring involuntary commitment to psychiatric wards. Some of the people who used drugs in East Asia were flown directly to mental health centres in Israel, after suffering a psychotic attack.

In light of the scope of drug use among backpackers, and in an attempt to minimize the damage caused by this phenomenon, two unique programmes for treating young drug victims were founded in the early 2000s; Kfar Izun in Kibbutz Sdot Yam and the Warm Israeli Home in India (in Manali and Goa, depending on the season). The rising trend also led to the formation of rescue companies that specialize in locating young Israelis abroad and bringing them home.

Stay Out of my Life. Growing legitimacy for soft drug use is also related to the popular notion in the western world as well as in Israel that the government should stay out of the personal lives of its citizens as much as possible. Furthermore, there's a general approach that people should not judge other people's behaviours and be as tolerant as possible. This trend gave birth to the Aleh Yarok (Green Leaf) party, founded in 1999. It did not reach the votes threshold, but its sheer existence in the political landscape has sent a message (most of its voters were probably young). Several Knesset members have already 'come out of the closet', admitting to smoking cannabis socially. MK Tamar Zandberg (Meretz) even submitted a bill that would permit self-use in small quantities.

An unpreceded event was held in April 2011 at Wohl Rose Park in Jerusalem, which was very symbolic for the status of cannabis among millennials. Several hundred youngsters demonstrated for legalizing soft drugs (some even claim there were thousands), in what became known as The Big Bong Night. Protestors blocked a road in Rabin Avenue and shouted various slogans in favour of legalization, such as 'the people demand legal cannabis'.

The Big Bong Night became a highly publicized event before it even began because it was produced and marketed using a new millennial-style format (the event launched a Facebook page with thousands of likes).

Route to Legalization?

The claim that cannabis is not harmful and perhaps even has health benefits emerged in public discourse back in the 1970s, but the number of studies that attempt to empirically investigate the issue has only grown recently. This is done in two different channels: one tests whether the drug is harmful and the other tests whether it has positive effects. It should be noted the media publishes a new survey of the effects of cannabis every other day, and the data is often inconsistent and confusing to the public. The reason is that the scientists themselves still disagree on the conclusions (the entire field is in its infancy). Another reason is that, in many cases, the information is published selectively and manipulatively, as per the publisher's worldview. Furthermore, if once the issue was divided between young people and old people, or representatives of 'the man' and ordinary folks, nowadays the people who support legalization and the ones who are against it come from all walks of life. Even the experts (medical personnel, scientists, lawyers, educators etc.) are not decisive in their conclusions, which adds to the confusion.

In any case, new data published, either in corporate media or on the internet, weakens the conservative approach and reinforces doubts over the time-old prohibition, which isn't being strongly enforced anyway. Those who support legalization present the following arguments: cannabis is no substantially different from cigarettes and alcohol, which are legal. It doesn't make you lose touch with reality, isn't addictive and doesn't lead to loss of control or violence. On the contrary, it soothes, lower social inhibitions and creates a friendly atmosphere. There are also no definite findings that conclusively prove cannabis use harms cognitive abilities. At most you experience slight memory damage after many years of use. Studies may have shown that cannabis could be dangerous to people with a genetic predisposition to schizophrenia, but this is a small group that can be warned in advance (much like people suffering from coeliac disease are warned about gluten).

Legalization supporters also claim that the law against cannabis use turns a considerable portion of law-abiding citizens into criminals. According to them, the moment cannabis is made legal, the criminal activities surrounding it will dissipate (smuggling, mixing the drug with harmful substances etc.).

Objection to legalization, according to its supporters, also comes from mega corporations trying to preserve their power, led by the global pharmaceutical industry, which is known to be centralized and aggressive. The fact that some countries have permitted controlled use reinforces the notion that legalization is already happening, therefore it is pointless to try to stop an ongoing global process at this stage.

Those who strongly object legalization speak of a 'slippery slope' that could lead to social loss of control in relation to drug use (they link the increase in cannabis consumption to the increase in chemical 'party drugs', which can be sold legally.) In their opinion, if you allow the use of one drug (soft as it may be), you pave the road for more destructive drugs. They also insist that cannabis has devastating effects on the body and mind and list multiple risks: short-term damage include disorientation, panicking, anxiety, decreased coordination and response time; long-term damage include sexual dysfunction, immunodeficiency disorders, growth disorders, cell and hormone disorders and cumulative damage to the lungs and brain (decreased memory and learning abilities, apathy, fatigue, lack of motivation, personality changes and mood swings.)

The rate of legalization supporters has grown over time, and the result of this revolution seems to be obvious. The legal and practical validation for medical cannabis, which peaked when the medical cannabis bill was passed in late 2013, had a major impact on public empathy for the drug. That year, the number of patients in Israel who received approval for medical cannabis was reportedly the highest in the world relative to the country's overall population.

Two more symbolic milestones were set shortly after: in a 2015 lecture, Police Chief Yohanan Danino amazed members of the Chamber of Commerce in Beer Sheva claiming that criminal law towards cannabis use should be re-examined. Several months later, deputy Minister of Health Yaakov Litzman announced his intention to allow the sale of medical cannabis in pharmacies.

Party Generation – General Features

The Goal is to Party, not to Work

Studies conducted in the western world in recent years suggest the beginning of a change in perception, mostly among the young generation: work is mainly perceived as a means for fulfilling life's ultimate goal: having a good time. In other words, you work so you can have fun, rather than have fun in order to clear your head, replenish your energy and go back to work.

Millennials perceive leisure differently than their parents for a number of reasons: first, they grew up with a massive selection of entertainment and got a high dose of fun. They expect this to continue in their adult lives as well. That's why many are prone to living in Tel Aviv and its environs – this area offers more entertainment than any other region in Israel.

The second reason is how they relate to the internet. The web surrounds you, offering many seductive attractions. You feel like you're the only one working (and suffering) while the whole world around you is having a good time. Millennials want to join the party, and right away, since they also haven't learned to delay the gratification.

Since many perceive work as a type of punishment, they look at the weekend as a vacation from prison. Tel Aviv bars are packed with groups of youngsters every Thursday night, as if to celebrate a 'Thursday holiday'; the work week is finally over, and now we can start doing what we actually love, i.e. party.

Full-time Party

It's interesting to watch how seriously millennials take every outing and try to get the most out of it. They will carefully review every hotel feature, spend countless nights planning a single party, have long discussions about past pleasures and treats, and obviously share these experiences in real time (through photos and text). Facebook is full of posts reporting every outing, followed by supporting comments such as 'you guys are adorable!', 'have fun!', 'kisses', 'I'm so jealous'.

When a Gen-X father and Gen-Y son go out to a restaurant together, the father will flip through the menu and just pick something without giving it too much thought. The son, on the other hand, will perform a thorough analysis of the menu and all of its options, consult the waiter, and only then pick a dish (this pattern coincides with their inability to make decisions and the fear of making a mistake). He will also send the food back if he doesn't like it, while the father will send it back only if there's something genuinely wrong with it. The son will also delve deep into the beer that comes with the meal, and might ask to get some samples before choosing. These differences aren't just because youngsters are more fluent in the world of luxuries, but also because they take outings very seriously. Furthermore, the father will likely finish up the entire plate, even if he's full (because he paid for it with his hard-earned cash). The son, on the other hand, will stop eating once he feels full, even if it means leaving a considerable portion of the meal untouched.

Not only have millennials developed far more sophisticated leisure skills than their parents, they also tend to completely lose themselves to the pleasures of the body. For instance, when they dance, their bodies move skillfully and devotedly (the brain sheds off any care and lives in the moment) and a blissful smile is seen on their faces. They moan in delight when eating something tasty, and are overflowed with joy when planning a vacation. This is why they need more and more treats, and the thought of the next activity or experience that might be waiting around the corner 'keeps them alive'.

The central role entertainment holds in millennials' lives and their hedonistic orientation also separate them from the previous generation when it comes to their willingness to spend money on these experiences. What parents perceive as a waste of time and mostly a waste of money is perceived by youngsters as a legitimate, if not necessary expense. They're willing to spend huge sums on a short, one-time experiences (eating out, travelling abroad), sometimes with money they don't actually have and with no guilty conscience. Many of the parents we interviewed admitted that although they often criticize their children's indulgence and rash spending, they can identify with them in many cases, and even feel jealous of them. The children often 'teach' the parents that it's okay to spend money on themselves, relieving them of their conditioned guilty conscience.

Generation Y's orientation for recreation is a massive engine for the development of entertainment areas around the world, mostly in major metropolitan cities. Many millennials have good instincts about parties and can spot potential and develop it as entrepreneurs as well as partygoers. It's impossible nowadays to imagine Tel Aviv without its large, young population.

Constant Hangover

Nowadays, fatigue is no longer a temporary thing, but rather an ongoing existential state, even borderline chronic at times. This is due to the demanding work world, the lack of clear distinction between work time and pastime and an intense lifestyle. When television broadcasts hundreds of channels around the clock, the internet is always available and businesses and places of entertainment are open till the wee hours of the night, it's very tempting to drag the day. The result is chronic fatigue that makes it hard to function at work and at home.

This phenomenon is particularly significant among millennials, due to their addiction to electronic devices, their need to always be connected to their friends and their love of parties and alcohol. You could say this generation has been suffering from a never-ending hangover since childhood.

Fading Boundaries between Work and Leisure

In the digital world, the boundaries between leisure and work are fading. For example, an office clerk can read emails for work while spending time on Facebook; a senior manager can sit in a café with her laptop, write a work plan while enjoying a good cup of coffee and the atmosphere of a club. More and more work places also provide recreational spots: break rooms with coffee and snacks, newspapers and even a gym. At the offices of one of the young companies we visited, one of the workers was appointed 'entertainment officer'. Her job was to choose the daily treat for lunch and produce weekly entertainment events for the employees. This is meant to unite them and mainly to make them feel like something good is about to come.

Wrapped in Music

Millennials grew up in a time of technological revolutions that completely transformed the way we consume music: the video clips revolution led by MTV, followed by YouTube; the earphones revolution (from Walkman to Discman to the smartphone), which allows you to listen to music privately wherever you go – even in public; the music app revolution, which allows you to download songs and create your own playlist; the digitization revolution, which has made commercial recording studios obsolete, allowing artists everywhere to create and exposes the masses to their music; reality TV shows that produce an endless barrage of young talent.

Naturally, these dramatic changes have had an effect on the entire population, but have left a substantially deep impression on millennials, since they were born into them and because they're more accustomed to using computers than any previous generation. These effects on youngsters can be seen in several patterns of music production and consumption:

Anytime, Anywhere. They listen to music whenever they can (mostly on the smartphone). They know many Israeli and international bands and artists and are the overwhelming majority of voters on reality TV shows (*Israeli Pop Idol, X-Factor, The Voice*). Many of them dream of becoming successful singers themselves.

A Visual Experience. They love music clips and the visual aspect is very important to them. Quite a few songs became popular hits among millennials not because of their musical originality, but rather thanks to visual spectacle (e.g. international hit Gangnam Style).

The Personal Playlist Replaces the Radio Playlist. The option of listening to your own playlist anytime and anywhere has made the radio less relevant, particularly for young people. In the past, people would listen to radio to enjoy the music. With all the alternatives nowadays, radio no longer fills this need. Without radio, there's less chance of discovering unknown genres and artists, and one is less likely to expand his or her musical horizons, reinforce curiosity or experience the unfamiliar.

Easily Bored. People used to listen to their favourite music through records, radio programmes and live shows. It was exciting because exposure was rare. Nowadays, listening to music has become so easy that it's pedestrian. Furthermore, when youngsters listen to a playlist comprised solely of their favourite songs, the element of surprise is gone too and satiation and boredom grow.

Multi-Cultural Musical Collage. Israeli pop music has gone through great transformations over the generations while promoting and reflecting deep social processes. Today we can look back at how Mediterranean music rose from the fringes into mainstream becoming the dominant genre and feel satisfied and proud. It reflects the cultural pluralism that has swept the media and turned Israel into a society of darbuka and synthesizers. Millennials were exposed to more diverse musical genres than any other generation, and this is reflected in the music they consume as well as create, which is more tolerant and pluralistic than any generation before. Eastern, or Arabic music may be more popular among Mizrahi youths, but it's less noticeable nowadays.

Junk Music. Many millennials are also attracted to music that comes with a shiny package, which often distract listeners from the lack of depth (widely caused by MTV's influence). Just like millennials struggle to read non-fiction books and prose, they also have difficulty listening to complex music. Only a select few nowadays sit alone in their rooms to listen to musical pieces without outside interference (smartphones, television, computers etc.) and even fewer millennials go to musical concerts of non-mainstream artists (jazz concerts, for example).

It seems most artists from this generation are also musically superficial (they mostly produce rehashed instant music with a short shelf life). It should be noted that the depleting Israeli music mine still produces a few musical diamonds from time to time, but these are rare incidents that almost get no media attention. Millennial artists are actually stuck in a tragic paradox: on one hand, music is very accessible to consume and easy to produce. On the other hand, the overabundance creates a sense of exhaustion, making it hard to be artistically innovative.

We might be seeing the beginning of the end of music as we know it. In this sense, millennials are not just the first benefactors of this technological revolution, but are also its victims.

The lyrics also display a general decadence. The classic Hebrew songs, which will live on in collective memory for generations to come, had lyrics written by the best songwriters and poets. Nowadays, inarticulate shallow lyrics are dominant in almost every genre.

In the past, when people wrote lyrics, they tried to achieve a higher form of expression. They would look for original metaphors or clever rhyming. Youngsters nowadays don't even try. Their choruses are less like poetry and more like a stream of text messages.

Gym and Spa Culture

Gyms with exercise and body-building equipment have existed in professional sports clubs, the army and educational institutions since the early 1980s. Over time, they have spread and become an essential part of hotels and health and sports clubs across Israel, often as part of the pool and spa complex.

With the introduction of fitness chains (Holmes Place, Great Shape, Sportan and others), the sports halls have grown bigger and more luxurious, and the equipment more diverse and sophisticated.

Group aerobics classes (spinning, Zumba, kickboxing etc.) allow participants to unload tension, improve their mood, develop a sexy body and engage in group solidarity. Meanwhile, awareness to health food has grown and, along with exercise, has become part of the new healthier lifestyle.

The health awareness revolution swept considerable portions of the Israeli population, but it is particularly prominent among the younger generation, which was born into it. A gym subscription is no longer considered a luxury, according to millennials. They love to work out (often with a personal trainer) because they can unload stress, work on their bodies and possibly hook up (in this generation the number of women at the gym nearly matches the number of men). Gyms also have a very social and lively atmosphere that appeals to young people.

Vacation Abroad as a Necessity

Many millennials travelled abroad with their families as children and as teens. Consequently, vacationing abroad became an exciting basic experience in their world. A survey published by British airline EasyJet in 2013 found that in the twenty years prior to the survey, over half the children in Europe (56.5 per cent) travelled abroad before the age of ten. One can assume that in Israel the data is even higher.

Clearing their heads outside of Israel is also very important to millennials because most of them went backpacking at least once in their lives, and there is something addictive about that experience. Other countries are also more appealing to them compared to previous generations because they're more globally oriented and are more prone to shopping and entertainment. Many have stated in our interviews that they need a least one trip abroad a year, even if it's a short 4-5-day vacation, otherwise they start feeling like they're suffocating and that 'they have no life'.

Better to Hang Out with Friends

For millennials, 'hanging out with friends' is the definition of fun, preferably in a party, bar, restaurant or café, but also on other activities such as trips abroad, dinner parties at home and even sporting activities (jogging at the park or working out at the gym). Even when they are with friends, it's important for them to share the experience with other people who aren't present (via Facebook or WhatsApp). Everyone needs to know they're having fun in real time, and everyone also needs to congratulate them on it, publicly, otherwise they're 'not really friends'.

Shared Interests and Hobbies

One of the characteristics of this generation is the division into groups and communities, focusing on a specific interest, expertise, hobby etc. These groups create their own platforms, where experiences, advice, ideas and identity accessories are shared. They focus on various fields, such as off-roading (bicycles, bikes, off-road vehicles); collectibles (vinyl records, comic books etc.); following a musical genre (like heavy metal); computer games; culinary; sports fandom; professional photography; wave riding and windsurfing; science fiction; paragliding; hand gliding; diving; martial arts; working out and body-building; ballroom dancing, hiking on the Israel National Trail and more.

Abandoned Traditional Activities

Millennials killed the classic pastime activities of previous generation: reading books, reading newspapers on Saturday (they don't have a subscription), going to classical music concerts and hosting friends and relatives for deep conversations. They're generally not particularly fond of serious conversations about real issues and would rather have a light conversation over drinks.

Even home lectures, which were a social institution for the Palmach generation and in the early years of Israel, are nowhere to be seen nowadays. After all, millennials don't like lectures and are unable to commit to prolonged stimulation. They would rather get together at a bar, for a party, in nature, for bicycling trips or on the beach.

7

Always Online – Digital Natives

Born with the PC

Millennials are the first generation to be born into the computerized world. Over the course of the personal computer revolution that started in the 1980s, they have been the pioneers and early adopters of digital devices: computers, apps, gadgets and all sorts of cellular uses. For example, they were first to inhabit social networks and first to embrace Facebook, YouTube, WhatsApp and Instagram as everyday tools. Being the first digital generation has had two sweeping consequences.

First, the effect the computer and subsequently the mobile phone has had on their way of thinking and lifestyle has been stronger than the effect on older generations, who entered the computerized world as adults.

Second, it has created a cultural gap between them and their parents and grandparents, which in time also affected their relationships with their teachers, commanders and employers. Thus, while young millennials developed advanced computer skills, such as the ability to quickly learn new programmes and to type fast, their parents and teachers lagged behind, and in many cases became dependent on them (similar to how immigrant parents depend on their native children). However, despite the generational gap, the internet's introduction to everyday life actually tightened the bond between millennials and their parents, since the web created a common point of interest, allowing digital children to help their struggling parents.

Researchers in the United States identified the differences between generations in regards to the use of digital tools back in the early 2000s. Youngsters born into the internet world – 'digital natives' – were compared to the first settlers who conquered the vast, wild American frontier, creating a new world with a new set of rules. Digital language is like a mother tongue for this generation, to all intents and purposes. The older generation, which had to learn how to use technology later in life, were defined as 'digital immigrants'. The language of the internet was indeed like a second language for millennials' parents and grandparents, i.e. unnatural and inarticulate, and there are still remnants of the 'old accent'.

Not only did digital natives in Israel (millennials) not lag behind their counterparts in other western countries, they were even ahead of them in many fields, due to the rapid development of computer culture in Israel. For example, Israeli millennials were the first to use instant messaging services like ICQ and Messenger. These services allowed users to have online conversations in real time as well as send files at the same time.

Instant messaging trained millennials to naturally accept Facebook, the social network which many become addicted to. Hence, an entire generation became accustomed to instant communication gratification from a young age: short text conversations became second nature and an acquired necessity for them. Millennials and computers grew together, progressing from one generation of computers to the next at an increasing pace.

Mobile phones also led to significant generational gaps. Youngsters got used to a wide variety of the functions that mobile phones offer even as children, while their parents and grandparents mostly used them to make phone calls. Young consumers were first to use programmes, websites, videos and apps. To this day, they send texts, images, videos and music much more frequently than older age groups.

Over time, parents also joined in on the digital party, and eventually every member of the family retreated to his or her own private electronic bubble. This phenomenon has been significantly prominent in Israel, which has been swept by the digital wave.

The Latest Addiction

There's a recurring question in science: does digital technology only amplify needs and common psychological and social tendencies, or does it have a deeper impact, such as biological and chemical? We may find an answer in evidence from recent years, which confirms the claim that using the internet causes changes to our brain.

What's Up, Dude?

Most scientific studies focus on extreme cases of addiction, i.e. people who are terribly addicted to dating sites, chatrooms, computer games, pornography etc. But as smartphones have become more and more widespread, we've all become addicted to some degree. Most people in the western world find it difficult to disengage from screens and a problem that used to mostly be typical among youngsters can now be seen among many age groups. But still, the young probably suffer the most.

Life in Israel has always provided an endless stream of interesting news, perhaps even 'too interesting'. So much so that people feel the need to travel abroad just to get away from the news. But in today's digital age, the news also travels with you when you go on vacation. Israelis' inherent need to catch up, exchange information and discuss current events has turned the online environment into a massively influential platform. If the average American or European use their smartphones mostly to exchange words with family and friends, the average Israeli also surfs on news sites several times a day just to see what's new in the vibrant Israeli scene. As a matter of fact, the interpersonal and social dialogue is intertwined in news updates, debates and updates about politics, national security and popular culture.

Sleeping with the Cellphone

This generation's attachment to their smartphone is one of their most recognizable traits. Millennials all over the world don't just own more cellular phones and advanced devices than older generations, they also care for them (with covers, ornaments, protectors etc.) and use them more frequently and for much longer periods of time than any other age group. They're also more addicted. A person can be labelled 'addicted' if they want to stop but are unable to, if they spend an increasing amount of time and energy on it, and if it disrupts their lives.

Many youngsters around the world, including those in Israel, don't even turn their phones off, and take them to bed when they go to sleep, like they used to take their favourite teddy bear or doll. A considerable portion of youngsters use smartphones in the bath, on the toilet, during family dinners and even while driving. They check for updates very frequently, indicating a serious dependency on the device.

Teachers describe teenagers who replaced talking on the phone with quick and compulsive texting during both recess as well as during class. Parting from their phones for an hour or two is a horrible punishment for them, similar to being sent to solitary confinement.

IDF boot camp commanders speak of the moment new recruits are prohibited from using their mobile phones. They become emotionally distraught, similar to how junkies act in rehab. It's so hard for them that IDF has dedicated specific breaks for phone use over the course of the day, and also installed makeshift power sockets in field tents.

Universities and colleges have long given up. Students come to class and just sit there, staring down the whole time. They are supposedly developing a sophisticated method for dividing their attention, but in reality their attention dissolves into a limbo of 'LOL stimuli'.

Fear of Missing Out

Cellphone addiction is undeniably the result of natural human curiosity, the need to know, be in the thick of it, catch up on things. People yearn to partake and share opinions, experiences and feelings, dish out advice and get feedback. The cellphone enables them to do this at any given time, from any place, through various medias (text, audio, images and videos) to multiple people simultaneously.

Smartphones have some significant benefits: they make information accessible, streamline the way we work, encourage creativity and emotional availability, connect people, expand the discourse, do away with awkward moments, provide entertainment and mostly add some spice to life (which is naturally monotonous and mostly uneventful). However, smartphone use also has some downsides, which only increase as time goes by. One of them is the fear of missing out – which leads to dependency.

An international survey found that nine out of ten respondents from around the world tend to put on their clothes, brush their teeth and check their smartphones as part of their morning routine. Two out of five admitted that they would 'feel anxious, as if a part of them were missing' if they couldn't use their smartphones to stay connected. They live in constant, uninterrupted stimuli, having developed a mental dependency similar to how athletes are dependent on endorphins. This syndrome was named FOMO (Fear of Missing Out) in 2004, and introduced to the Oxford English Dictionary in 2013.

The Young and the Restless

In addition to the fear of missing out, there are other symptoms of digital addiction which are considerably noticeable among millennials:

Lack of Focus. The constant fixation on incoming new information makes them absent-minded, nervous and restless. Studies have shown that people nowadays tend to change tasks at a high pace rather than focus on just one task. Technology may enable multi-tasking, but it also makes it harder to focus. Not only is the quality of work compromised as a result, it also creates stress due to failure to meet the deadline for assignments.

Hyperactivity. People who are exposed to constant stimuli become indifferent and joyless, mentally exhausted. They're sucked into endless chatter which drains them of energy. Ironically, the most democratic device in the history of mankind denies us of a basic liberty – the right for peace and quiet.

Superficiality. The addiction to short, instant messages creates intolerance to complex content. Fewer people are interested or capable of verifying information, delving deeper and appreciating a challenging thought.

Higher Excitement Threshold. The small screen can easily compete with the stimuli surrounding people, because it sends a perpetual stream of sophisticated visual imagery. When you can have a conversation with a large group of online partners, face-to-face conversations become boring. When you can watch thousands of amazing photos and fascinating movies for free, the view around you becomes monotonous and slow. When you can get countless dramatic news updates, funny texts and juicy gossip, life outside the screen seems poor by comparison. Our excitement threshold increases over time, as does the anxiety from becoming bored.

Virtual Reality Life. Smartphones save time and energy. You no longer have to go to the post office, buy a newspaper or even invite friends over to your living room. Everyone's already living in the same virtual apartment. Mobile phones diminish our mobility in time and space and allow us to live a full, rich life with the wave of a finger. So why even get up? We used to fill our world with stuff and mostly operate in a physical environment. Today we just create our own reality with the click of a button. Virtual life is comfy, and can easily compete with real life.

Lazy Passivity. Computer apps have made intellectual effort obsolete. You no longer need to memorize the multiplication table or phone numbers, spell words correctly or use a map to navigate. When you get used to things being done for you, which the younger generation has been used to since childhood, you become more passive and perhaps less altruistic, industrious or creative.

Living for the Experience. When someone reports or shares a meal in a restaurant or a certain moment in a party with his or her friends, they're not just documenting the joyous occasion, they're actually redefining the experience. The feedback ratifies their enjoyment, decorates it with (sometimes false) praise, amplifies the break from routine (you're having fun now while they go on with their everyday lives), immortalizes good moments, stretches the experience and mostly supports the hedonistic world view (material pleasures are what's important in life).

Millennials have become dependent on the constant echoing of thoughts and emotions, with smartphones acting as an extension of the brain, mouth, ears and eyes. There's great beauty in this pattern because it creates a new form of collectivism. However, it also creates an inability to experience things spontaneously and independently, as people have become dependent on what others think and obsessed with the need to impress. Today's youngsters are like a person who is unable to see the world without a camera. They live their experiences while documenting them and don't have their own natural memory of spontaneous experiences, but rather digital memories that store 'staged' experiences.

8

Bands of Brothers and Sisters – Friendship in an Age of Alienation

The Ethos of Friendship in Zionist Society

The Jewish people have always perceived themselves as more of an extended family than just an ethnic group. This can be seen in the open and warm interpersonal relationships prevailing in Israeli society. The fact that Israel is a small, isolated country has also helped enhance the feeling of community.

The code of solidarity and friendship in Israel is also based on unique social stratification – or more accurately lack thereof. Israel has always been a divided society with fundamental religious, ethnic, political and economic differences and tensions, but unlike European societies, it didn't create an aristocracy, whose lifestyle and circles of interaction are completely separate from the rest of society (like gated neighbourhoods and members only clubs, for example). Tycoons are a relatively new phenomenon in Israel, and one that has been subject to strong criticism from the media and the majority of the people, for good reason.

The socialist-pioneering code that shaped Israel before its establishment and during its early years may have died out, but the kibbutz atmosphere, where people are 'members' rather than 'residents', hasn't disappeared. It's deeply embedded in the cultural DNA of Israeli society and can be seen in everyday conventions and habits: in clothing, language, housing, art, politics and business. Even in Israeli courts, the language is less official and buttoned-up than in most western countries.

Military service (which for most Israelis is a civic duty) also helps reinforce the feeling of solidarity because it acts as a cultural melting pot, strengthens social skills and creates a sense of camaraderie among warriors.

The wars, terror attacks and the constant threats and pressures have also helped unite Israeli society, creating a folklore of mutuality and support. Israelis often affectionally refer to one another as 'my brother.' The Israeli art and entertainment worlds have also elevated the circle culture, in the spirit of youth movements and kibbutzim, through songs, folk dancing, cinema, fine literature and more.

Need Friends More

The Israeli friendship ethos has not passed over Generation Y. On the contrary, millennials have actually taken it one step forward (though some might say it's 'one step back') and given it a new, more global meaning. Friends are one of the main foundations of their lives, and they have a crucial influence on their decisions in a variety of fields, including choosing where to live, a profession, a workplace and even a spouse. This phenomenon isn't unique to youngsters in Israel and is common among all millennials around the world.

While 'keep in touch' used to be just something you'd say out of politeness, nowadays it has a practical application in everyday life. The bonds of friendship are so central to this generation, that for some youngsters their friends are as valuable to them as their own family. There are several reasons for this phenomenon:

Extended Bachelorhood. In the past, the older you got, the less important your friends became. With millennials it's the exact opposite: the older they get, the more they need their friends. Among other reasons since their replacement (a relationship) has yet to arrive or because relationships have become short-lived.

The Need to be Loved. The psychological need to be popular and loved also outside the nuclear family is universal. However, it seems to play a critical role for millennials, due to their upbringing and their insecurity.

Warm East Wind. You could say that the open and warm Middle Eastern culture has had a significant effect on Israeli popular culture. Restrained European decorum has been replaced with spontaneous expressions of warmth, affection and fun.

Overgrown Children. This generation's delayed adulthood adds a different angle to the camaraderie. Many millennials continue to act like teenagers throughout their twenties. In previous generations of those born in Israel, childhood friendships ended after the youth movement or military service. Millennials continue to act like a group of (overgrown) children for much longer.

Hanging Out Together. Many youngsters live close to one another (usually in the centre of Israel) and frequently go out together. The many available options, mostly cafés and bars, make it easier for them to maintain their friendships. Their digital fluency also provides more options for communication.

The Age of Sharing. The culture of psychological honesty, in which millennials were raised, makes it easier for them to share with one another. This led to a generation with fewer emotional barriers and more sophisticated interaction capabilities. This code has had a particularly strong impact on men, who are naturally more restrained than women. Millennial men are more open to discuss their intimate thoughts and feelings than men of previous generations. This changes the nature and quality of their relationships with other men as well as with women.

Support Groups. Many millennials have been raised in broken homes. The ongoing loneliness and pressures increased the need for support groups of empathetic friends with 'similar problems' from an early age.

TV Friends. Television shows about a group of young friends, broadcasted on Israeli popular channels – from the international *Seinfeld* and *Friends* to the Israeli *Florentine, Traffic Light* and *Naor's Friends* – create a role model that has also had an effect on young people in Israel.

Teamwork. Millennials were brought up in a sophisticated industrial world where individual inventors are a thing of the past. This is no longer a world of outstanding visionaries, but rather of task forces that initiate and develop things together. There is an increasing number of work teams and collaborations in industry as well as in the world of entertainment, art, medicine and science. Presumably, the message that teamwork is better than working alone has been internalized by the younger generation as well.

Family of Friends: Friendship Themes in Generation Y

Israeli friendship has several common themes that also apply to millennials. Some are traditional and may have weakened in this generation, and some are new and apply mostly to the younger generation.

Kiss and Tell

All secular Jewish Israelis know the symbolic time-old phrase 'kiss and tell', which reflects the need of many to be accepted by the group and earn their sympathy.

Sharing with friends has become an integral part of millennials' everyday life in a variety of ways. They whip out the smartphone to send a message or photo even in intimate experiences such as childbirth or break-ups as well as trivial experiences such as cooking at home, jogging in the park or buying a new outfit. The friends' involvement and their reaction to these private events are an inseparable part of the experience, creating a collective that experiences the world together.

They don't just share photos and videos remotely, they also do it when meeting in person. It's not uncommon to see them gathered around a smartphone, watching a funny video and cracking up.

Hivemind

Facebook and the smartphone fit right in with Israelis' basic tendency to consult one another. Since millennials are naturally less independent, they often seek out advice and send each other useful information. All you have to do is write a post about how you're searching for new roommates or ask for lecture summary notes and you'll immediately get a response.

Who Needs Favouritism when you have Connections?

Favouritism, i.e. the custom of cutting red tape for your family and friends, is very common in Israel. Religious, ethnical, gender and age discrimination are still very widespread in Israel, but have lost some of their strength among millennials. This is the most mobile generation in Israeli society, because the barriers of ethnic selection, which were prominent among Israeli hegemony (veteran-educated-Ashkenazic-men), have weakened in recent years.

Hospitality, But not as Much

Inviting guests to your home is very common in Israel, unlike Europe and the United States, where people usually meet in impersonal places. Furthermore, when a guest arrives at one's home for the first time, it's customary to introduce them not just to all of its residents but also show them every room in the house. The end of the meeting is a gradual ritual during which you walk the guest to the door, where you begin one last long conversation before the final departure. This pattern still exists among millennials, but has become less frequent due to the importance of cafés and bars as well as because rented apartments are smaller. Furthermore, since youngsters like to hang out in packs, the apartment is too small to fit everyone in.

Hugging and Kissing

Israelis are open, uninhibited, forthright ('dugri') and undiplomatic. They look each other straight in the eyes and have no qualms about asking personal questions. It is said that in Israel you always know what other people think of you, and this knowledge is the foundation of an honest relationship. This is also why it's very hard for Israelis to live abroad. They miss home, because they miss Israeli honesty, which is at the base of its camaraderie.

This pattern is a basic aspect of Israeli DNA, but it's even stronger among millennials, thanks to their emotional openness, their natural connection to Middle Eastern culture, their habit of being surrounded by love and their need for warmth. They touch one another, pat each other on the back, hug and kiss frequently (both men with men and women with women) and never shy away from public displays of affection.

No Secrets

Even the way millennials talk is different than previous generations. There's a traditional saying originating from Yiddish, which roughly translated to 'what have you heard?', demonstrates the Israeli tendency for sharing information. A typical Israeli conversation often starts with gossip about a mutual acquaintance, creating a friendly bond as well as a mutual exchange of information.

However, while previous generations avoided personal exposure and never discussed their problems in public ('you don't wash your dirty laundry in public'), millennials tend to over-share, with an emphasis on private matters. They don't just talk about themselves and their troubles out in the open, in many cases they share with a group of people rather than a single confidante.

Friendship without Depth or Sacrifice

Interpersonal openness doesn't necessarily demonstrate a relationship's depth or quality. Some claim that these over-the-top displays of affection actually reflect insincerity, or at the very least a lack of emotional and moral depth. During our interviews, we were told on numerous occasions of friendships that didn't hold up when tested, and the feeling that despite all the smiles, support and mutual sincerity, when the going gets tough, many simply disappear.

In other words, a friend in need is no friend indeed. This is a broad generalization, of course, as there are millennials whose friendships withstand difficult trials, like on the battlefield, dangerous situations, serious illnesses etc.

It's possible that millennials' inability to count on their friends in times of trouble is one of the reasons for their close relationships with their parents. They are their 'true friends' to a large extent.

Alcohol-infused Friendship

Millennials hang out together more than any previous generation, and are most skilled in creating a happy, friendly atmosphere. The restaurant, café, bar and club – which have become so common in their lifetime – make getting together easy and pleasant. Since they love drinking alcohol, smoking cigarettes and social drugs, dancing and chit-chatting, their companionship is easy-going and natural. Their togetherness is also linked in their minds to an elevating experience.

I'm So Cool

Humour is one of the main components of this generation's interpersonal relationships, because it alleviates tension and brightens the mood and because it's become a main component of western entertainment culture. Group humour also serves as social cohesion and promotes a good atmosphere, and has become far more accessible with the development of the internet, which is chockfull of funny bits.

It's important for millennials to impress one another and appear spontaneous and 'cool' like their favourite stand-up comedians. Their humour is mostly childish – gags and juvenile jokes. In previous generations, women loved to laugh but usually avoided trying to be funny. This gap has greatly narrowed in this generation, and comes into play with female sarcasm and 'dick jokes' that were mostly once the domain of men.

Never-ending Birthday Party

The birthday party isn't something new in the Israeli landscape, though it has become a grandiose event with a competitive element during millennials' childhood ('I can spoil my child more than you can').

The urge to hold a big, costly birthday celebration was also the result of working parents feeling guilty for working late hours and not spending enough 'quality time' with their children.

Since millennials experienced elaborate birthday parties as children, this event has become central in their lives. They hold a great significance for this occasion, and many celebrate it over the course of several days. In fact, the party starts online. When the joyous occasion finally arrives, the birthday boy or girl's Facebook wall is bombarded by warm greetings from close friends and casual acquaintances alike. And don't worry, anyone who forgets will quickly be reminded by Facebook or WhatsApp.

As this is a generation of broke partygoers, and because drinking is their favourite pastime activity, the birthday has become a celebration of alcohol in recent years. The bars are aware of this, which is why they offer youngsters special treats on this day. Many young women who pine over that sweet childhood memory come to the bar with a flower bouquet or crown on their heads. It's customary not to bring gifts, but rather buy the birthday boy or girl a drink. Only close friends, parents and spouses buy presents and usually give them in a separate, more intimate gathering.

Herd Mentality

People need to connect to other people not just for emotional support, but also so we can make educated decisions. However, while previous generations made decisions based on authority, knowledge or age, as well as facts and data, today's youngsters usually base their decisions on their friends' opinions.

The group had a significant impact on the individual in the past, but the use of social networks has amplified this influence. Herd mentality among millennials is very strong. If one member of the group decides to buy a product, travel to a certain destination or even get married this will have an infectious effect on the others. The first to lose weight, first to smoke, first to get married and the first to get divorced often serves as a catalyst for change among friends.

Childhood Friends

While social cohesion is created from an early age in every society, these bonds are very common in the small, familial country of Israel, and among millennials in particular. These friends are there for you in every moment of your life, and are considered more like family.

Many millennials have a strong bond with their childhood friends, even going as back as when they were toddlers. Social networks have played an important role in preserving these relationships, as they allow easy, continuous communication (even if it is on a 'backburner') with many people from different stages of life.

BFFs with Members of the Opposite Sex

Many millennial males have a platonic female BFF (mostly from their school days) and many females have a platonic male BFF. They share intimate issues with one another and dish out advice. This friendship is somewhat different from the same-sex friendships.

Male Groups, Female Groups and Mixed Groups

Feminism has been a bit sluggish with penetrating the heart of secular Israeli culture (in the late 1970s), but cross-gender camaraderie among youths existed in the Zionist tradition even back in the early 1900s: in new colonies, kibbutzim, moshavim, youth movements and gymnasiums. In photos and paintings from that period, girls often appear side by side with the boys. Even Nathan Alterman's defining epic, *The Silver Platter,* places a girl next to the boy. In this aspect, millennials continue this post-diaspora Zionist tradition of a mixed society, intentionally defying the Jewish tradition of separating men and women.

Millennials narrowed the gaps between men and women more than any generation before. This is expressed in worldviews, language, lifestyle and cultural capital (education, income etc.). Interestingly, however, millennials have also created a post-feminist view, which is reflected in a differential friendship culture: men cast themselves into their own support and pastime groups (a closed-off group, usually comprised of high school, army and university friends), while women create their own sorority. This happens for a number of reasons:

Delaying the inevitable. The notion that women are trying to establish a stable relationship as quickly as possible often deters men and sends them into a 'support group' that delays the inevitable. The decision to hold on to a group of men-children is also a type of escape from commitment and settling down.

Uninterrupted Male Bonding. Many young men feel as if their interests differs from women's and that the presence of a woman disrupts their openness and intimacy (which mostly revolved around complaints and gossip about women and sports talk). Nobody is on their backs and no one gets offended. Popular Israeli TV series *Traffic Light* is based on this motif. Many preserve the youthful atmosphere of their old school and neighbourhood through traditionally male ballgames (mostly soccer and basketball) and social activities (bridge, poker, sports betting etc.)

Sociable, Feminine Discourse. In the past, women had to be invited and escorted by men to go out. Today they can do it on their own. They even dance alone and travel to South America and the Far East by themselves or with a group of independent women. This create a sort of 'girl power' that reinforces the bonds of friendship between young women.

Meanwhile, the interaction between the men of this generation is more 'feminine' than before, and therefore more sociable. They tend to touch each other, hug in public and open up to one another.

Furthermore, if men used to be more goal-oriented and have short, purposeful conversations with a competitive hierarchy (to determine 'who's right'), millennial men have developed 'soft' discourse skills and have learned how to chat to achieve closeness as well as for support. Unlike their fathers who would mostly exchange their views on politics, the army and sports, young men today also enjoy 'girl talk', which is naturally friendlier. It involves personal issues such as clothing, pastime activities, love, food and dreams.

Beyond these segregated groups, there are also mixed-gender meetings, mostly in cafés, bars and clubs. It's not uncommon to see groups of loud men and women enjoying a beer or some other drink. Their flow is natural, and unlike previous generations, who usually separated men from women, here everything is mixed and the conversation is interesting to everyone.

Brothers in Arms

IDF has always served as a unique social framework for Israelis, and its impact on the code of interpersonal relationships in Israel has been tremendous. The strong bond with army friends is usually common among combat units, who also go through meaningful experiences during their reserve duty.

Relationships with army friends are particularly common and long-lasting among millennials, mostly because the service is a more traumatic experience for them and they need more support from their friends. Many have had rough experiences during their regular and reserve duties, in policing activities in the West Bank and the fighting in Gaza. The fact that everyone is on Facebook, Instagram and WhatsApp helps maintain the relationship.

The Big Trip

An important and unique source of Israeli camaraderie is the traditional big post-army trip. This used to be common only among a selected few, but today it's a particularly widespread pattern, with far-reaching implications for the friendship code.

The most popular destinations are India, Thailand, Nepal, United States, Central America, South America, Australia and New Zealand. Many travel alone and encounter other Israelis while abroad, forming relationships between individuals as well as groups. Many also seek out partners for the beginning of the trip, in order to manufacture a 'soft landing' for themselves upon arrival at their destination. They find them on Facebook or through ads and meetings at backpacker shops. These are usually ad hoc friendships based on a common interest, and don't necessarily evolve into a long-lasting relationship. They travel together as long as it suits them. The trip goes on for several months, during which they get together with new groups and disengage from old groups, if it 'fits them' at the time. Facebook is very helpful in this manner, since it allows you to follow people at any given time (most report when they change locations as well as their coming plans). Upon returning home, some friendships last, mainly in Israel, while others dissipate.

Roommates

The habit of living in rented apartments with roommates has given birth to a new kind of friendship. Living together can bring two-three strangers closer (men and women alike), which often turns them into close friends who share their world with one another. Some friendships continue even after co-habitation ends.

This pattern has become particularly common among millennials due to their extended bachelorhood and high rental costs (they're forced to share an apartment with others).

Cross-ethnic Relationships

In generation Y, the role of ethnicity in the formation of social bonds has become rather insignificant compared to previous generations. Millennials have more cross-ethnic relationships than any other generation, be it everyday friendships, romantic relationships or marriage.

The Bond of First-time Parents

Many young parents become friends with the parents of their children's friends. They connect over the kids' activities, in kindergarten, school, after-school activities etc. This kind of relationship tends to centre around the issue of raising children. Unlike previous generations, millennial fathers also form friendships with other parents, due to their increasing involvement in their children's upbringing.

Parents as Older Siblings

There has been a clear distinction between parent-children relationships and same-age relationships in previous generations. The generational gaps and distance drew clear boundaries, created a buffer and quite often even led to mutual estrangement. Millennials, however, were brought up in an informal, less authoritative atmosphere, resulting in a friendly relationship with their parents. This is reflected in open dialogue, daily updates, advice and shared leisure activities. It should be noted that millennials used to spend time with their parents throughout their childhood, and even watching TV was a family activity, much like watching with friends.

Many parents also have a long-standing friendly relationship with their children's friends, and it is not uncommon to see parents joining their children on a night out or even the long trip in South America or the Far East. A comparative study has not been conducted, but one can assume that the percentage of parents in Israel who are friends with their kids on Facebook or on WhatsApp groups is among the highest in the world.

Young people used to be ashamed of having a warm relationship with their parents. It was considered diasporic and immature. The 'Jewish mother' is a recurring character in Jewish and Israeli mythology – an overbearing, loud, vulgar, over-protective, aggressive and manipulative person, who has no reason to exist except through her son. She sacrifices her life for him, instills guilt and pushes him to material success at any cost and marriage with her doppelganger.

Today's Israeli mothers aren't less anxious, and perhaps are even more so compared to the 'Jewish mothers' of the past. The struggle of letting go of the child isn't easier either. But the alienation and hostility between mother and son have been replaced by a strong friendship.

Adult men of previous generations would blatantly shake off their mothers. Being a 'mama's boy' was considered an insult. Men were proud of the macho bond they had with their fathers and pushed their complex and meaningful relationship with their mothers aside. These days, this bond has become a status symbol, a source of pride rather than something you hide.

Millennials boast about their relationships with their parents – mothers and fathers alike – and describe them as their best friends or older siblings. They have daily conversations with their parents, sharing, asking for advice or simply providing them with updates.

Young people are very proud of their 'pet parents' and often discuss their parents with one another ('my dad did that', 'my mom likes that'). Usually, parents are not criticized, but rather function as close friends. This is also declared publicly on Facebook.

Parents also perceive and boast about their relationships with their kids as a friendship of sorts and they take pride in it. This forms a new type of friendship for mutual outings and trips. The parents provide the funding and their kids provide companionship.

The blurred line between parenthood and friendship in this age has received a special term: Peerenting. This phenomenon can be attributed to several factors: the lack of distance (inspired by humane psychology and encouraged by the media); the legitimacy of staying young (particularly in Israel); the high divorce rate, creating a fraternity of suffering between parents and children; and the tense security situation, which makes it feel like every day could be your or your children's last. Millennials' immaturity and lack of independence also play a role in the background.

Pets for Pet Children

Pets are increasingly establishing their new social status as the typical Israeli youth's best friends. This is predominant in Tel Aviv – the city of youth, where dogs have become a substantial part of the urban landscape. It's nearly impossible to walk down the street without running into a dog walking on a leash, running beside their owners or a bicycle, lying next to them in cafés and bars, or patiently waiting outside stores.

The population in Tel Aviv has grown by some 10 per cent in the past two decades, while the population of dog owners has grown by over 300 per cent. We have no method for counting the number of house cats, but assume that the rate is similar.

There are approximately 40,000 stray cats in Tel Aviv today. They are mostly being taken care of by 'cat people', who feed them at regular hours, provide them with water and often even spay or neuter them, a service offered by the city for free. Some 5,000 of these 'cat people' are registered in city hall.

Meanwhile, the number of veterinary clinics in the city has grown from 6 to some 100 in the past two decades, and the number of pet stores has gone from 10 to 80. These stores don't just sell pet food now, they also sell different kinds of accessories and decorations. The number of dog grooming shops has also risen, and they offer a new variety of services. There are over 40 fenced dog parks across Tel Aviv – shaded spaces where dogs can run as they please, while their owners rest on a bench.

The presence of dogs is more observable than that of cats, as cats don't go on walks. However, polls conducted in the western world show that cats have surpassed dogs as the most popular pet, and the gap in favour of cats has continued to grow in the past decade. This might be tied to cats being more low-maintenance. Some claim the cat is a reflection of the new generation: self-indulgent, self-centred and prone to mood swings.

The affection for pets has also been prominent in international digital culture, fascinating young people in particular. Cats and dogs star on the internet with hundreds of thousands of presentations and videos shared from screen to screen. People upload photos of their pets and share funny and sweet videos that can even compete with photos of babies and children shared by parents.

What is it about pets that makes so many low-paid youngsters living in small apartments take on the responsibility of raising them? The answer becomes obvious when considering that this is a self-centred generation who's not rushing to settle down. The phenomenon has several explanations:

Yuppie Upbringing. Millennials were raised in Yuppie families where both parents dedicated much of their time to their careers and the children spent many hours at home alone. These families tend to adopt dogs that can serve as companions for the children and provide them with a sense of security. Millennials have grown used to having a pet around, and they maintain this pattern when moving out to live on their own.

Sense of Familial Stability. Pets also provide a soothing break from a hectic schedule. Even workaholics have to come home sooner or later to feed their dog or cat. This creates a routine in a chaotic world, and the daily ritual of taking care of a pet relates to the feeling of order and stability – often even more than relationships with other humans.

Four-legged Friend in the Big City. In a competitive world that holds individualism very highly, pets help make up for this cold, alienating feeling. Since single life in the city is becoming longer and more common, the role of pets in this generation has become more substantial and they've become an important partner in life. Furthermore, in a world of mistrust and betrayal, loyalty, predominantly among dogs, is an important anchor.

Efficient Tool for Dating. Dogs are tools for social interaction and dating: many dog owners meet new people during their daily walks in the neighbourhood or park. These are usually short, one-off encounters, but there have been many reports of casual conversations between dog owners that developed into romantic relationships.

The Humane Aspect. Animal rights awareness has expanded in recent years, and many consider raising a pet – particularly one saved from the pound or from the street – as a type of ideological and political statement. An affinity for pets displays sensitivity for rights and humanity, as well as environmental sensitivity.

Playmates. Millennials also love pets because they love playing and fooling around. Many play with their pets at home, in parks and even at the café, restaurant and workplace. It has become so common that more and more workplaces allow employees to bring their dogs, and many restaurants and cafés in Tel Aviv have become 'animal friendly'.

Dogs as Practice Babies. Pets often provide a (usually temporary) substitute for a child. This creates an interesting new pattern, in which a young couple who are moving in together establish their relationship by buying or adopting a pet together. The new tenant helps them create a shared identity and independence and review their teamwork before going for the 'real thing'. This cat or dog is sometimes used as an excuse to postpone the birth of an actual child.

Tel Aviv Attraction

Youth Capital

Since its foundation over a century ago, Tel Aviv has gradually evolved according to global, national and internal trends. However, the municipal breakthrough that is turning the city into what experts refer to as an emerging 'world city' has only started at the dawn of the twenty-first century. This accelerated change started when the Israeli market was opened up to the world, and Israel embraced an entrepreneurial market economy. Tel Aviv stood at the forefront of this change, practically leading it. This change was so fast and dramatic, that it seems Tel Aviv is leaving other cities in Israel behind, leading to its nickname, 'State of Tel Aviv', used fondly by some and derogatively by others.

Tel Aviv has always been a party town, though not nearly close to the reputation of recent years. The city has regulated the process of getting a business licence, simplified bureaucratic procedures and encouraged entrepreneurs, designers and chefs to start up new businesses. Commercial zones have been expanded and a map was drawn to mark areas where businesses can be opened at night. Tel Aviv has gradually turned into a metropolis with a young, cosmopolitan chic.

The growing Israeli market has created a new real estate culture, with Tel Aviv at the centre. Contractors, renovators, realtors and speculators have all recognized the potential of real estate, and abandoned homes and apartments have been bought, renovated and turned into attractive rental properties. Gray commercial centres, low-priced streets and crumbling neighbourhoods have turned into real estate investments, gradually changing their appearance. Meanwhile, a process of gentrification emerged: the old people left, replaced by young people. Youngsters who spent long months in the Far East, South America, Europe and the United States, have brought new ideas home and founded hundreds of world-class cafés, bars and restaurants. Israel has also given birth to a generation of architects and designers, who have imported materials and perceptions and implemented them in the growing Tel Aviv bubble.

Tel Aviv is definitely the capital of Israeli millennials, and this generation contributes more to its unique nature than any other age group. Some live in it (mostly in rented apartments), while others arrive there every day to work, study, meet friends and hang out.

According to the Central Bureau of Statistics, as of 2011, the young population (ages 20-44 – Generation Y and Generation XY) in Tel Aviv constitutes approximately half of the population. In fact, the number of youngsters living in the city is far higher than the official data, since most of them are renting apartments and still registered as residents of a different town on the population registry, mostly where their parents live. According to Tel Aviv Municipality data, every third resident in the city is 18-35 years old – overall some 140,000 young residents.

As for its urban character and dominant lifestyle, young people's influence in Tel Aviv far outgrows their numbers. This is because most club-goers, pedestrians and café, restaurant and bar dwellers (including the waiters) are young. They are also a majority in neighbourhoods located at the heart of commercial centres, as they prefer to rent apartments close to these centres. Many also work in the area as service providers. Youngsters are also a majority in the fields of hi-tech, art, media and entertainment, which are concentrated in Tel Aviv and its environs.

Living in the Tel Aviv area has become a stage in the lives of many youngsters, similar to the big trip to the Far East or South America. How and why has Tel Aviv become the capital of young people in Israel? There are a number of milestones and reasons:

Big City Myth. The New York metropolis, emulated by many cities, has become an international myth thanks to popular television shows centred on groups of young people. Youngsters from all around the world, including Israelis, are attracted to the big city because they also live this myth. Israeli series such as *Florentine, Traffic Light* or *Naor's Friends* have turned this international experience into something more local and another part of this is due to the fact that it enhances the 'big city' attraction in Israel.

If I can Make it There, I'll Make it Anywhere. The media has always loved Tel Aviv's charm, and most of the people working in the media either live in Tel Aviv or in the vicinity. The Tel Aviv myth has been developed and enhanced in various local newspapers, entertainment magazines, cinema and TV shows. Celebrity culture, which was also developed and leveraged by the printed press and online media, has fuelled the myth and charm of Tel Aviv. For young people around the world, living in a major metropolis is the key for fulfilling your global dreams. If you dream of becoming a successful artist, model, journalist or business owner, you need to live in the big city, which is at the centre of it all, meet people, make connections, see and be seen.

Not a Dull Moment. Millennials have become accustomed from an early age to strong, constantly-changing stimulation. They find life in the rural periphery boring. With all due respect to the view, nature and local businesses, young people need 'action', different experiences, and a busy, aesthetic and visual environment. That's why they're attracted to the big, rich city, where everything is dense, frenetic and ever-changing.

Places to Go, People to See. Leisure and dating culture is so developed among millennials that it requires having everything concentrated in one place. This is why many cities in Europe attract young people. For millennials, Tel Aviv is the only option in Israel, since that's where most of the music, restaurants, clubs and bars are.

Shopping Galore. Millennials are ultra-consumers who shop recreationally. Tel Aviv and its suburbs have the most stores and variety of products and brands in Israel, including boutiques, fashion stores and big malls. A considerable portion of stores and markets are dedicated to vintage and second-hand products, which youngsters are particularly fond of.

Open 24/7. One of Tel Aviv's advantages is the many convenience stores and neighbourhood mini-markets that operate around the clock. They hold great significance for youngsters who party all night and maintain more flexible study and work hours.

Urban Village. The white, modest and visually pleasing architecture, the intimate, vintage nature of the streets and houses, the friendly beach and the dense vegetation grant Tel Aviv a peaceful, rural nature. Many of the city's inhabitants are young people who returned from the big trip to the Far East and South America and didn't want the celebration of youth to stop. This unique combination between a major city and a rural atmosphere is also important to them due to their small apartments and the need to take out the dog.

Easy Mobility. In Tel Aviv – like other cities in Israel – there's currently no subway that allows people to travel from one side of town to the other quickly and efficiently. There's also no light rail above ground. Tel Aviv makes up for this absence with its size. It's big enough to be considered metropolitan and small enough to allow people to get around on bicycles, scooters and on foot. This is also aided by the multiple bike lanes and 'Tel-Ofan' bicycle rental service.

Big LGBT Community. Tel Aviv attracts thousands of young LGBTs who see it as a tolerant and embracing safe haven. The local LGBT community, which is reinforced by tourists from abroad, contributes to the city's young, vibrant and dynamic nature.

Loads of Temp Jobs. Tel Aviv is a national business centre and the scope of people working in it is large. The city is also home to several international corporations as well as hundreds of hi-tech companies. It also offers a variety of flexible temp jobs suitable for youngsters: waiting tables, babysitting, cleaning, deliveries, sales, investigative journalism and more.

Study and Party. Tel Aviv and its environs have the largest concentration of higher education institutes – Tel Aviv University, Kibbutzim College, Shenkar College, Beit Zvi School for the Performing Arts, Academic College of Tel Aviv-Yaffo and more. The advantage for young people lies beyond the convergence of institutes (which creates a student atmosphere) but also in their proximity to nightlife hotspots.

Urban Tribes

Young people have always loved spending time together and rubbing shoulders, but in the age of extended bachelorhood, this need has grown. The large-scale metropolis expands the potential for gatherings, alleviates loneliness by walking among big crowds and provides an alternative for family in the form of groups of friends. Tel Aviv is basically a city of young packs, living in urban fraternities, maintaining the backpacking atmosphere and experience to some extent.

This phenomenon of 'Urban Tribes' can be seen in most dynamic cities around the world. It bears dramatic significance in possibly foreshadowing the degeneration of the traditional family.

The interesting, weird and troubling aspect of this lifestyle is the fact that the way these young packs behave is somewhat similar to groups of vagrants. You see them riding around on bicycles, sitting in cafés, bars and parks. Walking the dog, meeting each other, hugging and kissing, mooch off each other or off their parents, buy, sell, borrow and lend. Their life in the urban bubble is played out one day at a time, from fling to fling, from party to party, from temp job to temporary unemployment, from rented apartments to sublets, burning their cash on cigarettes, beer and junk food as if there's no tomorrow. Their friendships are essentially the only anchor in their unstable lives.

Depletion of the Periphery

When they're single, young people rent apartments in the city or its outskirts (some 5,000 young people in ages 15-29 are added to Tel Aviv every year), and when they get married (and particularly after the birth of the first child), they move to communities adjacent to the major metropolitan areas, which offer lower cost of living and housing as well as high quality community services, but also allows them to work and spend time in the big urban environment (in the past decade, more and more couples choose to remain in the city after getting married and raise their children there).

The process of the populace converging in major metropolitans while the periphery thins out and withers is happening in most western countries nowadays. All of mankind is converging in major cities, and experts predict that by the mid-twenty-first century, three quarters of the world's population will live in them. In recent years, more and more parts of Europe have started to suffer from the symptoms of abandoned ghost towns, and according to the Central Bureau of Statistics, most peripheral cities in Israel are also losing their population in favour of cities in the centre, especially new cities or ones with extensive building plans.

Tel Aviv-Jaffa was the first municipality in Israel to draft a comprehensive policy regarding young people. Out of respect for young people who live in the city and shape it and as part of Tel Aviv's strategic plan, the city founded a youth unit, entrusted with promoting projects for the younger population within the municipality. The unit has been operating for only a few years, and already runs dozens of large-scale innovative projects.

New Social Network

Living Online

Facebook wouldn't have succeeded in the way that it has, especially among young people, had it not met a deep, human need and offered a social aspect that was missing from previous generations. Facebook allows you to always look your best, appear happy and post well-crafted comments. You can instantly share any experience with all of your friends, and you can always find someone who'll laugh with you, sympathize and support you. It seems as though the most basic need Facebook fills is the need to belong. On Facebook, you're always part of a group of friends, and the level of your relationship is not as important.

It is known that every new technological medium penetrates the younger populace first. Older people tend to be suspicious and hesitant and lag behind. Still, one has to wonder how it is that most social network users are under the age of 34. Why do older people shy away from using a social network that's so easy to use and offers such clear advantages? Why did the use of Facebook create such an outstanding generational gap – so much so that it has turned its use into one of the main characteristics and cultural brands of Generation Y? Here are some possible reasons:

The older generation tends to see Facebook as a hollow activity – a useless conversation and a total waste of time (many mistakenly assume that in the case of emails, for example, they are required to respond to every comment.) They also shy away from the medium due to the technological difficulty, which creates psychological inhibitions and the fear of showing oneself up in public. Posting on Facebook exposes the users to unpredictable and often even spiteful criticism. They prefer to write personal letters or settle debts behind the scenes.

Perhaps the thing that deters these 'geezers' the most is the way worlds are colliding. The digital social network creates an interesting social process with serious implications: it opens social circles and loosens traditional boundaries and barriers. All of a sudden, work and professional circles are merged with the family circle, as well as friends, leisure culture and more. This process feels more natural for millennials than it does for older generations.

However, as Facebook use has expanded in recent years, the age of social network users has consistently increased, so much that it drove waves of youngsters away from the network to the open arms of Twitter, Instagram or Tumblr, simply because they felt Facebook has become too 'old', though this phenomenon is more relevant to the US than to Israel.

Wide Range of Friendships

In the early days of social networks, there were some who claimed virtual friendships came at the expense of actual (face-to-face) friendships. Some went as far as claiming that communicating with the keyboard teaches people to have superficial, non-committal and even utilitarian and egotistical relationships. According to this argument, writing a supportive status or clicking 'like' are no substitute for a real hug and practical help for a friend in need (which usually also requires sacrifice).

In practice, virtual friendships do not contradict physical relationships, but rather co-exist – alternately online and in person. This actually creates a wider variety of social ties, with the face-to-face meeting being just one of them. One's Facebook friends vary from close friends to people they've never even met.

The ability to get constant updates about people's daily lives and sharing experiences, joys and grief with others creates a new kind of partnership, whether around a specific interest, such as support for a social initiative or sports fandom and sometimes around a wider idea.

Facebook has created a situation where youngsters (who are its heaviest users) are no longer chained to one group as they were in the days of youth movements. They have a diverse network of relationships with a variety of options. This is a vibrant world in which the word 'friend' can no longer sum up the range of a relationship. Sometimes, it's the people you only know casually who can offer a new perspective on a problem and provide opportunities you wouldn't normally get. These distant friends are also free of prejudice and feelings of jealousy and competitiveness that close friends often have.

And most importantly: with the social network you're never disengaged from the world and your ability to connect and communicate with new friends increases immeasurably.

Online Support

Israelis aren't known for their capacity to offer genuine compliments. We are, however, experts of criticism and gloating. The aggressive discourse and the joy of gossip can be found in the virtual space as well, but at the same time, there's an interesting transformation in Israeli discourse culture that has left a considerable impression on the world of youngsters: Israelis have started being genuinely happy for one another, and they bless almost as loudly as they curse. Everybody's a sweet-talker now, dishing out compliments and gushing praise.

The 'like' button definitely represents Facebook's supportive climate more than any other button. It sends a short, concise message of sympathy and approval. If smileys were a pleasant convention that mostly marked the end of a conversation in emails and text messages, Facebook's Like button expresses an entire cultural code.

The number of likes a post gets is indicative of the user's popularity, creating a feeling of satisfaction in a game with addictive elements. It also creates a 'quid pro quo' mentality, where if I like your post, I expect you to return the favour.

The rules of Facebook essentially translate American and European communication rules, according to which compliments are offered in public and criticism is voiced in private. Voicing negative feedback publicly is considered rude and even offensive. The social network also generates strong peer pressure. When many people write positive comments, it also affects those who are usually not prone to dish out praise. The online discourse's availability and shareability allow people to generously give out compliments and encourage everyone to join in.

Youngsters have grown used to compliments, and some argue they've even become addicted. Generally speaking, millennials tend to produce a friendly environment (be 'positive') and push all negativity away. That's why they shower each other with greetings and praise. This phenomenon has great beauty, though in many cases it originates from a herd instinct, shallowness and hypocrisy. There's also a certain amount of self-glorification, as they compete over who's the most generous and supportive.

Out in the Open

Facebook is a stage and a giant mechanism for attracting mutual attention, perhaps mostly because it allows people to expose themselves emotionally and make public confessions of unprecedented magnitude. To some extent, Facebook posts are akin to reality TV, reinforcing the media psychologism that has transformed into mass psychosis. In fact, our personal lives have become public domain practically without us noticing, and intimacy is displayed in every street corner with our full consent.

As mentioned, youngsters are less inhibited, which makes it easier for them to quickly fit in with this environment. They tend to encourage one another to share distresses and intimate details about their lives, and always offer empathy and a shoulder to cry on. They appreciate openness and honestly and express empathy towards the person opening up to them, exposing his or her weaknesses and woes.

It is a generation that grew up on the New Age culture, which encourages 'opening' and 'release'. Young people have no problem discussing issues that were once considered taboo, fully-knowing their friends would respond to it respectfully. The sharing of emotion can be attributed to the effects of psychology, media and human education that reigned during their upbringing, as well as their inert insecurity and immaturity, and their constant need for support on every matter.

Sharing intimate experiences on Facebook has another aspect. It's not just about reporting after an experience. It is about making your Facebook friends full, active partners in real time. For example, many write love letters to their spouses on their walls. They're written in second person (i.e. addressed to a person's spouse) but are actually intended for all to see. In many cases, the post includes intimate details that one would normally only share with his or her partner. Through this post, they turn their friends into spectators – bringing them closer into an intimate situation.

Flexible Friendship

Millennials live a dynamic, highly mobile life. This also projects on the way they bond with one another and disengage as quickly and as easily. They actually never cut off ties completely but rather put them on the 'backburner' or simply on hold. This is done so they can keep the option of tightening the relationship, as well as because they know today's world is small and you can never really cut someone off completely.

Facebook serves as an 'amplifier' of sorts, which allows one to control the volume of the relationship. On one hand it allows you to rekindle relationships from the past (school, army, college etc.) while on the other hand it allows you to minimize the relationship with the Ignore, Hide and Unfriend functions. Some claim that the fact Facebook allows you to remove friends with the click of a button naturally contributes to the creation of a selfish society that sees everything, including emotions, as disposable products. On the other hand, most millennials agree that unfriending someone on Facebook is a rather aggressive step – an unnecessary declaration of war. Since their relationships are flexible and superficial, and because they prefer to avoid confrontation, they usually opt not to unfriend even the most obnoxious people.

WhatsApp

WhatsApp began as a genial app for unlimited free texting, but the group chat feature has turned it into the fastest growing alternative social network of recent years. WhatsApp's group chat function is used by groups of friends, families, school and college students, work colleagues and more.

The app is slightly similar to sharing on social networks, only here you know exactly who's being exposed to the content you're sharing, and the chances of it leaking and ending up in the wrong hands is as low as the chance of an email sent to a few recipients becoming a viral post. WhatsApp is also completely ad-free and easy to use.

As in the case of Facebook, the first to adopt the app were young people. Many took parts of their activities in the social network to WhatsApp and a great deal more use both tools simultaneously. They actually complement each other: WhatsApp is used more for personal (as well as discrete) updates and relationships around the clock while Facebook is used more as a stage for expressing one's opinions publicly and conveying more complex information.

WhatsApp groups can be divided into the following categories: ad hoc groups – created for a specific purpose like bachelor parties or joint trips. This allows a group of people who don't know each other to coordinate without having to call everyone in person; functional groups, such as university study groups or parent groups for their children's after-school classes, enabling a pick-up or carpool; professional work groups, for organizing and sharing issues concerning work; regular friend groups – everyone has a number of groups for their various social circles; family groups – here too, everyone has several groups, divided by a certain hierarchy, like the nuclear family group, cousins group, extended family group etc.

For many youngsters, WhatsApp has not only replaced emails and Facebook posts, but also actual conversations. They often have over twenty groups and one can assume there's a reverse correlation between the number of groups and the age of users. This online friendship comes at a price. The quality of a face-to-face meeting declines when there are constant distractions from online friends in the background, who from time to time might write something that requires an immediate response.

The ease of use and multiple groups have taken the culture of mutual updates to the next level, and the fear of missing out has become more irksome than ever. 'I don't know whether I love or hate WhatsApp groups', one interviewee told us. 'I can't live with them – they're a time-consuming hassle, but I also can't live without them –they're very useful, and sometimes amusing. I'd probably never shut them off because I'd be afraid something is going on that I'm not a part of. I don't want to be left out of the loop, so I actually have no choice...'

It should be noted that WhatsApp is also used for one-to-one communication, not just for group chats. This app has replaced SMS to a large extent thanks to two clear advantages: first, it's free – the app is internet-based, enabling you to send unlimited messages (this feature is crucial when friends travel abroad and want to communicate with one another or keep in touch with their friends in Israel). The second advantage is real time information – on WhatsApp you can know whether a friend is 'online' or 'Typing' (i.e. responding to the message and not ignoring it) at any given time and in real time. You can also know when was the last time your friend was 'online' and deduce whether they chose to ignore the message. Supposedly, this is a violation of one's privacy, but through the millennial glasses, transparency and constant trackability are an obvious plus.

Community on the Horizon

Plague of Loneliness

Some claim loneliness is the deadliest plague of the twenty-first century, in spite of social networks and perhaps because of them. They help people connect but create shallow, less meaningful social connections.

According to a study, 40 per cent of Americans declared they were lonely, twice as many as 35 years ago. 16 per cent of Australians reported feeling lonely, the loneliest of which being under the age of 30. In New Zealand, 40 per cent of youngsters (ages 15-29) feel lonely, more than any other age group. 60 per cent of young British people (ages 18-34) feel lonely.

The 'urban tribes' don't provide a full response for the city's shortcomings, and in many cases just manage to sweeten the bitter pill of loneliness, alienation and financial insecurity.

Is the individualistic lifestyle about to completely take over our lives and push the community to the curve? Is this what millennials are going to face when they are old? Not necessarily. Something new is on the horizon, and it's reflected in many surprising ways.

The New Kibbutz

Although the privatization of kibbutzim is still in full swing, researchers have recently described an opposite trend. Communities that have completed the process are now asking: what's next? As it seems, at the end of the movement's successful struggle to liberate the individual and family, the desire for fresh models of communal life is actually growing stronger.

In the past few years there has been a constant increase in the number of people from the outside seeking to become kibbutz members. The demand for living in expansion neighbourhoods in many kibbutzim is soaring (mostly in the centre). The applicants are usually people who have come to the conclusion that they would rather live in a community. At least some of these young people are joining not just out of comfort, but rather because this way of living truly interests them, on a moral level.

Kibbutz members who spent many years in the city are rediscovering its advantages and returning home. They don't want to live by the old model, in which the community encircled all fields of life and smothered the individual, but rather create a corrective experience and an improved model that combines socialism, community and personal liberties. This could lead to social reform for Israeli society as a whole.

Sharing Communities and Co-op Revival

The rise of dozens of sharing communities, spanning a variety of ideologies and lifestyles, is another expression of the increasing yearning in Israel for 'togetherness'. From old-timey vintage communes through neighbourhood communities and student and youth movement graduate communities, to purchase groups that create a safe space for themselves. All of these frameworks strive to achieve balance between 'togetherness' and 'individuality', creating a life of spiritual and altruistic meaning. All of these communities create mechanisms of mutual support and aid (all of which are voluntary) as well as platforms of leisure that create a shared experience: singing, conversation, sports, hiking, dancing and studying. Even allegedly small phenomena such as parent communities (education associations), neighbourhood communities or community gardens in urban neighbourhoods (neighbours from different backgrounds meet while working the land) reflect this trend.

Following the collapse of the co-operative concept in the 1970s and 80s, there has been a gradual awakening. In the past four decades, the number of co-ops has grown by 50 per cent around the world and the number of unionized members has more than tripled. Israel is still very far from the global co-operative movement, but the awakening is already felt in many fields.

In recent years, co-ops have gained popularity (mostly among youngsters), dealing in a variety of arenas – from health and welfare through food to art and entertainment businesses. They are formed in an attempt to deal with the high cost of living and reduce mediation gaps as well as due to financial (business partnerships), social (being together) and ideological (justice and fairness in marketing and profits) motives.

The digital world holds great potential for promoting the communal code, thanks to the development of social networks and apps that allow people to join forces (e.g. carpooling), help one another (e.g. job searches) and exchange useful information. It is likely that this trend, which essentially combines digital technology, millennials' sharing orientation and the yearning for a sense of community and mutual aid, will only grow stronger.

Back to Sanity

Are we on the verge of a post-individualistic age? It is perhaps too soon to tell, but it seems many youngsters are looking for a calmer, saner existence that also involves mutual responsibility.

The high cost of living and real estate prices require a new way of thinking. People understand it's better to work together in order to survive. Many are frustrated by life in Israel, both practically as well as emotionally. They've experienced layoffs, divorce, the death of relatives and the rat race in a cold world and have not found solace in some great ideal. Exhaustion and boredom systematically ruin any chance of excitement. The naivety of Zionism is dying, leaving a big vacuum.

Since the age of leadership is about to die out, there's no father figure or figures for people to look up to. It's every man for himself and the burden is heavy.

Life expectancy is rising and young people are realizing that they will face exile in their twilight years. They see what's happening to their grandparents and it scares them. They want to grow old in a community rather than be tossed away like a useless object.

But above all, millennials are living on shaky ground: they have no steady job, no stable income and many also don't have long-lasting anchors like intimate relationships or family. They depend on their parents and know this can't go on forever. Therefore, it is natural for them to want to look for mutual support. Many have already created support groups, and they wish to expand and deepen them.

Furthermore, this generation is unable to find meaning in work but rather in leisure. They don't want to be slaves to their bosses, like their parents, or eternally enslaved to the job. They want to breathe. They want to be together, hang out together, drink together. Therefore, it's only natural for them to gradually build their own custom-made community frameworks.

9

Youngsters in Pink – Flexible Femininity and Masculinity

Fluid Gender Roles

Signs of a change in gender conventions, and particularly in the model for masculinity, started to appear with the flower children of the 1960s, when rock 'n' rollers started letting their hair grow long, shake their booty and sing in falsetto, while the women picked up guitars and started taking birth control pills. The Yuppies of the 1980s (Generation X, parents of Generation Y) took this change one step further. This is reflected among other things in the countless television shows that millennials were exposed to throughout their adolescent years. They presented the model of a sensitive man who isn't afraid to talk about his weaknesses and troubles next to a more assertive, liberated and independent woman.

Therefore, it was no surprise that the differences between the 'weak sex' and the 'strong sex' faded even further among millennials, but few predicted just how far it would go and what kind of sociological implications it would have.

It's not that the old masculinity, and even male chauvinism have become a thing of the past. Not at all. Men still talk about getting laid, watch sports and enjoy graphic pornography with a domineering nature. However, patterns that used to be considered 'feminine' – such as colourful clothing, dyed hair, crying, physical closeness and words of affection among men, admitting weakness and asking for help – have become common among today's tough guys. The range of behaviours has expanded, ranging from the old-fashioned rugged men to the new breed of sensitive men. Most men, as usual, are somewhere in the middle, but the trend generally tends to the softer side of the scale.

Likewise, the basic feminine model still exists among young women, but patterns that were once considered 'masculine' – such as tattoos, piercings, motorcycles, beer, cursing and sexual initiative – have become common among young women these days. This trend may affect all age groups in the secular population, but it is far more dominant among the younger generation. This comes into play even in the slightest nuances of body language and talking style.

Why is Generation Y narrowing gender gaps? We propose several reasons for this phenomenon:

Price of Rugged Masculinity. From an early age, millennials have been exposed to the psychological message that the model of a tough, rugged man may entail a personal and social price, since it leads to ego-driven conflicts, over-competitiveness and sometimes even violence. Many men are also unable or unwilling to embrace this extreme model, and have a natural tendency for softened masculinity.

Rise of the Nerds. The touchy-feely upbringing, which delayed their maturity and created a 'nerdy' code of behaviour, has helped soften gender roles. Boys were simply taught to be less 'husbandy' and girls were taught to be less 'motherly'. The nerd is a post-male figure because he does not need the physical strength of the man of old (the hunter-warrior) to survive in the competitive world. He can get control and money using only his wits (hi-tech).

The Metrosexual Man. Softened masculinity, which led by the Yuppie model, brought forth a prototype model called the 'metrosexual'. The metrosexual is an urban man with a disposable income who's meticulous about his grooming and appearance: muscle toning at the gym, massages, facials, hair removal and hair transplants, manicure and pedicure and fashionable clothing. Millennials have been widely affected by the metrosexual model, due to its wide prevalence in the media and their tendency to live in urban centres.

In Touch with their Emotions. Some cite the rise of New Age culture as an influence on the primal male instinct. Under the New Age culture, young men have learned to be more open and sensitive, or, essentially, more feminine.

A Matter of Hormones. Some take it one step further and offer a biological explanation for the narrowing gender roles phenomenon. In their perception, the root cause lies in Generation Y's mothers, who consumed foods and medicine with high levels of oestrogen, resulting in boys with a feminine appearance and behaviour.

The medical world has indeed found a sharp decline in testosterone levels in recent years. However, scientists don't attribute the change to mothers but rather to the evolution of the human race. Since men are no longer required to fight for their existence on an everyday basis as they did in the past, they tend to produce less testosterone. On the other hand, there has also been a decline in oestrogen levels, which is attributed to women's growing independence and their entrance to the male-dominated employment world.

Evolution on the Aegis of Technology. There are some who claim that as the focal points of human activity move from the physical to the virtual; as the battlefields, commerce and games are relocated into computer environments; and as science and technology succeed in perfecting automatic alternatives to physical labour, the global and western human body is becoming more durable, more efficient and more good-looking, but also less manly to some extent. The technological revolution that provides direct access to information while cutting out the authoritative middlemen (politicians, religious leaders etc.) undermines traditional male power, making it essentially redundant.

The old model of management was based on hierarchical thinking, control and obedience, and it was only natural that men were the ones who served in managerial roles. However, in the new age, the keywords of leaderships are cooperation and attentiveness, which are more feminine traits. And indeed, although men still have a majority in most power centres, there is a consistent trend towards change in favour of women.

The younger the age group, the more women are taking the reins of leadership away from men. The change is noticeable mostly in middle management of organizations and commercial companies, while some even have a female majority. Young women have proven to be more efficient and responsible than men, therefore management tend to let them take the steering wheel more and more.

Wanted: A Manly Man

Much in the same way that they manage to get in touch with their feminine side, millennial men have also managed to overcome or at least tone down the difficulties of the 'old style man'. The problem is that drifting away from the macho model generates new problems.

While women are gaining power, men are becoming 'weaker' – particularly when it comes to millennials. They are less motivated to rule, lead and win the race, and tend to display a sense of helplessness that wasn't typical among previous generations. We've already discussed the weakened mental strength that characterizes this generation, a phenomenon that is possibly more noticeable and significant among men. If manliness means making decisions, taking responsibility and leading, there's no wonder that immature millennial men are having trouble integrating into the world of adults, making them 'pussies', in street terms.

This phenomenon has become so prominent in this generation, leading to a stream of books that mourn 'the downfall of manhood' in the United States. A 2010 article in *The Atlantic*, titled 'The End of Men' by Hanna Rosin, reviewed the change that occurred in the past century in the world of western economics, which has turned women into the largest group in the American work force, as the unemployment rate among men rises, while the average income of young men drops. Women have also surpassed men in academic graduation rates.

The subject of weakened men has come up more than once in our interviews, particularly among millennial women. They described impotent men who can't even change a light bulb. They may be softer than their fathers and proficient in what used to be considered feminine skills, but they struggle to serve as a stable anchor. This has led to the creation of websites that offer men advice on how to perform everyday functions: from instructions for the perfect shave to proper behaviour in a new relationship with a woman who has children.

What are the repercussions of the change in gender roles, as reflected in Generation Y? It's hard to tell. Some researchers claim that the necessary synergetic balance between femininity and masculinity has been breached. They claim that the weakened feminine man has upset the balance of the family unit, and is one of the causes for its ongoing erosion. Today's man is no longer able to provide for his family, while the woman also struggles with juggling work and motherhood.

Even if that's true, the means may justify the end: an end to wars. If men are so feminine, it's likely that their motivation to conquer and kill will also diminish. That may be another reason why this generation isn't too interested in politics or in the army. In short, the deal is this: less violence, compulsiveness, subjugation, crime and wars in the world and more empathy and emotional discourse.

Mild and Smiling Post-Feminism

It's not just women who miss the macho age but also some of the men, resulting in the creation of 'retro gender roles' with a tongue-in-cheek vibe. Men can still be manly and women can be feminine, to some extent, while feeling at peace with their gender. Ideologically speaking, they understand that biological differences should not be translated into social inequality. Moreover, biological diversity enriched humankind. The new approach, which is common among many millennials, is that you can and should have equal resources (wages, social status, power, education etc.) and still recognize the fact that men and women have different biological characteristics (such as in John Gray's popular book *Men are from Mars, Women are from Venus*).

'Retro gender roles' can be implemented since the younger generation has already been brought up in a feminist age and accepted gender equality as a complete social fact (not that the gaps have been completely closed, but the principle has become sacred). Therefore they don't have the urge to be extrovert about their feminism at any cost. They take it for granted and don't require any proof. They have no problem with male bonding, where you curse, fantasize about blonde women and worship soccer stars. The same thing happens on the female side. They too feel like they can dress well, wear makeup, remove unwanted body hair – in short, work on their 'sex appeal' and still be 'kosher' feminists.

'Retro gender roles' also come into play with the new legitimacy for mocking uncompromising feminism and for using broad generalizations and old stereotypes about men and women. This generation is more ironic and sarcastic than its predecessors, which is why millennials can also laugh about moral conventions that were wrapped in a thin veil of political correctness. This approach basically says, let's not be too prudent and let's not emasculate ourselves in the name of unrealistic ideals.

Millennials Come out of the Closet

In the formative stage of the State of Israel, Israeli society was puritanical with limited sexual awareness and tolerance. Even masturbation was considered filthy. Back then, members of the LGBT community were invisible to their immediate environment and lacked a sense of individual or group consciousness. Many had a hard time coping with being different, repressed their sexual orientation and identity and felt guilty. Public disregard for homosexuality was also rooted in the prevailing and utterly false view at the time that this was an esoteric and marginal phenomenon with no significant demographic presence.

The media also silenced the phenomenon and only mentioned gays sparingly (usually as faceless and nameless figures) and almost always in the context of crime and delinquency. The stereotypical homosexual was described in the media as well as in court rulings as a pervert who sexually abuses the weak, harasses helpless minors and has his way with them in the dark. In short an abnormal, dangerous person who subverts the foundations of social order. Most LGBT people in Israel lived at the time in social and sexual solitude and in fear, forced to meet each other in secrecy.

In the late 1970s and early 80s, internal tension in Israeli society grew, expanding the rift between left and right and between religious and secular. Meanwhile, the media became more critical and aggressive (mostly due to the shock of the Yom Kippur War), preparing the ground for gender protest and for a hesitant yet more organized coming out of the LGBT closet.

The late 1980s opened a new era for the LGBT community in Israel, with the founding of Klaf – Feminist Lesbian Community, and the publication of the first issue of monthly magazine *Magaim*. However, the pinnacle of change was the annulment of the section of the penal code that prohibits homosexual intercourse.

Sexual discourse in general became more legitimate at the time due to the influence of the global sexual revolution, and phenomena that were once considered taboo – such as masturbation, orgasm or erectile dysfunction – were openly discussed. The legitimacy for criticism and development of political protest culture (emergence of the social left) helped soften the attitude towards homosexuality (mostly in the media, academia and the arts) and paved the way for more and more assertive claims for gender equality of all kinds. The feminist revolution also had a substantial contribution in this process.

The early 1990s gave way to a stream of new laws and regulations regarding civil rights in general and LGBT rights in particular, changing the status quo and slowly legitimizing the phenomenon. One by one, LGBT students started organizing in universities and in 1996 the Geot Forum was founded within the political party Meretz, which led the process of change in the political arena.

Tel Aviv, the most vibrant and pluralistic city in Israel, has always been considered the natural meeting place for LGBT people. However, it only established an official, organized gay culture in the mid-90s, including services for the community as well as in entertainment and leisure. The gospel from Tel Aviv gradually flowed to other places across Israel and support organizations were formed one after the other in Haifa, Jerusalem and other cities.

The early 2000s gave way to a 'judicial production line' of laws, court rulings, provisions and procedures that have expanded LGBT rights (in regards to labour, finance, personal and marital status, social rights etc.), making Israel a relatively LGBT-friendly place, from a legal viewpoint.

When gay people started appearing on talk shows during the 90s, they were usually portrayed as the 'other', the different, intriguing guest. However, nowadays their image in the media has been 'normalized'. What seemed like a fantasy only a decade ago – LGBT people becoming popular megastars – has become reality.

Secular media has become so confident of its positive attitude towards gays and lesbians, that it even allows itself to take jabs at them and laugh at their expense (mostly in satire shows and stand-up). In the past, jokes about gays had a layer of hostility and loathing while today they express empathy and acceptance (according to the sociological principle that laughing at someone means that they're included).

It should be noted that media representation of LGBT people is still plagued with considerable stereotyping and the common tendency is to treat them according to what sociology calls a 'master (overshadow) status' (a person is gay or lesbian first and only a regular human being with a variety of attributes and qualities second). Meanwhile, the tail wind from secular media, academia, the courts and the art world reinforce the status of the LGBT community and diminishes prejudice. More and more members of the gay community can live full lives out in the open, even beyond their immediate surroundings, and an increasing percentage of them are surrounded by feelings of love and acceptance in their immediate social environment at the very least. The number of LGBT married couples is also growing, even outside of Tel Aviv, and many children are brought up in a world where it's natural to have two moms or two dads.

The day when LGBT advocacy groups could finally be dismantled as their members become integrated in all groups of Israeli society (most ultra-Orthodox and Arab LGBT people are still forced to live a lie) is still far from our reach. Millennial LGBT people, though, are born and raised in a different reality than their predecessors. Most of them did not experience the dark ages of Israeli society (they were only children during the intermediate period), therefore the process of shaping their gender identity and sexual orientation was naturally different than previous generations.

The formative age in which a person's sexual orientation (including the age of coming out of the closet) has decreased over the years, thanks to television among other things. For example, *Queer as Folk,* an American-Canadian series which ran for five seasons and was also broadcast in Israel in the early 2000s, has had a deep impact on many. A great number of millennials were raised on a gay series, with gay characters, gay terminology, gay situations and, above all, they watched the show with their family and friends, who were also exposed to these ideas/characters/situations, so they could know what their gay friend or relative was going through.

Most media outlets nowadays have no qualms with dealing with LGBT issues, under the general discussion of relationships, gender, sexuality and civil rights. The change in the media also comes into play in the status of LGBT celebrities. Most celebrity gays and lesbians from previous generations came out of the closet at a later age, often after the media basically forced them to declare their sexuality out in the open. Most of them were also careful about promoting LGBT agendas and preferred to keep their personal relationships away from the limelight. Meanwhile, millennial LGBT celebrities aren't just comfortable with announcing their sexual orientation, many actually wear it proudly.

The internet has also played a particularly crucial part in the world of LGBT millennials. The web alleviates adolescent misgivings and saves many from loneliness and estrangement. If once LGBT people only had limited access to information about their kind, today there are countless websites with information and discussions relating to their world. The web also provides practical advice on relevant fields in their lives – from support programmes to sexual information – as well as information about youth organizations, meetings and events for the community across the country.

It should be noted that despite this tremendous progress, there are also difficult coming out processes and personal and social redemption is still ahead of us. It is likely that most LGBT people who are completely out of the closet these days come from a higher education and economic background and most are also secular. In contrast, LGBT people from lower socio-economic backgrounds and traditional homes have fewer social resources and perhaps are less confident about revealing their LGBT identity to their surroundings. Furthermore, the tough reality of a tormented gay person is not as familiar to most of the general public and gets less representation in the media.

The moment of coming out of the closest is something that LGBT people and their families will never forget. For some, this is a moment of release on the road for being accepted and accepting one's self, while for many others this is a seminal trauma that opens up a chasm between them and their parents, leading to exclusion and disownment. Nonetheless, polls conducted in recent years show that the situation is improving – the number of parents who support their LGBT children grows every year (mothers tend to be more open than fathers). Educated parents also fear they will be looked down upon as 'primitive', therefore they demonstrate a more supportive approach, at least on the outside.

The characteristically warm and friendly relationship between millennials and their parents, and the tendency of many parents to protect their children in any situation, obviously also push things in this direction.

From Grindr to Tinder

In the past, legal limitations and stigma forced gay people in Israel to meet on the outskirts, in dark places, behind trees and bushes, in apartment building staircases and abandoned rooftops, just for the sake of sexual contact. Everything was done in haste and out of anxiety and dread. Many even avoided revealing any information that could identify them and would usually flee the scene immediately after, out of fear of being betrayed (as they were considered to be criminals).

The parks culture reflected an age of exclusion and disrespect for LGBT people and their sexual needs. Most young LGBT people nowadays are not familiar with the park as a concept and place, because more comfortable and legitimate alternatives have been created during their lifetimes.

The internet's expansion in the late 1990s opened a new era for LGBT culture. It allows everyone to communicate with others anonymously in a manner that's not as awkward or dangerous.

The digital revolution of LGBT life in Israel was led by the Atraf Dating website, launched in early 2002. The website was originally an online entertainment magazine, providing updates on parties and concerts across Israel as well as photographs from selected events. It consequently developed into a rich social site with many mini-sites: Atraf Layla (a party, concert and nightlife index), Atraf Blogs and, above all, Atraf Dating. Since its launch, Atraf has become the only medium through which Israeli LGBT people communicate for dating, friends or sex. As of 2014, over 400,000 surfers were registered at the website, mostly LGBT, and thousands were online at any given moment.

The recent decade has seen the rise of location-based apps that allow smartphone owners to meet other users based on their geographical location (the world's most popular and well-known of these apps is Grindr), thus upgrading the virtual ability of finding a partner for casual sex. All you need to do is randomly walk down the street and the smartphone will notify you when a potential partner is found nearby.

Fast-paced encounters are very suitable for millennials who are known to be impatient, prone to immediacy and prefer instant gratification. Therefore, it's no wonder that the immense popularity of the digital medium is raising concern among some of the community's activists – particularly the older ones. They believe that addiction to the digital medium leads to superficial interpersonal relations (sorting people according to limited, external criteria). In their view, it also reduces the need to go out and consume culture outside of the home, thus hindering the community's social development.

All of our LGBT interviewees have agreed that this has created a 'meat market' and an alienated 'production line', which turns sex into a superficial thing and makes it hard to achieve a meaningful human connection, but at the same time all of them also agreed that this is a legitimate activity that should not be forfeited. In this sense, LGBT millennials are no different from straight millennials, perhaps simply radicalizing the phenomenon of mechanical, hedonistic sex that separates intimacy and emotion from sexuality. The one-night stand has become the name of the game in the sexual culture of the twenty-first century, due to new cultural codes as well as due to the effect digitization has had on our lives.

In this sense, LGBT sex culture is perhaps a type of social avant garde that leads the entire secular camp. No wonder that nowadays there is also an app called Tinder which is based on the same principal of Grindr, except it's also open to straight people.

Young Symbiosis between Straights and Gays

Studies conducted in recent years in the world (mostly the UK and US) on the relationship between straight and LGBT youths indicate a considerable, possibly dramatic improvement in the level of tolerance. A comprehensive study that investigates the relationship between young straight and gay millennials has not been conducted yet, though the findings of a research report by Hoshen (the gay community's tolerance education centre in Israel) give room for optimism.

Obviously, straight Israeli millennials are more open to the phenomenon of LGBT, accepting it more naturally than any previous generation. In all of our interviews, polls and focus groups, we haven't encountered one negative opinion about LGBT people. Most of them were indifferent to any sexual preference, stating that everyone has the right to 'do what they feel like'. This worldview matches up with the general tolerant attitude among today's secular youths – 'stay out of my business and I'll stay out of yours'.

Straight millennials' relative tolerance for the LGBT phenomenon is connected to their open attitude towards sex. This pluralism in which they grew up and which shaped their worldviews softens dichotomous perceptions, giving way to intermediate models. For example, if anal sex was once attributed mostly to gay people, today it is also a legitimate alternative in the straight world, even one that's recommended by sex therapists. Even threesomes aren't that rare anymore – many people have sexual experiences that aren't considered to be strictly heterosexual without having to define them that way, and the grey 'middle ground' is legitimized and expanded. It should be indicated that scientific research is very beneficial in softening gender dichotomy, supporting the notion of 'sexual fluidity' among both men and women through new findings, which are subverting deeply-rooted social conventions. Scientific literature that deals with the nature of sexual identities or sexual orientation claims that there are many more subgroups of sexual orientation than we have grown to believe. In fact, today it's more common to place sexual orientation on a spectrum rather than on two dichotomous opposites: straight or LGBT. All that reinforced the sexual pluralism of the Y generation.

The fact that many millennials have been exposed to sex from a young age (mainly on the internet) also helps soften prejudice about various expressions of sex. Almost every pornography site has an LGBT sex category, and that sends the message that we're all living today in the same world. Or more precisely at the same party.

Another reason for straight millennials' empathy towards their LGBT counterparts is the fact that more of their contemporaries are coming out of the closet. Empirical research shows that the level of homophobia is in negative correlation with one's knowledge of LGBT people around them. The more gay friends straight people encounter, and at an earlier stage of their lives, the more tolerant they become towards the phenomenon. This is reflected in gay and lesbian Facebook pages and blogs. Many write openly about their partners and get likes and warm comments from all of their friends, including the straight ones.

This symbiosis between young straight and LGBT people also comes into play in their social frameworks and pastime activities – particularly in Tel Aviv. Straight and LGBT friends party together and have warm relationships, regardless of their gender identity or sexual orientation. It's simply a non-issue for them. Their motto is: your sexuality is your business. Furthermore, many young women have found a kindred spirit in their gay friends. They particularly enjoy hanging out with them, since they are companions who don't see them as sexual objects, know how to give a compliment, know how to have fun, know and love the feminine world and reinforce their sense of sexiness and femininity. This is a pure friendship for them, without the typical competitiveness and tensions that usually come with relationships with other women friends.

Some claim that young LGBT people are gradually shedding social stigmas, among other things, and perhaps because these days it's not as easy to tell gay people and straight people apart. On a socially subconscious level, this entire generation is gradually undergoing a process of transgenderness. In other words, the traditional differences between genders are weakening. If pioneering feminism demanded equal rights for men and women, the new wave of feminism actually has more far-reaching demands – to change the deeply-rooted behaviour and lifestyle of gender roles. It turns out that this claim has ideological as well as practical implications. The boundaries of masculinity and femininity have indeed become more blurry over the years, and millennials are actually the first generation that can produce clear results of this dramatic transition.

Since straight millennial males have embraced certain behaviours and lifestyle choices that are considered feminine (according to the old conventions), and straight millennial females are embracing behaviours that used to be considered more masculine, the actual differences between LGBT and straight people have narrowed in this generation, resulting in a weakening stereotype. Young Israelis (mostly men) tend to display expressions of affection in patterns that were once considered 'gay'. They kiss and hug each other often, touch each other and use terms of endearment.

The central change lies in how the image of the ideal Israeli male has been reshaped, so 'feminine' gay men are no longer perceived as weak, inferior people and are no longer required to convey 'masculinity' in order to prove they're still men. Similarly, lesbians can also act assertively without being suspected of manly behaviour.

$$10$$

Sleeping Crosswise –
Singlehood as a Way of Life

The Crumbling of the Modern Family Unit

The evolutionary changes experienced by the family unit in the western world have stemmed from moral, scientific, political and technological developments. They've made an impact on three main aspects: subversion of the power balance between parents and children and the development of a new model of softened authority; a decline in fertility; and the undermined sanctity of romantic relationships, which expresses itself in longer-lasting singlehood, the rise of single (unmarried) people and in the divorce rate.

Millennials are actually the first generation to be born and raised into the new familial age, accelerating and establishing phenomena that started with their parents (Generation X). Behaviours and worldviews once considered marginal are becoming part of the mainstream, not only affecting the family unit but also many overlapping phenomena in the fields of education, economics, politics and more.

Marriage on the Decline

Up until only a few decades ago, marriage and starting a family were considered the highest social ideal. Young people were raised to search for a partner and get married as part of the natural process of growing older and settling down. In the past two decades, though, marriage has been on a drastic decline, particularly among young people. One of the reasons for this phenomenon is that being single has been legitimized. Not that many years ago young people, and particularly women past the age of 30, were considered to be damaged goods and miserable, suffering from stigma and prejudice. This norm is still common in the western world and more distinctively in Israel, which is considered a very traditional and familial society. However, the negative labelling of single people is growing weaker, slowly but surely.

If once, young people, mostly in the secular-Jewish sector, tended to get married in their early 20s, nowadays it has become more common to get married in the late 20s, and sometimes even after that. Millennials prefer to have fun, see the world, study, experiment, and only then get married, if at all.

Children and Parents are Single Simultaneously

Besides those who choose to remain single, more and more divorced people who are either in no rush to get remarried or are having trouble doing so are added to the status. The singles phenomenon started expanding back in the 1980s, but it seems to have spread as far as to become a cultural characteristic in recent years.

In 1950, 22 per cent of American adults were single, and 9 per cent of households were comprised of a single person (with no children or other adults in the house). Nowadays, over 50 per cent of Americans are single, and 28 per cent of households are comprised of just one person. In major cities the numbers are even higher.

The situation in Israel is similar. A look into private households (not including people living in kibbutzim or institutions), reveals that from 1970 to 2010 the number of single households grew by some 30 per cent, reaching some 20 per cent of Jewish households in 2010.When looking at strictly secular-Jewish households, this rate is much higher. This change is especially dramatic among young people of the traditional age of marriage (25-35). Thus, in Tel Aviv, the 'capital of young people', the rate of single women in ages 25-29 stands at some 70 per cent, while the rate of single men of the same age group is over 80 per cent.

Another factor that makes today's youngsters unique is that many of them enter committed relationships and get married while their parents dismantle their own marital package. This creates a weirdly dramatic crisis: just when their children need support and guidance while trying to adapt to their new lives as adults, the parents get caught up in their own crisis and find it hard to support their children both emotionally and financially. Not only that, the exhausted parents actually expect in many cases to get emotional support from their adult children. They open up to their children about their everyday struggles and reveal vulnerability and helplessness.

Prolonged singlehood generates a great deal of suffering and pain. Many speak very honestly about feeling lonely, the financial and emotional struggle of living alone and the frustration caused by endless dates that never lead to the desired results. The fear of missing the train and ending up childless also creates anxiety and depression.

Why are They in No Rush to get Married?

There are several possible reasons for why millennials postpone marriage:

Increased Life Expectancy. People's decisions over the course of their lives – when to study, get married, have children, get divorced and more – are directly and indirectly influenced by their estimation of how many years they have left to live. Therefore, it is only natural that when life expectancy is getting longer, the age of marriage is also pushed backwards.

Less Pressured by their Surroundings. In the past, young people, and mostly young women, were under social pressure to get married by the time they hit thirty, even at the price of compromising. Many people have suffered emotional scars as a result, leading to the decision to avoid pressuring their children on this matter. The pressure indeed still exists to this day, but its frequency and velocity have been greatly diminished.

Lessons from TV. In older times, only young students were expected to live with a bunch of strangers in a rented apartment. Over time, popular television shows such as *Three's Company, Seinfeld* and *Friends* convey a message that this kind of framework is possible and perhaps even preferable to a committed relationship, mostly in the interim period. And as we stated earlier, this period is only getting longer for millennials.

Informal Relationships get Legitimized. The common view in Israel is still that marriage is the natural state for human beings, and the majority of Jewish people in Israel institutionalize their relationships by formally registering for marriage. However, the scope of people in a committed relationship who live together in Israel without getting married is consistently on the rise.

Trouble with Decision-making and Tendency to Procrastinate. One of generation Y's characteristics is constant indecisiveness as they wait to the last moment, and sometimes even past the last moment. This syndrome also affects the question of when to get married and to whom. Since they want to keep their options open, they constantly postpone making this decision.

Lack of Maturity. When the transition from childhood to adulthood grows longer, it's only natural for the age of marriage to be delayed as well. Generally speaking, in the secular world people can decide to marry whomever they please, which requires a certain level of independence, maturity and mental preparedness. However, many people in their 20s and even in their 30s still feel like they're not ready to enter the world of adults – i.e. get married and have children.

Fear of Commitment. Many millennials also postpone the decision out of fear of commitment and taking responsibility as well as unwillingness to cut loose from their protective parents. Since many young people feel comfortable with their delayed maturity, they postpone marriage, consciously or not, in order to 'clock some more childhood years' and enjoy all worlds as much as possible. Even when they enter a committed relationship, fear of commitment (mostly among men) often cuts the relationship short.

Bored Now, Time to Trade Up. Millennials tend to get bored quickly, which leads them to seek out new thrills. Furthermore, the technology world has taught them that they don't have to stay faithful to the same product and can trade up once in a while. This habit has also seeped into their relationships, creating a value of 'disposable relationships'. The mere thought of getting 'stuck' being married to the same man or woman for their entire lives is dreadful to them. So when the relationship stops being as exciting as it once was, many just bail and move on.

Can't Let Go of the Guys. Since millennials have a strong bond with their friends, many try to avoid cutting the group's 'umbilical cord' as long as possible, making their singlehood last longer.

Free and Happy. If once marriage was perceived as breaking loose from one's parents and starting an independent life, today it is often perceived the opposite way: starting to serve a 'life sentence', or entering a dead-end street (or as they put it: 'fun time is over'). Many millennials enjoy the intoxicating and deceptive feeling of freedom of the 'in-between' period. Their basic view is that there's no point in taking on the burden of life before you exhaust the experience of freedom, which among others involves travelling abroad, going out often and multiple one-night stands.

Must Do More. For many years, secular society has adapted the norm that the 'right' time to get married is shortly after military service, or during one's studies at the very latest. In recent years, however, the pre-marriage 'must do' course has grown longer and the list also includes working for a year in order to pay for the big trip, the big trip itself (spanning for about a year, sometimes even longer), a period of settling in back in Israel and a period of adapting to student life followed by work. These years are characterized by searching for life directions and financial instability, which makes marriage less appealing at this point in their lives.

It's 'Me' Before 'We'. By nature, marriage involves giving up personal advantages (personal freedom, flexibility etc.) in favour of bigger advantages (true love, financial stability, children etc.) In other words, this is somewhat of an engineered social exchange. However, it seems something has gone wrong with the traditional trade-off in recent years, and question marks have been raised regarding its value and feasibility. These question marks have grown particularly strong among millennials, since this self-centred generation isn't keen on making personal sacrifices. When the 'me' comes before any type of 'we', institutionalizing one's relationship is postponed 'until it feels right to me'. It should be noted that more and more articles that rationalize prolonged singlehood and even avoiding marriage have been published in the popular media in recent years. They point out the irrationality and futility of making this sacrifice for someone else, thus reflecting a general state of mind of personal utilitarianism that western culture promotes.

Incapable of Intimacy and Meaningful Relationships. Psychologists we've talked with made the argument that this generation's lack of maturity makes it hard for many of them to develop intimacy with other people. It seems they haven't 'figured themselves out', making it harder for them to create long-term relationships. The dating scene also adds an 'instant' aspect to relationships, turning the process of getting to know people into a somewhat mechanical thing that erodes innocent romance.

Digital technology, which prefers textual over verbal communication, also affects the ability to develop a stable, meaningful relationship: since a healthy relationship is based on open discourse and a shared interest, a generation that hasn't developed any verbal abilities is likely to face obstacles in creating relationships.

It is also possible that the inability to develop intimacy is actually 'one example' of a wider phenomenon of estrangement and mistrust of other people, which is common nowadays in general and among millennials in particular.

Looking for 'The One'. The culture of abundance also projects on the choice of one's spouse. Since there are many options, the fear of making a mistake has grown. There's also the feeling that somewhere over the horizon there's a better option waiting for you on 'one of the shelves'. This view also leads to second thoughts and constant doubts over whether this is the right person for me, or whether there's someone 'better' waiting at the next date.

These doubts are supported by the myth of the knight in shining armour. The media blasts its consumers with the notion that romantic relationships are the ultimate goal that everyone must strive for at any price. Everyone is required to find their 'perfect soulmate', as one young woman defined it. Some young people are aware that this is merely an unrealistic fantasy and try to 'sober up' in time, not always successfully. The problem is that with sobriety also comes disappointment and sometimes even crash, which dissolves the relationship as well as the marriage in some cases.

No One is Good Enough for Me. Some link this generation's narcissism to their inability to find a stable relationship and start a family. According to social exchange theory, every person 'prices his or herself' in the dating marketing before falling in love with a potential candidate. This process of subconsciously calculating one's advantages and disadvantages based on personal and social metrics has crucial significance in fulfilling the potential of marriage. Actually, people who seek out a partner with a higher 'value' than their own value in the market, are prone to fall in love in vain.

Millennials, who have been raised as princes and princesses by parents who boosted their egos with countless compliments, are likely to develop an unrealistic 'market value'. Many youngsters prepare a list of qualities they look for in a mate, disqualifying potential candidates for the slightest deviation from their (often unrealistic) checklist.

Women Don't Need Men as Much. In the days of old, it was customary that the man was the head of the family, primary provider and the one making the decisions when it came to finances and other issues related to the household. A great majority of women were housewives, thus depending on their husbands. Unwed or divorced women suffered from stigma. Therefore, single women were not picky about who they married, and married women weren't keen on breaking up the marriage, even when the relationship turned sour. This changed along with the changing status of women in the world. These days, they are more independent (both financially and professionally) and are less anxious about divorce or being alone.

Prolonged Trial and Error Period. Since the 1970s, the secular-Jewish population in Israel has established the norm that a successful relationship requires a long trial and adaptation period that includes two consecutive stages: experimenting with different partners, followed by living together under one roof (while renting with the one you chose). The 'preview marriage' tradition started to settle in the 1980s, but has become a basic norm among millennials while its typical duration grows longer and longer. Many couples tell themselves that they function as a married couple for all intents and purposes, therefore there's no real need to rush to the Rabbi. In many cases, the decision to get married comes when a couple who have lived together for a long period decides it's time to have a baby, while both partners have already been accepted by each other's families.

Time Goes By Too Fast. Life in the present era is very intense, particularly for young people. Many of them are living the moment, with no plans, routine or daily schedule. This makes time fly faster, until they suddenly 'wake up' one day and discover they're 30 years old, and the advantages they once had when they were young and single (good looks, confidence, optimism etc.) have faded away. The psychological pressure grows, undermining the necessary nonchalance required for searching for 'the one'. Single people start to lose their confidence and this is projected on the environment, making potential spouses nervous. Nobody wants to connect to a desperate person and the 'I'm looking' label is the polar opposite of sex appeal. Research has shown that love is a delicate balance between a partner's over-accessibility and lack thereof.

Let's Get Married after we get our Acts Together. Many young people are afraid of settling down out of fear of lowering their standard of living. In previous generations, young people got married first and only then did they find financial stability together (while pooling their resources). These days, the formula has flipped: find financial stability first, then get married.

Having no financial or occupational stability makes millennial couples wary of marriage. Many of them don't have steady jobs and are concerned about sharing a financial responsibility with another person, let alone get a mortgage and have kids.

Everyone Either Cheats or Gets Cheated on, so Why Get Married? As a result of the growing divorce rate and general instability of relationships nowadays, many people get into a fatalistic state of mind according to which even if they find someone they want to marry, chances are it will end in divorce. Some youngsters even experienced this as children when one of their parents was cheated on. As a result, many believe that infidelity between spouses is the norm, which increases their mistrust of the institution of marriage and their reluctance to tie the knot.

Alone and Comfortable. Having their own room and parents who work long hours, millennials have grown accustomed to spending long hours by themselves. The habit of living alone mitigates the need to find a life partner. Furthermore, the longer the chapter of singlehood gets, the more comfortable they become with the concept of being alone, and over time it deteriorates into a 'chronic state', making it harder to let a permanent partner enter their personal space.

Legitimacy for Staying Alone. More and more people feel like the marital and family framework isn't right for their character and lifestyle, and the options available for having children without a husband or wife (artificial insemination, surrogacy, adoption) have contributed to the beginning of the legitimization of giving up the traditional family.

The notion that marriage isn't worth it has found a voice in an increasing number of recent articles in the popular media about the glamour of singlehood. For example, 'you can flirt with whoever you like, whenever you like, with no guilt'; 'you can sleep diagonally (the bed is mine and mine alone!)'; 'you don't have to worry whether he's going to like your friends'; 'all the stuff in the apartment is actually your stuff!'; 'my money is always spent on a worthy cause (myself)'.

It's true that in many cases, these articles are meant to comfort the many single men and women who are supposedly unable to find true love, essentially creating post factum rationalization for the 'problem'. They are also written in a tongue-in-cheek tone. It seems, though, that there's also a serious statement here behind these smiles, reflecting the spirit of the times.

Perhaps it echoes a new perception that seeks to replace the old institution with something that allows love, intimacy and joint parenthood on one hand, and greater flexibility on the other. Is it possible? Time will tell.

11

Dating Around – Meeting Places and Dating Markets

Long Road from Matchmaking to Dating

Zionism's secular revolution sparked important changes in Jewish matchmaking culture. At the dawn of the State of Israel, secular parents became less involved in the process of choosing their children's spouses, shifting to an informal supervising role ('what does his father do?', 'what are his parents' ethnic backgrounds?') and ratifying the child's choice. Professional matchmakers have been replaced by relatives, friends and acquaintances. Going to a matchmaker or posting an ad in the newspaper were considered disgraceful and embarrassing at the time, and single people were ashamed to admit to using such means to find a mate.

Personal ads became more common in the late 1970s, with newspapers dedicating full sections for this purpose. They were short (15 words or less), dry and businesslike, and included just a few details about the person posting the ad, such as age, height and several personal traits (for example: 'handsome man, financially well-off, 173/35, seeks delicate, pretty and friendly woman under 30').

Over the years, the dating industry has expanded under the influence of the telecommunications revolution. For instance, the use of videos, teletext, computerized databases, phone services and voice mails gradually replaced the traditional mailboxes.

TV also hopped on the matchmaking bandwagon, led by Rivka Michaeli's show *Blind Date*, which went on the air on Channel 2 in 1995. Many dating shows were broadcast over the years, the most popular of which being the Israeli *Take Me Sharon,* the international *Paradise Hotel, The Bachelor, The Bachelorette* and *Who Wants to Marry a Millionaire?*

The indirect message of these shows, which millennial teens watched devotedly, is that singlehood is a common and not necessarily negative social phenomenon, romance is just a façade and it's okay to play with other people's feelings. Another problematic message assimilated by the young viewers is that choosing a partner is like picking out merchandise from a shelf where there is infinite variety. In other words, singles should try more and more, until they find an exact fit.

Meeting and Dating Circles

High schools, youth movements, regular mandatory military service and academic studies used to act as settings for romantic encounters. With the exception of youth movements, which have lost much of their allure among millennials, the other settings still provide romantic opportunities for youngsters to this day. However, other scenes have developed in recent years, far outweighing the aforementioned scenes when it comes to millennials.

The normalization of sex, the utilitarian nature of sexual relations and hedonistic culture's takeover of our lives have helped develop the club and bar culture, particularly in the Tel Aviv area. They are used both for casual sex and for romantic involvements. The 'pick-up bar' holds particular importance since it's usually dark and loud. A great deal of sexual encounters takes place in the bar's bathroom.

Another central dating scene is the big trip to South America and the Far East. Young people who go on these trips usually travel in same-sex groups. They meet many young people during this trip – from Israel as well as from other countries. This leads to the development of many friendships and romantic encounters. Our interviews have shown a very interesting pattern that's typical among millennials. Since the big trip is an ideal period in which you can make all your dreams come true, since many relationships are temporary and superficial and since this generation's self-interest is usually stronger than other considerations, many couples decide to proactively break up before the trip. This is done so the relationship can't prevent them from getting the most out of the journey as well as out of the mutual understanding that the experience abroad also includes romantic and sexual encounters. Even when both partners want to travel at the same time, many prefer to travel with their closest friends rather than with their girlfriend or boyfriend.

The internet's development has led the matchmaking market to shift its focus onto the virtual space, and the popularity of online dating has consistently increased over the years.

Millennials are on social media, which naturally plays an important role in the romantic field. It starts with approving a friend request at the beginning of the relationship, allowing the other party to investigate and discover as many details as possible about you, browse your photos, see where you work, who your friends are and your likes and dislikes, continues with the announcement of being in a relationship – which slaps an official stamp on the new couple. Then follows the stage of reporting your shared romantic experiences, which of course include photos and likes by both sets of your friends.

Dating Culture

A date is a romantic meeting between two participants considering a potential relationship. A typical date may entail meeting at a restaurant, café or bar. Most dates are 'blind dates' between two prospective partners who've never met before, or made initial contact via the internet (on dating sites, social media etc.)

The date has become very commonplace among millennials, due to their low inhibitions as well as their prolonged singlehood. It's also technically easier for young people to go on dates. Many of them spend at least some of their time in the Tel Aviv area (for living, work, or leisure), which allows them to meet one another without having to plan a long drive in advance.

The 'perfect relationship' myth drives young people to try to get to know as many prospective partners as possible, in an attempt to find 'the one'.

The dating world has been extensively covered in Israeli media in recent years. The multiple articles on the subject demonstrate how important dating is for the young generation and showcase recurring patterns, some of which will be described as follows.

Dating Anxiety

Stress, anxiety, uncertainty, disappointment and failure are an inseparable part of dating culture, and perhaps it contributes to this generation's chronic insecurity and skeptical and cynical worldview.

Meeting someone you don't know face-to-face in an intimate setting and the fear of being rejected, insulted and embarrassed produce constant pressure. The more you go on dates, the higher your anxiety levels, the shakier your confidence and the more you become skeptical and cynical about the concept of being in a relationship.

Due to the great importance attributed to beauty nowadays, many youngsters are concerned that their looks will be their downfall, particularly after being turned down a few times. Being introverted and shy is also a problem, as the short, intense encounter requires a quick first impression, supposedly giving the more assertive and chatty people an advantage.

Anxiety often takes root when the date actually goes well. Will there be a second date? And if there isn't, then what? Should I tell my family and friends about my failure and disappointment? Maybe the other person is waiting for me to give them the go-ahead?

Many young women are afraid of being used by people who are looking for one-night stands or even just for a place to crash.

Masquerade

The dating world greatly reflects the importance of a person's image nowadays. Young people commonly believe that the key to success in life lies in creating the right image and marketing it successfully. If you keep having bad dates, the problem isn't you but rather the persona you've created.

Since dating involves 'self-marketing', it also generates awkwardness and confusion. Many people agonize with themselves after the date for being too quiet or talking too much, being boring, saying something out of place, not being clear enough etc.

Popular media provides its consumers with various rules and do's and don'ts. These superficial recipes actually complicate things, creating a reality of deception and mutual suspicion. Dating has become a game of masquerade in which everybody is trying to figure out what's under the mask.

One phenomenon that amazed us was the fact that articles, comments and blogs about dating have not produced even one discussion about the value of intellectual conversation. According to this notion, the meeting isn't supposed to be used to exchange opinions on politics, religion, ideology – as if the two people have no worldviews. Everything boils down to making an impression, communication problems, potential shortages and questions about personal taste (favourite food, TV show etc.)

Women Taking Charge

More and more women are taking on roles in the field of dating that were previously only reserved for men. For example, if traditionally the man would ask the woman out and even propose the time and place, nowadays the woman often is the one to do these things, and more frequently the two decide together. Women are even more assertive during the date and on more than one occasion initiate first sexual contact.

Picking up the Cheque

In the not so distant past, the man would normally pay for the woman he asked out on a date. One would expect a generation raised on the teachings of feminism to change this tradition, specifically when taking young people's financial hardship into account. In reality, this is not that common. Even this generation usually expects the man to pick up the cheque. The difference between generations deals less with actions and more with how they feel about said actions. Many men complain about the financial burden of dating, and many women feel uncomfortable with this situation. A few even insist on splitting the cheque.

The Transparent Cellular Wall

Before the age of cellphones, personal encounters forced people to partake in an actual conversation. Nowadays, cellphones make it hard to concentrate on the person sitting opposite you and the conversation often gets interrupted by calls and messages. Many dates look as if there's two people randomly sharing a table, each of them immersed in his or her screen. Even when they decided to focus on their dates, the cellphone does not get turned off and the eyes continue to nervously wander. The problem here isn't just with the lack of concentration and mutual attentiveness, which leads to very superficial encounters, it's also inconsiderate and rude.

The Wingman

Since millennials are naturally open and live in packs, many young people hook up their friends with prospective mates. Members of this close-knit group often share dating experiences and ask for advice in the event of a misunderstanding or crisis. It isn't unusual for a man to consult a female member of the group (who isn't his partner) on such matters.

Many youngsters go out on group dates that involve several couples. The best friend often comes along for the date. They serve as a 'wingman', i.e. help put the date in motion, fill in awkward silences and make sure everything run smoothly.

Gender Gaps

Even when there's no spark, the date can still end with sexual intercourse, as young people feel it is a legitimate and desirable part of their time together. Though both men and women tend to refer to the date as a sexual arena, our interviews as well as various online statements (blogs, Facebook etc.) show that men tend to be more focused on this goal ('getting laid'), obviously due to gender gaps and delayed maturity (men are more childish and more self-centred). Many men come into the date expecting a one-night stand, and any indication that the woman is looking for something more drives them away.

Many men boast of their sexual conquests and complain about women being 'too talkative', 'clingy', 'frigid' or 'a drama queen'. Women experience more heartbreak, when after intercourse the man loses interest and disappears (or asks them to 'disappear').

Abandonment Issues

When the date doesn't go well, a polite, considerate person would elegantly avoid giving a date his or her mobile number (if they haven't already), for instance by saying 'hit me up on Facebook' (the friend request is never approved). Less sensitive people would use all sorts of excuses, most of which have been rehearsed in advance. Youngsters have become very skilled in this way, amassing an arsenal of excuses designed to avoid an unwanted date or simply to end a disappointing one. As we all know, no excuse can mitigate the feeling of rejection and humiliation that almost everyone experiences at some point of their lives.

Due to the 'blind' and therefore unpredictable nature of the date, and due to millennials' tendency to be self-centred and impolite, many dates end on a bad note, i.e. someone gets discarded like a useless object. It's not uncommon for a series of dates to be cut short by one party via text message or on Facebook.

Our interviews consistently brought up stories that demonstrate the cynical nature of dating culture. We got the impression of a self-fulfilling prophecy according to which relationships are superficial to begin with, which are destined to burn out at some point, even when they do start out as true love. This notion lowers their expectations, creating a somewhat fatalistic acceptance of their impending abandonment.

Reality dating shows have definitely played a central role in cultivating the culture of instant dating. Young people who watch these shows without the proper filters are taught not to trust anyone, not even people who appear to be affectionate (including body language and compliments). The indirect message of these shows is that love is superficial and temporary, intimacy is a fabricated illusion, trust between people is nothing more than just laughter, relationships are a manipulative exchange of goods, and separation is a kind of dismissal.

On the other hand, perhaps there is something slightly anachronistic and ritualistic about the old conventions of courtship. Perhaps this short, disposable instant dating culture does have something more direct, purposeful and free from hypocrisy and complication, a kind of shortcut more suitable for the age of openness and instant gratifications, much like tasty fast food.

What About the Ex?

Since a typical Facebook friend list can be broken down into different degrees of friendship, a dilemma arises when one has to decide what to do after a relationship ends and you're still friends on Facebook. This dilemma is complicated due to the concern that the break-up would be too public, as this is a generation that tries to avoid direct confrontation and fears drastic measures. Since the action of removing someone from your Facebook friend list is considered extreme, it leads to a serious conundrum between the emotional urge to 'get this person out of my life' and keeping him/her as a passive friend. People usually opt for the latter, creating a new kind of problem – stalking exes and trying to make them jealous.

Free, Awkward Sexuality

Born in the Post-Puritan Age

Millennials have grown up in a time where all restraints have been lifted. The media, art world, academia and healthcare system started talking more openly, and bedroom secrets that were repressed and concealed by previous generations were released into the world. Their parents had already benefited from the fruits of the sexual revolution in the west and were far less puritan than their previous generations. However, when comparing the status of sex in Israeli society during the 1970s and 80s (the formative years of Generation X) to its status in the late 1990s onwards (the formative years of Generation Y), the differences are quite noticeable.

The public space has been overloaded with erotic messages in recent years, with sex appearing in every corner. Written and spoken language has become more cheeky and unrestrained, and the way people present themselves has become more revealing than ever. Things that used to be considered crude, vulgar, slutty or even delinquent, have now found a place in the mainstream. No one in secular society makes a big deal out of talking about sex, essentially creating an understanding that talking openly about it helps remove prejudice and promotes personal liberties and happiness.

The internet revolution, which took place during millennials' childhood, turned the sexual revolution up to eleven, basically starting a new sexual era. In this reality, children of nearly all ages can watch all sorts of uncensored sex acts on their personal screens.

Furthermore, in the ultra-consumer age, the end justifies the means, allowing for blatant as well as covert use of sexuality for the purpose of selling a product. The most popular television shows – watched by both children and adults – focus on erotic messages to get more ratings. Advertising firms use minors to convey sexual messages, creating twisted role models.

Having Sex at an Early Age

Studies from around the world show that the age for having sex (i.e. the wide range of physical relations such as cuddling, not just the act of penetration) is constantly dropping. The trend in Israel is similar. According to data, many teenagers start having sex at 14-15 and the bar keeps getting lower and lower. Sex counsellors and therapists speak of the peer pressure teenage girls and boys are under to experience sexual relations, even when they don't really want to.

Clinical studies show that having sex at too early an age (the exact age still being debated) can potentially lead to difficulties and problems a person will have to face for the rest of his or her life. People who are emotionally immature might develop warped perceptions of their body and the bodies of others, are more likely to experience sexual abuse and are more emotionally vulnerable, particularly when it comes to developing healthy intimacy and establishing steady relationships. This is particularly true when they have bad experiences, which is a common phenomenon among teens. Furthermore, young people are more susceptible to influence from their environment and manipulation by people who don't necessarily have their best interest at heart.

Moreover, since sex is an emotionally revealing and demanding act of intimacy, and since childhood experiences tend to make a strong, long-lasting impression, sexual traumas can have repercussions beyond the issue of sexuality, particularly in regards to people's self-image and interpersonal relationships patterns.

The problem is heightened among millennials because of their delayed emotional maturity. This creates a tragic paradox: the generation that was supposed to postpone their sexual activity due to their delayed emotional development, actually found themselves having sex at a younger age than their parents.

There are several more reasons for this generation's sexual issues and difficulties:

First, this generation has no secrets and has been taught to impress their peers. When eroticism and sexuality become a metric for social prominence and success, it's naturally translated into competition and social pressure. When everyone around you believes that anyone who doesn't try sex is a nerd or a loser, even those who don't want to do it or are not ready for it are forced to fall in line.

Second, this generation started drinking a lot at an early age. Alcohol tends to make people sexually active, leading to a whole other set of issues. Legitimacy for drug use has also increased and plays a part in sexual relations.

Third, this generation tends to be fatalistic. They live in the present much more than youngsters in previous generations, and 'to hell with the consequences'.

Despite all this, the Ministry of Education still hasn't drafted a proper sex education programme for children of various ages. The discussion (if one even takes place) usually revolves around the functional and technical points, focusing on human anatomy, warnings and risks.

And what of the parents? Although millennials are known to have a warm and open relationship with their parents, it seems that the 'responsible adults' weren't really around. Millennials may have not been raised by puritan parents or had to fight for their freedom, but their parents' humanistic and pluralistic approach has actually abandoned them, forcing them to do 'whatever feels right' and learn from one another, for better or worse, as well as from scattered pieces of information on the internet.

The defensiveness of parents and the shaking off of their responsibility gets terrifying expression whenever there's a sex scandal involving minors.

In many cases, the parents of male minors who are accused of violence against their female counterparts are protective of them, pointing the finger at the girls who supposedly 'seduced' their sons. They refuse to accept that their sons have a twisted perception of sex and that they fell asleep while on duty.

Porn Generation

Society's attitude towards displays of sexuality has changed over the course of history (and continues to change). For example, nude or semi-nude photos that once only appeared in 'men's magazines' in the 1960s and were considered 'indecent' nowadays appear in legitimate popular media.

In the past, consuming pornography boiled down to keeping *Playboy* magazines under your mattress, watching sex films in dark cinemas, and in later years renting pornographic movies from the video rental machine, preferably without being seen by the neighbours. Nowadays, porn is one mouse click away. People are exposed to erotic material on a daily basis, and the digital medium facilitates this exposure, comprised of various layers and diverse human needs.

In the early 2000s, shortly after the internet's big break, people would joke that if porn were to be taken off the internet, there will be no more websites left except for one with a petition to bring back porn.

Millennials are the first generation to be intensively exposed to porn from an early age, and this has definitely had an influence on their sexual perceptions. Many researchers believe that exposure to sexual content online has considerable positive influences. For instance, exposure to nudity and sexual acts is an important educational tool. It provides important information about human physiology, pleasure centres and the range of sexuality. It improves performances and increases attentiveness among partners. Porn has definitely taken sex out of the closet and released many restraints. Erotic content also serves as a very efficient tool for satisfying sexual curiosity and legitimate self-pleasuring. The ability to masturbate to images and videos allows people to discover their own needs and sensitivities, relieves stress (therefore decreasing the potential for sexual violence) and provides important experience. Watching sexual content also relieves loneliness and helps spread the important value that people are essentially equal, with similar needs and desires.

The world of pornography has helped establish millennials' liberal attitude towards sex, remove the typical sanctity and hypocrisy of previous generations and allowed many of them to practise natural, shame-free and uninhibited sex.

However, porn has also had some disturbing influences on this generation:

Too Early Exposure. Easy access to porn has exposed millennials to sexual content while they were minors, even before their first sexual experience. Studies show that too early exposure raises the potential for sexual distortions and anxieties.

Negative Body Image. Watching pornography videos also hurts young people's body image, due to the differences between them and what they see as the 'right model' for the male and female body on screen. Many are disappointed by their bodies and fear they will not be 'in demand' in the market.

Addiction to Thrills. Studies have shown that watching porn makes changes to the brain's neurochemistry, leading to lust, obsession and occasionally addiction. There have been multiple reports in recent years of the growing rate of youngsters who have become addicted to the thrill of pornography and struggle to achieve sexual release. The problem is with the dosage of consumption, which leads to erosion. When you can watch dozens of videos at any given time and your thrill threshold is constantly on the rise, it becomes more difficult to become sexually aroused and have sexual relations with real partners. Most young people are afraid to talk about the problem and are unaware of how widespread it actually is. There's nothing wrong with them physically, but their emotional distress is strong. The addiction to sexual excitement also makes it hard to establish a steady relationship, making them more likely to grow tired of it quickly.

Distorted Image of Sexuality. The porn industry is operated mostly by men and marketed primarily to male consumers. This is also one of the reasons that the common sexual model is fundamentally chauvinistic and delivers misleading and often dangerous and immoral messages to young men. A lot of porn is based on sexual exploitation of women, humiliating and sexually degrading them. Many young people, unaware of the context of the material, get a false and completely twisted image of women's sexuality and the nature of sexual relations between partners. It is therefore no surprise that there is a growing rate of incidents in which a group of young males take advantage of a young female who is emotionally vulnerable, while being completely oblivious to the fact they are being exploitative, sometimes going as far as conducting gang rape. They're just implementing what they see on porn sites in real life. It should be noted that the models presented in porn also affect the twisted concepts of sex by the young women who are exposed to them.

Incidentally, sexist models don't just come from the world of pornography but also from the world of video and computer games.

Mechanical, Immature Sexual Model. Porn is usually the first sexual model youngsters get exposed to, pushing aside the more responsible sex guides that were popular in the 1990s (such as *The Lovers' Guide* tapes). In many cases, young people learn to deal with sexual activity in a childish manner, making it hard for them to establish meaningful relationships.

Normalization of the Sex Talk

Throughout the course of history, sex has been classified as a private, intimate affair you don't really talk about. For millennials, though, it seems that all of the walls have been torn down, and what was once considered too revealing and blatant has been legitimized.

Young people today are more sexually open than their parents (when they were their age) and tend to approach sex as something mundane rather than something sacred. They define intimacy differently and have no qualms about revealing very personal information, which used to travel by word of mouth, if at all.

The free sexual discourse on relationships, loneliness, love and passion for one's spouse is particularly prominent on Facebook. What's particularly interesting and different about this generation is that men and women both partake in this dialogue, including dirty jokes. In the past, when the boys told dirty jokes the girls would be quiet and blush, whereas today, sexual gags are exchanged freely between girls and other girls, boys and other boys and between girls and boys. Issues that once made people uncomfortable are now naturally discussed among young people.

Even when they're married, it's relatively easy for young people to consult friends or go to counsellors and therapists as well as talk openly about problems and difficulties within the relationship and the family unit.

Say Goodbye to Discretion

As society becomes more permissive, the clothes one can wear in public becomes scantier. This phenomenon is particularly noticeable among women: short, tight and transparent clothes, as well as deep cleavages that don't leave much room for the imagination. The manicure, pedicure, make-up, tattoos, piercings, swimsuits and thong bikini (lingerie has become a very important issue for millennials), push-up bras, breast augmentation and the shaved pubic hair trend (among women and recently among men as well) also send out a message of sexual extraversion.

It should be noted that erotic clothing like miniskirts and high heels isn't something new in western countries nor in Israel, but in the case of Generation Y, unlike previous generations, this is the norm rather than the exception. It has become so common and normal, that few secular families even deal with this issue, which is perceived nowadays as obsolete and irrelevant. Parents usually don't even notice that their underage daughters are leaving the house with an appearance that transmits sexuality and sometimes even blatant sexuality. Furthermore, many even encourage their children, and particularly their girls, to obsess over their appearance (buying fashionable clothes, going to the hair salon, beautician etc.), while the emphasis is no longer just on 'does it suit me?' but rather also 'am I sexy?' They don't just do it in the name of the free choice ethos (not meddling in their children's lives), but also because they themselves have been brainwashed by effective consumerist propaganda that puts people's appearance in the at the centre of it all.

'Make out' culture also gets an eccentric emphasis in this generation. While previous generations would cuddle away from the public eye, millennials feel comfortable making out in public, in front of their friends and parents. Many have loud sexual relations while their roommates, guests, siblings and even parents are in the other room.

Millennials don't fuss over keeping a low profile because their threshold for embarrassment is higher and because they fail to tell private and public spaces apart (partly due to immaturity). They're also less attentive to the feelings of people around them and to the fact that blatant sexuality might make other people with different sensibilities and values feel uncomfortable.

Women 'Fuck'

Successful US series *Sex and the City*, which ran between 1998 and 2004 (also in Israel) follows the lives of four best friends that among other things, represent four models of sexuality: Charlotte is the old-fashioned needy woman, Miranda is the career woman who's not as interested in sex, Carrie is searching for a sensitive man for an equal relationship and Samantha represents the new model – the woman who 'eats young men for breakfast'.

As it turns out, Samantha's character wasn't so uncommon, actually paving the way for younger girls who aren't afraid to express their sexuality. This is reflected in recent television series, particularly the aforementioned *Girls*. Much ink has been spilled on the unconventional appearance of Lena Dunham, the show's protagonist, and particularly about how freely the show presents her 'misshapen' figure. In an interview for *New York Magazine*, Dunham stated that her desire to show nudity is fundamentally political (showing women as they really are). However, this statement seems more anthropological than ideological, representing how this generation actually behaves.

In the past, young people who were very sexually active and switched partners frequently (particularly girls) were considered slutty or 'cheap'. Nowadays, this is the standard for millennials, and most of them don't see anything wrong with it.

Although studies have shown that men are still more active, there are multiple signs that women aren't just more sexually active, they also take more initiative, demand more, and some young women even go as far as using men to satisfy their needs (in the past a distinctively male phenomenon). Many young women carry condoms and 'morning-after' pills in their bags or purses and the age of using contraception seems to be on a decline. In crude terms, one could say that today's woman also 'fucks' rather than just 'gets fucked'.

This phenomenon has manifested in slang: the term 'fuck-buddy' is used to describe both male and female friends who meet up strictly for the purpose of intercourse with no strings attached.

Open to New Experiences

The sexual openness of millennials (both male and female) is manifested among other things in their willingness to try out various positions and have sex in untraditional places (including public spaces).

Oral sex is seen as nothing more than a sexual hors d'oeuvre and is likened to a casual contact, the same as a hot kiss. The sheer use of the term 'going down' reflects this phenomenon.

Anal sex, which was once mostly attributed to gay people, as well as sex with multiple partners (orgies), have become more legitimate and are not as rare in this generation. Many millennials have no qualms about having steamy, spontaneous sexual activity in 'unconventional' places such as public restrooms, the beach (where any bystander could watch) and staircases.

'Cum and Go'

Most millennials agree – male and female alike – that 'fucking' is just a pastime activity, an 'instant pleasure' which doesn't require long periods of courtship or even any meaningful emotional investment. Casual sex reflects and promotes the creation of a different sexual model, in which the stability of a sexual relationship as well as deep feelings towards one's partner are no longer necessary.

One could say that this is the dawn of a new age, where sex is about to be completely separated from love, relationships and family. A strong expression of this phenomenon is the 'pick-up bar' – bars that serve as meat markets for the purpose of delivering the goods. On one hand, this reflects the release from shackles and inhibitions. On the other hand, young people pay a hefty price for this way of thinking. Studies have shown that men find it easier to treat sex mechanically than women. This is because it's easier for them to separate their emotions from their urges. When sex is mechanical and disposable, under the influence of alcohol, the 'aftertaste' for women is usually sour and even bitter. Many young women get frustrated by their sex lives, and often feel cheap and even violated.

We've heard about cold sexual relations and the inability to reach healthy intimacy from our interviewees as well as from couple's therapists. This is also reflected in blogs and online comments where young women discuss negative experiences. One woman wrote: 'there was one guy who asked me to get out of bed and go home immediately after sex, because he felt uncomfortable falling asleep next to a stranger. There was something exciting about having a quickie, but I'll admit it was also depressing. I asked myself: 'is this the kind of sex I'll have for the rest of my life? Will I ever find a sex partner who's also capable of love?'

12

Happily Ever After, For Now –
The New Relationships

Might as Well Get it Over With

As the age of marriage gets higher and as it's more acceptable in this generation for couples to live together without getting married, marriage often comes not because people feel like they've found 'the one', but rather due to more pragmatic considerations (though not always consciously). For example: the pressure to have children (more common among women), the urge to be 'like everyone else', the need to please one's parents and relatives and the financial benefits. Many young people admitted to us that the decision to get married was based on the feeling that 'we might as well get it over with'.

This often happens under a phenomenon that experts refer to as the 'wedding chain'. Several members of one social groups get married one by one, often completely oblivious as to why all the dates are so close together. It turns out that some of them are afraid to be left out of their social circle and be the last single people of the group. This motivates them to make it official and continue with the group under the new status of newlyweds.

East Meets West

Every society has its own mechanisms to monitor the choice of spouses and ensure the 'interests of the tribe'. Two such powerful mechanisms operated in Israel: one based on nationality and religion and one based on ethnicity. The common convention was that Jews only marry other Jews, Ashkenazi Jews mostly marry Ashkenazi Jews, and Mizrahi Jews mostly marry Mizrahi Jews.

The Jewish society in Israel is still quite strict about endogamy, although the young secular generation has shown a slight increase in the rate of interfaith relationships. More and more Israelis stay abroad for long periods (travel, work, studies etc.) and fall in love with non-Jews. Social media also creates accessible meeting points between young people from various countries, and the global marriage market is rapidly expanding. Another reason is the rise in tolerance towards the other and the increasingly popular myth that 'love conquers all'. Moreover, due to the rising marriage age, many parents are simply overjoyed that a wedding is finally taking place that they don't meddle much with the actual choice of bride or groom.

Integration has been far more prominent for cross-ethnic marriage. Generation Y's parents were the first to tear down the walls of ethnicity, resulting in a considerable number of mixed families. However, in quite a few cases, this choice led to struggles and confrontations with their narrow-minded parents. Millennials mostly manage to avoid this trauma, as their parents are less prone to ethnic stereotyping. They also tend to agree with their children's choices and keep criticism at a minimum. There is a popular convention that everyone has the right to choose his or her partner, which contributes as well. In any case, it's actually not that easy to identify young people by their ethnic origins nowadays, since many of them were raised in mixed families and ethnic background has been less influential on or relevant to their lives.

Consequently, the rate of ethnical 'intermarriage' (Mizrahi and Ashkenazi) among millennials is much higher than all previous generations. They don't ignore their friends' ethnic background and it is still part of their identity, but they're far less prone to label people according to their ethnicity (except of Ethiopian Jews and Russian speakers, to a certain degree) and tend to judge people based on their personality and achievements.

Furthermore, while Mizrahi Jews used to be ashamed of their origins, millennials have replaced this shame with pride and a return to their roots. Most were born in Israel and relate to their family origins merely as an added 'spice' to their personal identity. Mizrahi and Ashkenazi youngsters enjoy cracking jokes at each other's expense, with no inferiority complex, out of the understanding that every culture has its pros and cons.

Light Jewish Chuppah

Most millennials hold traditional views on religion, so naturally the vast majority get married according to the time-honoured secular tradition, i.e. registering at the Rabbinate with an orthodox Rabbi performing the ceremony. However, in recent years there's been a surge of young people opting for an alternative within the orthodox framework (that is, the traditional model with 'illustrations'). This process has come into play with, for example, the growing demand for Tzohar Rabbis as officiants.

Over the years, couples who wish to avoid the Rabbinate have also grown in number, opting for other alternatives such as secular Jewish ceremonies (selected passages from religious texts with various additions as per the couple's worldview and taste), a reformed or conservative religious ceremony, a secular ceremony (civil wedding with no religious characteristics) and a legal contract.

These alternatives are still rather rare on a demographic scale, but demand is on the rise. The variety of ceremonies is also increasing.

The Grand Marriage Proposal

Many millennials have an ambivalent take on marriage: on one hand, it's the end of freedom and fun, while on the other hand it's a dream come true.

Since a considerable portion of this generation comes from broken homes (more than previous generations), and some of them carry baggage from their parents' divorce, the wedding is perceived by many of them as an opportunity to turn over a new leaf.

The marriage proposal is usually extravagant, reflecting the idealization of the event. It has to be romantic, creative, theatrical (and public, in many cases), unique and distinctive. This pattern is led by four factors: naivety; the yearning to be at the centre of attention (which is why they immediately report it to their friends with text and photos); exhibitionism; and the wedding being perceived as a carefully planned party production.

Over the years, people have been trying to outdo one another and come up with the most unexpected, grand proposal (in the style of 'candid camera' or a 'surprise party'), while some proposals are performed in front of a cheering audience and go viral on the internet. Such a proposal is supposed to portray the groom as cool, original, creative and dedicated to his spouse. Ironically, these grand gestures are plagued by childish insensitivity (the bride is forced to partake in the spectacle woven together by her partner, express her feelings in public and immediately agree to this life-changing proposal), expressing this generation's typical focus on self and insensitivity.

Under the sharing culture, a great portion of millennials post an initial announcement of the engagement on Facebook, followed by a photo of the ring – an announcement that obviously rakes in a series of cheers and compliments.

Bachelorhood Parties

The concept of a bachelorhood party was not very well-known in Israel until the 1990s, at which point it was imported and spread mostly by millennials. They use the services of a wide-ranging industry that specializes in this type of party. This generation is particularly fond of bachelorhood parties because they meet some of their deepest needs and fit their worldview and lifestyle.

First, the party is their last chance to experience the 'freedom' of single life. The bride or groom are taken on one last night of pure indulgence, and in many cases the location of the party is kept secret until the last moment.

Second, this party is an opportunity for friends to make their own contribution to the production of the wedding. Since they're sociable and like to share and because they're always looking for a reason to party, they go out of their way to organize an unforgettable entertainment experience for their friend – whether it's a resort, restaurant, adventurous hike, spa, strip show and of course lots of alcohol.

Third, young people tend to stretch the wedding party ('the biggest production of their lives') to the maximum possible. In this sense, the bachelorhood party is like a teaser or an aperitif.

Fourth, this party serves as an opportunity for the bride and groom to share their feelings of excitement, mixed with anxiety and pain, with their closest friends. It helps the bride and groom say goodbye to their childhood, among other things by going on 'one last ride' (drinking etc.) and having heart-to-heart conversations. This farewell to childhood also indirectly serves as a departure from their old buddies. This is their last party before 'giving away' their old friends. From now on the married couple's relationship will overshadow the relationships within the peer group and perhaps even break away from them.

Bachelorette parties have a distinct feminist component that expresses women's liberation. While in the past, men controlled the wedding ceremony ('paying' for the bride, losing their virginity), today's young women openly declare that this is a 'girls only' production, with no men allowed. Women also get drunk (which is traditionally a male thing) and also enjoy sexual content, such as hiring a male stripper, playing party games, talking dirty and joking about intimate subjects.

The party's guestlist is comprised of girlfriends approved by the bride. The bride's best friend will know whether she prefers an intimate gathering with five to ten girls, or an extravagant event with as many as thirty guests. The event is held at a friend's home or at a bar. Occasionally, they'd rent a special location for the night, whether it's several cabins or a villa (preferably with a swimming pool). One of the more recently added options is a 'party bus' that enables them to take the party on the road in Tel Aviv.

The wedding industry's development has paved the road for an entire field that specializes in bachelorhood parties and includes producers, sections in newspapers, blogs, Facebook pages, websites and portals that offer discussions and share experiences, as well as 'ideas' and 'suggestions' for the party.

The bachelor party has most of the basic elements of the bachelorette party, with an additional emphasis on 'male fun': ATV rides, card games and of course lots of alcohol. A particularly large group of men usually rents a villa in the countryside. The owner provides the young men with the perfect setting for a party: leather sofas, mattresses, a fully-equipped kitchen, a bar, a surround sound system, a jacuzzi, Wii station, professional pool table, dance floor and more. The pool and backyard are most important, so they could 'play in the water, barbeque and just sit out in the open'.

The strip show has become more and more common at these parties, due to millennials' promiscuity as well as their urge to go to extremes. Its purpose is to allow the groom to experience his freedom one last time and go on one last night out with the guys, doing stuff his partner might not approve of after they are married.

The Dream Wedding

Decisions, Decisions

Starting in the 1980s, the wedding event became a commercial project that requires families to invest a lot of time and money. At the same time there evolved a trend of designing the wedding party with an original personal seal: the invitations, location, decorations, food and drinks, artistic programme, 'wedding song' (with which you enter the chuppah) are all meticulously planned.

Millennials put a particularly strong emphasis on being unique as they are socially encouraged to break the mould, express their freedom and design their lives, including certain rites of passage. A wedding for their generation is a manifestation of the young couple's creativity, good taste and healthy sense of humour. Above all else, though, it expresses the growing importance of the ideal (some might say myth) of romantic love.

The wedding is perceived today more as an event for the couple and less for the extended family. This change is reflected in the couple's central (and often exclusive) role in planning the event and the choices this entails. Even the nature of wedding invitations has changed accordingly: in the past, the invitation was from the bride and groom's parents, whereas today it comes from the couple. Furthermore, while wedding invitations used to follow a certain format that included mostly practical information (the time and place), nowadays the goal is to convey style and generate empathy. The digital world (email, WhatsApp etc.) provides invitations with a new interactive aspect: guests are welcome to comment – express their enthusiasm and share congratulations – as well as send photos and videos before and after the wedding.

Wedding preparations used to be a breeding ground for family conflicts. Nowadays, with the symbiosis between parents and their children, this seems to be less of a concern. Although most parents still pay a significant portion of the wedding costs, they tend to let the couple do 'whatever they want, after all, it's their wedding...'

For many young people, the wedding is a dream production, i.e. a onetime opportunity to fulfil the ultimate experience, the party of all parties, all according to their personal taste. This is also an opportunity to treat and impress their friends. That's why they spend so much time 'shopping' for every part of the event. They also enjoy this phase very much, because they get to play the part of the 'rich customer'.

The decisions phase is long, exhausting and often a source of tension between partners, for three reasons: first, the high expectations from the event and social pressure to succeed; second, this is young people's first experience of managing a complex project; third, the market's supply is infinite and confusing. Millennials, who struggle with making a decision on any matter, suddenly find themselves having to make a lot of seemingly fateful decisions – from the event's concept (indoor or outdoor venue, beach, forest) to planning the smallest details: the menu, wedding dress (often more than one), the groom's suit, make-up and hair design, photography, lighting, music, bar service, wedding rings, the bouquet, flower arrangements, table dressing, chuppah design and more.

Over time, online forums offering guidance and tips on preparation for the event have appeared. Unsurprisingly, there are almost no grooms in these forums, as the wedding is perceived by most people around the world as well as in Israel as the bride's night. Polls show that the bride is indeed more dominant than the groom when it comes to making decisions about the event.

The urge to be unique converges with commercial motives, generating an extensive industry of wedding production professionals offering various services.

As one would expect, the need to be original and produce an unforgettable event, results in all 'onetime' weddings being unique in the exact same way. This happens for three reasons: the fact that it's all been done before, the urge that still exists in young people to be like everyone else (at least on the most basic level) and the fact that the event is produced by commercial companies that offer the same services to everyone.

Bulimic Parade

The basic menu used to be comprised of an appetizer, main course and dessert. Nowadays, the wedding feast is a bulimic parade, offering a variety of fine dining dishes and gourmet morsels. Young people consider food and drinks to be the key to the event's success, which is why the bride and groom go back and forth tasting and consulting in order to come up with a 'winning menu'. The 'tasting dinner' has actually become a whole ritual also attended by the bride and groom's parents.

In most weddings the amount of food greatly surpasses the guests' stomach capacity. Everyone is aware of the utter wastefulness and the unnecessary showing off, and yet they keep caving in to the social edict of more, more and more. Some young people occasionally post reservations about this contemptible norm, though very few of them, if any, are willing to go against the tide.

Active Bar

Whereas once the guests would raise one small glass to toast the bride and groom, nowadays the wedding is a real banquet with a variety of drinks and professionally-made cocktails. Young people, for whom drinking culture is part of their lifestyle, put a lot of thought and money into the alcohol served at their wedding. Many are willing to 'upgrade' the basic selection of drinks provided by the venue or caterer, even at significant costs, since this is one of the criteria that determine the quality of the wedding and the memories it leaves behind.

Millennials are particularly fond of the 'active bar' concept: the waiting staff leave their posts and come to the dance floor holding trays of shot glasses for the guests. In addition to alcohol, smoking weed has also become popular in recent years. It's meant to help the guests bond, lower their inhibitions and fuel the joy.

Bang your Head to the Beat

Millennials and music are inseparable; therefore, it is only natural that the DJ leading the wedding would be carefully selected as would the musical repertoire – including the song played while they're walking down the aisle and the song played after the groom breaks the glass (these songs usually have sentimental value).

Big weddings often include a performer, whose cost is set according to his or her popularity, usually making the wedding significantly more expensive. In some weddings, the bride and groom even put on a little show inspired by *Israeli Pop Idol*, with their friends sometimes accompanying them as their backing singers.

The party depends on the music's quality and over the years the quality and volume have improved. This is where the guests are divided in two: young people who dance and (grumpy) old people who can't even hear themselves think.

The dancing stage is the climax of the wedding and a very important measure of its success. As the hour draws late, the older people abandon the dance floor and the young people take over. The DJ and lightman lead the alcohol-infused dancers into a whirlwind of rhythm (usually dance music with a Middle Eastern flavour), and everyone becomes devoted to shaking their hips, stomping their feet and waving their hands in the air. They hug each other fondly, shower each other with compliments ('I love you, man'), sing along with the well-known chorus, smile blissfully and roar in delight, like wild animals who have just been released from captivity. Every once in a while, they go to the bar and 'refuel' while raising a toast together. Although everyone is immersed in his or her spontaneous movements, the main theme is togetherness and solidarity. The best friends carry the bride and groom on their shoulders, dancing in a circle or a row in a collective celebration of senses that lasts until the wee hours of the night, even when most of the older people have left (truly good friends don't leave the party until it's over).

Documentary

Since the invention of the camera, the wedding was one of the most important scenes for family photos. The emergence of video photography in the late 1970s changed the tradition of documenting weddings as well as the nature of the event itself. Thanks to video, weddings have become a staged production with the young couple as its stars.

The development of digital photography and the increasing pool of photography and film school graduates have built a blooming industry that offers high-quality photography services. The well-equipped photography crew blends in with the guests and captures the moments of joy, happiness and relief on stills and on video.

The photo shoot actually begins on the morning of the wedding day (and often even earlier), as the preparations and the journey to the venue are also documented. On their way there, the bride and groom naturally stop to take tacky postcard-style photos against the background of the appropriate landscape.

The artistic photo gallery will serve as colourful proof of the party, its protagonists and stages, demonstrating its success (who came, who danced with whom and how excited everyone was).

Professional photos from the wedding as well as spontaneous smartphone photos are uploaded to a dedicated website and occasionally to the photographer and the couple's Facebook page, expanding on and echoing the touching event.

Another recurring custom in recent years is a short video presentation usually prepared by the young couple's closest friends. Sometimes the video is more humorous, while other times it's more like an episode of *This Is Your Life*. It should be noted that millennials are the first generation to be visually documented in their cribs and even prior to that, which is why it's easy and tempting to prepare a montage of moments in their lives, which are also moments in the family's history.

When Fun Becomes a Fine

Up until a few years ago, all wedding venues had a kind of 'tub' for storing presents, though nowadays this item is more of an archaeological artifact, as there's unlikely to be anyone out there who dares to bring something larger than a standard envelope as a wedding gift. There is an implied contract between the hosts who've spent so much money on their wedding, and the guests who are required to 'at least cover the cost of the main course'.

Receiving a wedding invitation has therefore become more like getting a fine, which leads people to avoid weddings and other events using all sorts of excuses.

The wedding's financial burden is particularly heavy for millennials, who are already struggling to make ends meet, especially since they are surrounded by friends, and therefore are invited to a lot of weddings. This creates a paradox, in which they expect to receive cheques from their friends when they get married, but when they're invited, they bitch and moan.

One interviewee framed it like this: 'when you see a couple announce they are getting married, you start thinking how much is this going to cost me'. When there's no choice, only one partner attends the wedding (not to mention the kids, who are no longer welcome anyway), in order to 'minimize the losses'.

Since couples know that the gift is a burden for the guests (mostly the young ones), they feel the need to give them their money's worth. This inflates the cost of the wedding and forces them to invite hundreds of guests (in order to cover the costs and 'turn a profit'), to the point where in most weddings the bride and groom don't even get a chance to greet all of the guests. In many cases the wedding's costs surpass the profits, essentially making the couple start their lives together in 'overdraft'. Recently, public criticism of the phenomenon has increased, describing the extravagant weddings as an outcome of a materialistic and hedonistic culture. In the meantime there is no apparent change on the horizon, except from a few nonconformist-alternative modest wedding parties.

When the Party's Over

Honey, Honey, Honey

Since falling in love has become a status symbol, and since millennials are an exhibitionist generation that's used to echoing their feelings and experiences onto their friends, engaged couples and newlyweds tend to showcase their 'amazing relationship'. It's important for them to show everyone how in love they are and get 'likes', so they tend to share sweet personal messages with friends.

Birthdays and anniversaries also provide an opportunity for showing their friends how romantic they are. They write a mushy post on each other's Facebook walls, while their friends quickly 'moo' back, expressing their admiration for the lovely romantic gesture.

The Hangover

Many young couples (more commonly women) experience an emotional crisis after the wedding, exhibited by depression, decreased sex drive, fatigue and introversion.

The crisis happens when they come down to reality after the party's euphoria, anxious about starting an adult life with commitments, concerned about losing their freedom and the gap between high expectations prior to the wedding (including expectations from their partner) and the dull, everyday reality.

Many couples experience a strain on the relationship. The fireworks from the honeymoon and from before the wedding are replaced with bitterness and mutual accusations, leading in some cases to a break-up.

This is Farewell

A high percentage of millennials come from broken homes, which has left them with a bitter perspective on the institute of marriage. Furthermore, as the age of divorce drops, they also get the impression from their divorcing friends that marriage ends badly and quickly, increasing their distaste for it. One interviewee said: 'even those who are madly in love when they get married make huge compromises! How many perfect couples do you know? Many of those who have found great love will find themselves divorced with great hate'. This theme is also occasionally discussed online.

It is so symbolic and indicative of the spirit of the times that when you type ' the decision to get' into Google, the search engine first suggestion is 'a divorce' and not 'married'.

The global divorce rate is constantly on the rise and the same goes for Israel – particularly in the secular Jewish population. Studies have found several background variables that increase the potential for divorce (according to statistical correlations): getting married at a young age; a previous marriage; when the wife is significantly older than the husband; different levels of education; different ethnic origins. Studies also show that the longer people are married, the less they are likely to get a divorce.

Some of these variables raise the potential for divorce among millennials, but there is another, particularly significant variable at work against them: their parents' divorce. Statistics show that people who experienced their parents' divorce as children are more likely to have difficulties with relationships as adults (the younger the child is during the divorce, the greater the damage in adulthood).

Consequently, millennials are more prone to divorce than their parents. 'Fast-track divorce' – i.e. within three years of marriage – is already a phenomenon. Some even don't last one year.

This creates a tragic paradox: the generation that strives to recover from the negative marriage experience of their parents, are actually more likely to get divorced.

In addition to family background, there are other cultural factors that raise millennials' potential for divorce:

Expectations of Marriage are Too High. The myth of love and relationships, which has grown much stronger since the late 1970s due to the influence of television and cinema culture, has led to excessive expectations. These expectations lead to disappointment, which often leads to a break-up.

Till Doubt Do Us Part. Many young people enter the marriage 'not sold on themselves', and the first real crisis amplifies that doubt, which eventually increases the chances of the marriage falling apart.

Honest with Themselves. Millennials are prone to admit weakness, hardships and mistakes and therefore are quicker to wise up and recognize they've made a mistake. This is unlike previous generations who weren't keen on admitting their faults, not to themselves and least of all in public, which is why they would often continue to stay in a failing marriage.

Increased Life Expectancy. Some claim that the institution of marriage isn't suitable for today's life expectancy. Acknowledging the high probability that the marriage won't last for many years is a self-fulfilling prophecy. Many feel (and rightfully so, statistically speaking), that there will be other opportunities for a new romantic relationship.

Late Marriage. Psychologists claim that marriage at a later age – which is more common nowadays – makes it harder to adjust to life in a committed relationship and deepens the longing for their previous single life. Married couples above the age of 30 also have to have babies quickly, which may increase the potential for entering a whirlpool of difficulties even before their relationship has managed to take root.

Self-Fulfilment. In the past, the goal of a stable relationship and parenthood overshadowed the pursuit of happiness and self-fulfilment. Today, questions like: 'is this what I wanted out of life?' have become legitimate, and therefore more common. In many cases, the answer brings forth inner turmoil, leading to a drastic change, including a change in marital status.

Never Learned to Give. Millennials were never taught how to give, share, make concessions or please other people. The focus on one's self weakens married life, making it more vulnerable.

Nothing is Irreplaceable. Millennials were raised in an ever-changing environment where everything is temporary and replaceable. As a result, even the institution of marriage is seen by many as a product with a limited shelf life. When it gets worn out or becomes less desirable, we can try upgrading to a new 'product'.

The Curse of Routine. Routine, children, the accumulating fatigue, the demanding job – these are all things that couples from previous generations had to face as well. The difference is that in this fast-paced age of stimulation and temptation, people get bored more quickly and seek out new thrills. For millennials, who have grown accustomed to having a wild sex life before marriage, the crisis of routine is probably more destructive.

Online Temptations. The virtual world offers opportunities at the click of a button. On one hand, a secret online relationship with a man or woman could 'air out' the marriage and prevent affairs. On the other hand, it challenges and endangers it.

Prone to Giving Up. Some psychologists believe that lack of resilience is the main cause for marriages falling apart quickly. According to their perception, young people these days are quick to give up and abandon ship, because they are unable to deal with crises and stand the 'pressure cooker' of living together. When they realize that being in a relationship in a shared household is harder than they'd expected, the collapse begins. Instead of stepping up and working on improving the relationship they would rather call the whole thing off.

Modern Parenting. Couples of this generation most commonly get divorced when a baby is introduced to the family. This phenomenon started with Generation X but grew strong in Generation Y, particularly due to the new female assertiveness and the new expectations about the male's role within the family framework. The tension between high expectations from the young father and his inability to actually perform undermines the relationship and increases the potential for divorce.

The Pressures of Livelihood. Millennials have to work long hours to make a living, so it's only natural that this attrition would affect their relationships. Furthermore, many millennials work odd jobs and struggle to make ends meet, which heightens the tension at home. Many also enter into matrimony in a poor financial state. Despite the feminist approach, many young women still expect their husbands to be the primary breadwinners. When this expectation turns out to be false, it leads to disappointment and disillusion, undermining the relationship.

Girl Power. Whereas in the past couples stayed together for economic reasons, these reasons are not as substantial nowadays, and many young people prefer to 'cut short' to avoid 'getting caught up with property and kids'. Furthermore, in the past, when considering a divorce, many women were concerned about the repercussions due to their absolute dependency on the man who was the sole provider. These days, more and more women are financially independent and capable of providing for themselves and for their kids.

Studies show that the active force in breaking up a relationship nowadays is usually the woman. Women are no longer willing to tolerate cheating, mistrust, lack of control over property and obviously violence of any kind. They're also no longer willing to stay in a marriage that isn't physically and emotionally satisfying. Furthermore, the internet provides women who have doubts about their marriage with accessible sources of information and support on the different aspects of divorce.

Social Benefits for Single Parents. Social legislation in recent years offers benefits to single parents, making the decision to get a divorce easier. The chances of a single mom (most single parents are women) falling into financial problems and even poverty may be very high, but the support of the state and local authorities make it easier to survive.

No Longer Stigmatic. In the first decades of Israel the integrity of the family unit was usually above all other personal considerations. Even couples in unstable relationships weren't quick to get a divorce due to the social stigma that would befall them and their children. This stigma has weakened through the years, while tolerance for different lifestyles has increased. Divorce is no longer an unusual phenomenon and being a divorcee is no longer a badge of shame. Divorce is even associated nowadays with freedom, courage and independent thought and many people see it as a phase, en route to turning over a new leaf such as in a career move.

(Not) Staying Together for the Kids. Children used to serve as a substantial obstacle for divorce, as parents were concerned about the damage it might inflict on them at an early age. Nowadays, more and more psychologists encourage couples to break up a bad marriage, claiming that having two functioning families is better for the children than one dysfunctional family. According to this view, toddlers who get used to living with just one parent or with someone who isn't their biological parent, eventually take it for granted. Furthermore, being children of divorce is no longer perceived as something unusual or particularly traumatic, while parents' willingness to sacrifice their own happiness for their children is constantly decreasing.

Weaker Ties with Extended Family. In traditional families, the bonds of matrimony went beyond the husband and wife and also included their families. The living space contained the extended family, who covertly supervised the couple. Nowadays, many couples lead their lives completely separate from the extended family, making it much easier and simpler to part ways.

Monkey See, Monkey Do. Beyond all the aforementioned reasons, there's definitely a normative process of emotional contagion which affects the divorce rate. When young couples see that the people around them are breaking up their marriages, it encourages them to follow in their footsteps (after some cracks have already formed).

What will Become of the Family?

How do millennials deal with divorce? Since this is a young generation, we currently don't have any statistics on the phenomenon. However, based on a basic understanding of their general characteristics as well as interviews we held with several divorced couples of this generation, we can make some assumptions. On one hand, the experience they gain during their single life is supposed to make their divorce crisis easier. On the other hand, the financial instability, dependency and low resilience increase the potential for damage. Many millennials live from hand to mouth, without a steady job; hence, a divorce could seriously worsen their situation and increase their dependence on external forces (mainly their parents and other members of the family). Divorce can also cause serious damage because the men of this generation are more sensitive and more involved in raising their children, making it harder for them to deal with the broken parenting structure.

However, this deep crisis in the family institution could serve perhaps as a precursor for a structural change that will solve the problem of divorce in the future. Up to this point, society assumed that long-lasting marriage was the correct state and divorce was a 'malfunction' that should be amended or a 'disease' that should be healed. Meanwhile, we're approaching a point at which divorced people are no longer the abnormal. The day when couples who only part in death are the minority isn't very far away. Even today, over 40 per cent of all families are defined as 'non-normative', with a growing number of alternatives to the framework of a married couple that raises their children in one home.

Meanwhile, the long-standing taboo on non-monogamy is also weakening. In fact, there are already quite a few young people living non-monogamously, with romantic relationships becoming narrower and more short-term.

Generation Y might be indirectly signalling to society as a whole that we need to update the norms and create more flexible alternatives. This naturally leads to difficulties, due to mankind's basic need for stability, security and a consistent intimate relationship as well as the functional role long-term relationships play in raising children and grandchildren.

In our estimation, the tension between the long-standing convention and the ongoing development will only worsen over the years, and millennials will play an important role in this process. It's not coincidental that an increasing number of young people are interested in living in a kibbutz (including former kibbutz members who are now returning). The next phase might be bringing back the communal children's house through the backdoor (with some obvious tinkering) in an attempt to offer an updated parenting alternative.

13

Helpless Parenting – Millennials Raising Kids

Birthrate and Procreation

Fewer Children Per Family

The dropping fertility rate is a global trend that's creating a new demographic reality. The main reasons for this phenomenon are the growing importance of material wealth (fewer children = fewer expenses); the rising cost of raising a child (clothing, computers, after school courses, moving to a bigger apartment etc.), the growing importance of the paedocentric ethos, which requires parents to spend more time with the child (more children = less time per child) so they can be 'the best parents ever'; and the fact people get married and have their first child later in life (partly because women want to acquire an education and build a career before starting a family). The rising divorce rate and lower divorce age have also made an impact: many couples get divorced after the first or second child, leading to no more babies.

There are two additional important reasons for this: the desire to bring a child into this world and raise the child together is an expression of deep love. But in a world that puts selfishness above all, marital love weakens, consequently weakening the mutual desire to create new life. Egocentrism also weakens the altruistic urge that's the primary motivation for having children. Many people are simply concerned that a child would rob them of time and energy and lower their quality of life. The other reason for the reluctance to have children (adding to fertility statistics) is the concern women have over losing their job following pregnancy and childbirth.

Israel is somewhat different than the global trend, because it inhabits large traditional populations (mostly ultra-Orthodox Jews and Bedouins) which typically have high fertility rates. Nevertheless, even here, mostly in the non-religious Jewish sector, the past few generations have shown a considerable decline in fertility rates (due to the aforementioned reasons). It is particularly prominent among the younger population, dropping below replacement level.

Childless by Choice

One out of five women in the western world chooses not to have children (compared to one out of ten women in the 1950s). This is the extreme expression of the drop in fertility, entitled 'childless by choice'. This choice, whose mere existence was ignored up until recently, is becoming a social trend with far-reaching repercussions on western society. *Time Magazine* dedicated a special issue to this trend entitled 'The Childfree Life', which polled the lowest birthrates ever in Europe and the United States.

The phenomenon of childless couples led to a growing market of services. From self-help books (e.g. *Childfree and Loving It!*), through support groups (like the Vancouver-based No Kidding! Group or the The British Childfree Association), to products made especially for these families (for example, Honda designed a dog seat that is a substitute for the child seat).

There are many reasons for choosing a life without kids. Some declare they don't feel the passion to become parents; some are not willing to pay the financial and emotional toll of parenting; others would rather avoid it out of ideology, like the concern of bringing a child into a world of misery and suffering or the refusal to succumb to society's norms.

Experts note that most childless couples didn't make a conscious decision not to have children, but rather simply postponed the decision to start a family until the reality of being childless at some point became an irreversible fact. Only about a third of them make a conscious decision not to start a family.

Millennials are also motivated by anxiety: the fear of taking on a huge physical and emotional responsibility, fear of failure, and sometimes fear of pregnancy and childbirth. Some even have concerns about having kids because of their negative experience as children of divorce.

And what of Israel? Most Israelis (90 per cent as of 2013) still consider children to be 'the greatest joy in life' and over half (57 per cent) believe that a life without children is an empty one. However, in light of the processes experienced by Generation Y, it's likely that in time more and more single people and couples will choose not to have children. Public statements that defy supreme family values in the media are indicative of the upcoming trend.

The lessened motivation for having children and the growing social legitimization for the trend are also reflected in the voices of parents who dare for the first time in history to publicly admit having regrets about bringing children into this world.

Terrified Male in the Delivery Room

Childbirth used to be the sole domain of women. The older women in the family (mother, grandmother, aunt, big sister) would be there to guide the mother-to-be. When the delivery was moved from the home to the hospital, doctors and midwifes replaced the women of the family. However, it was customary for one female member of the family to be there during the delivery.

The husband's presence at the delivery room started to gain momentum during the 1970s, becoming more common in the 80s, with the ascension of the sensitive man figure. By the early 2000s, it had become the sweeping norm. This is essentially the 'grand finale' of the 'new man's' involvement in pregnancy and childbirth – from the ultra-sonography through childbirth preparation courses to being there at the actual delivery.

For most millennial couples, the husband's presence in the delivery room is elementary. It is commonly believed that if you created a life, you don't just enjoy the 'fun' part of conception and sit out the rest of it. You need to be part of the entire process, including the 'hard' part of actual childbirth. This norm creates several problems, which are usually disregarded.

Many young men experience childbirth as a stressful, traumatic event, mainly due to the gap between romantic expectations and the bleeding reality (excretions, squirming and screaming from pain). Because of their low mental resilience, not only do they not help the woman in labour and the medical staff but in many cases they actually make the experience more stressful.

Studies have shown that for some men, seeing the birth of a baby later causes them to avoid having sexual relations with their partner due to the negative association. This phenomenon might have had an impact on the increased divorce rate among millennials.

In recent years, men have taken on another role in the delivery room – documenting the event. What started out as random shots on the smartphone has turned into a millennial trend – photos posted in real-time or sent to friends shortly after.

The Cult of Parenthood

'My Everything'

Parents have always talked fondly and proudly about their children, but millennials seem to have completely lost a handle on things. Affectionate parenthood has become such an important status symbol for this generation that public spaces (social media included) are full of open and often excessive displays of affection towards children: kisses, hugs, songs, compliments and words of endearment. More than the need to inform the environment of 'how precious and special my child is', this behaviour is intended to showcase the parent as dedicated and attentive. This is also the reason why birthday parties for children of millennials are blown out of proportion, accompanied by sappy posts on Facebook about the offspring: 'my beloved, today you are two years old. Thank you for the great privilege of being your father, thank you for two extraordinary years, during which I understood what it's like to have someone who's more important to me than I am.'

Primal Parenthood

The provocative *Time Magazine* cover from May 2012 showed a photograph of a three-year-old child who stands on a chair in order to suckle from his 26-year-old mother's breast. The headline was: 'Are You Mom Enough?' The article, which made a lot of noise about the legitimacy of public breastfeeding, introduced Dr. Bill Sears' 'attachment parenting'. This is a trend of 'vegan parenting' that encourages the mother to return to her primordial roots. For example, carrying the child on her person throughout the day and breastfeeding them until a late age.

American 'whims' usually arrive in Israel in small doses, and the first people influenced by this approach were young parents. A community called 'Like Nature Intended' was established recently in Israel, with an active and lively website that publishes articles about the 'continuum concept' – raising children 'naturally' the way human beings have been raised since the dawn of mankind. Externalizing breastfeeding and others expressions of closeness between a mother and her children is part of the externalization of parenthood, and to a great extent the result of a general cultural atmosphere that encourages people to express their emotions publicly.

My Little Genius

Most young parents have been swept by psycho-capitalist propaganda, which focuses on the message that in order to succeed in life, one must get an early start as quickly as possible. That's why you shouldn't let the baby just stare at the crib. You need to stimulate his/her senses, teach and train them. Every toy and game has an educational purpose and every class serves as a step for the next competitive stage.

When the young parents' naivety, dogmatism, guilt and insecurity face a sophisticated marketing mechanism, it leads to a massive market of educational toys and enrichment courses ('Baby Yoga – from birth to crawling', 'Sounds for Toddlers – from crawling to walking', 'Sibling Relations Workshop', 'Music and Stories' etc.). These things empty the young families' already depleted wallets and increase the pressure on the family. Over time, it leads to the perception that money buys all, including good parenting.

Many parents develop an obsession for promoting their children, which is manifested in the search for unique educational institutions, pushing them to centre stage and accompanying them on every class and practice. This can also be seen in the numerous WhatsApp parent groups dedicated to kindergartens and elementary schools, where criticism and protest directed at the teachers are the norm, leading to constant pressure on the system.

Branded Children

The parental status symbol is also acquired through gift culture. Whereas in the past children expected modest birthday gifts, nowadays, parents and grandparents shower their children and grandchildren with countless expensive luxuries. Ironically, this actually makes the children appreciate materialistic gestures less. They become demanding and incapable of gratitude. They also get tired of things quickly and become increasingly enslaved to outside stimulation.

Furthermore, instead of playing with the toys their parents bought for them, they turn to their exhausted parents leading to their eventual collapse.

The pressure of pleasing one's child also comes from the advertising world that parents and children alike are exposed to. Children who don't wear the right brand of shirt or shoes, or carry a branded backpack and pencil case, are labelled as 'outsiders' among their friends and are doomed to suffering and distress. Their parents are tormented by guilt. What used to be reasonable when millennials were children is now out of control, as they themselves are now parents and the overbearing advertising mechanism strikes at them from every direction. The tyranny of brands currently has a stronger impact on parents who are older than millennials, i.e. with children in kindergarten and elementary school. However, as time goes by its impact extends to younger parents as well. These days, babies leave the hospital surrounded by brands, with the most advanced baby carriage, matching diaper bag and fashionable clothes.

Documented Love

Millennials' parents had to carry around big video cameras in order to commemorate exciting onetime events in their children's lives, such as birthdays and kindergarten parties. Millennial parents have smartphones, and they document their children and their parenting experiences on a daily, borderline obsessive basis, as they've grown used to document and share every other experience in this way. Every smile, every new hair, every new outfit or graceful sneeze are recorded and uploaded for viewing and feedback. This is the silent cause for the next generational problem: toddlers who are used to posing for the camera from the day they were born and might become self-centred and disengaged at a whole new level.

Why is so much Emotional Weight Attributed to Parenthood?

Expanding the Tradition. Millennials were raised by over-protective parents, who educated their children according to the paedocentric ethos, so it's only natural for them to continue along this path and expand on it. Since they never acquired the authoritative language and because many of them are very immature, they tend to treat their children like a little brother or sister or like a pet and talk down to them (in content as well as in tone of voice).

Alternative Career. The cult of parenthood that has swept western society has leveraged the ethos of child grooming to a new level of worship, pushing millennials to become the supreme parent. The urge to excel and develop a 'parenting career' sometimes serves as an opportunity to make up for the parents' personal failings, particularly in the world of employment.

Escape from a Full-Time Job. Quite a few young women choose to be 'full-time moms' out of an either conscious or unconscious desire to escape the career rat race, which wore them down earlier in life. Once they choose to devote themselves to raising their children, they do it wholeheartedly, among other reasons in order to justify their choice to themselves and to the people around them (some also take on part-time jobs).

Late Parenting. Total, externalized commitment to the parenting role is also derived from the fact that many young people become parents at a relatively late age, making it the fulfillment of a lifelong dream.

Maternal Fatherhood

Fathers of previous generations saw their primary role as providing for the family, supporting and protecting the mother and disciplining the children. Men would come home tired after a long day's work, and quickly sink into the living room couch to watch some TV. They didn't spend much time with their children and were barely involved in their personal lives.

These days, however, men's parental awareness has changed since society expects fathers to also step into traditionally 'maternal' roles. Western media encourages men to 'open up to their maternal side' and shows countless demonstrations of 'new dads' excelling at their job.

This new concept of fatherhood is spreading due to the equality ethos as well as the common notion that parenting is essentially an acquired skill. Men used to be 'exempt' from everyday childcare and were encouraged to focus on providing for the family. For women, being a mom was life's purpose. Life within extended families allowed for a flow of information and life experience from grandmothers and older aunts to young mothers, while also passing on gender role expectations. People used to say half-jokingly that parenting was the only profession in modern society that doesn't require any training or qualification. Nowadays, however, when every parental action comes with an instruction manual, they can also be passed on to men, much like giving instructions for home cooking.

The results are in: studies show that the number of hours fathers dedicate to taking care of children and housework has nearly tripled in the past fifty years. The tightening bond between fathers and their children is also manifested in their participation in activities that were once women-only, such as waking up at night to take care of the baby, changing nappies, dropping the kids off at kindergarten and school and taking them to the playground.

Millennials try to implement the 'maternal fatherhood' model more than any previous generation, since they themselves feel like they were raised by more sensitive fathers (including divorced fathers who naturally felt the need to be more 'motherly'), because they're more exposed to this model than in the past (through the media), and because they are fundamentally more 'feminine' and pluralistic in their views and lifestyle. Israeli society is starting to recognize the cultural change, and even the establishment is starting to accept this new fatherhood. In June 2013, the traditional 'jobs for moms' in civil service was changed into 'jobs for parents'. It allows both men and women to leave work early. As of May 2015, some 8 per cent of the people who requested this benefit were men.

In the past few years, young fathers have been given a platform on blogs and forums for sharing the challenges of parenting with their friends. They demonstrate Generation Y's softer model of fatherhood as well as the openness and collaborative nature of this generation. For instance, Facebook group 'Papazone', established in February 2012 by journalist Or Barnea, three years after his wife founded 'Mamazone' (which became immensely popular, quickly turning into a platform for thousands of mothers to discuss everything related to raising their children). According to Barnea, the dad group was founded so 'we could also share our world, talk and consult about our children and everything else that's on our minds'.

In January 2014, Omri Imbar formed the 'Dad Parliament' on Xnet's family section – which was defined as 'the first dedicated platform for dad blogs'. In an interview with Liat Schlesinger for *La'Isha Magazine,* he said: 'the idea was to bring the issue of fatherhood into public awareness. You can't throw a stone without hitting 300 mom bloggers. And I thought: "what about the men?" I think it used to be harder for people to say "I'm an active father", and now it's said. There's a revolution here.'

Despite identifying with the 'parental father' model, millennial men are still confused and concerned about the burden of expectation from them as parents. Alongside the joy and personal satisfaction that engaged fatherhood brings, it also gives rise to signs of distress, anxiety and frustration, which are also expressed in these blogs.

Since this is a direct and open generation that has no problem with expressing weakness, they publicly express their woes. Many men admit to their awkward function as parents and mock themselves on a variety of online platforms. This phenomenon is also prevalent in popular sitcoms and TV shows such as *Mother's Day, Arab Labor, Super Nanny* and *Traffic Light.* A well-known illustration of this phenomenon can be found in the amusing and cynical children's book by young American author Adam Mansbach. The author puts his son to sleep by reading him a story about animals who go to sleep, and the child is asked to follow their lead. Unlike the typical children's books, however, the request here is direct and blunt (and therefore authentic and funny): every verse ends with the punchline 'go the fuck to sleep', reflecting the desperation of men who have no patience for this annoying task.

This creates a tragic paradox: the generation that identifies with the new model of manhood more than any other generation, is also the least equipped to implement it. Most of them are just too needy and weak to stand up to the task. Millennial fathers face difficulties for several reasons:

Confusing Double Standards from Society. On one hand they are required to play the classic role of the strong, resilient, authoritative and invulnerable man, who sets boundaries and teaches his child to 'fight back' in kindergarten and provide for the family. On the other hand, they're expected to show kindness and love and connect to their 'feminine side' and partake in household chores.

Overbearing Employment World. Most workplaces don't give men enough leeway and require them to work long hours, which makes it harder for them to create a balance between their role as breadwinners and their role as parents. The challenge of being a good employee and a good parent leads to guilt and occasionally to some form of escapism. Many young dads avoid their responsibilities at home and find refuge in artificially prolonging their office hours and taking on more responsibilities. Over time, they even regress to the original concept of manhood, which sees the woman as the primary caretaker and the man as someone who's mostly supposed to support her emotionally and financially. The result is that the romantic idyll seen during the pregnancy clashes with reality.

Lack of Male Authority. The biggest challenge new fathers suffer from is the lack of leadership skills. Many young fathers were raised in pampering houses with no discipline, and some of them also believe you should never confront your children. Everything has to be done pleasantly and nicely. Consequently, male authority disappears from their children's upbringing, and the father, who is supposed to teach, make demands and plot a path for the child, is often managed by the child and struggles with his role as a parent.

New Parenting is Unnatural for Men. Some believe the maternal father model, which generates excessive expectations, actually traps young fathers, because supposedly it's biologically 'unnatural' for men. They have a 'shorter fuse', making them lacking in the required patience for raising children.

Meanwhile, others claim that biology is simply a sexist excuse and that inequality is a social prison. Therefore, in their mind, the new model will eventually bring men more joy.

The Difficulties of Functioning as a Divorced Father. The rising divorce rate has introduced another difficulty. Studies show that divorced fathers – whose numbers are increasingly growing – have a sense of freedom on one hand (released from the burden of raising children which is now rests mostly on the mother) and a strong sense of guilt on the other hand.

The difficulty they experience following the divorce also includes a financial burden as they are required to pay for child support as well as a mental challenge due to the imbalance (between the father and mother) when it comes to custody rights. In recent years, protest among divorced fathers has grown over gender discrimination in the eyes of the law. The government tried to promote a reform at the time, which among others dealt with automatic custody granted to mothers of young children (outraging many men), but it still isn't being implemented, while tensions ensue.

The Single Parent

In the past decades, the traditional family structure (a married couple and their children) is slowly giving way to other types of families. One of the most common alternatives is the single parent family, i.e. a family led only by a man or (usually) a woman, who runs the household on his or her own.

From the mid-1990s until 2010 the number of single parent families in Israel more than doubled. This growth is due to the rising divorce rate as well as the rate of women who choose to have children without a man (by means of artificial insemination or with a partner). The immigration wave from the former Soviet Union has had a substantial impact on this trend, as nearly 20 per cent of immigrants arrived in Israel as single parent families. The immigrants not only changed the statistics, but also helped legitimize the independent family unit (which has also been reflected in the media).

Millennials have expanded this phenomenon in the past few years, with the high rate of single women, this generation's general openness to alternative family models and the fact that their parents are involved in their lives, making it only natural for them to help raise their grandchildren as well. In 2012, 20 per cent of single mothers were under the age of 34.

More men have become single parents by choice in recent years as well. At the moment, this includes mostly divorced men rather than single men, but one can assume this trend will only expand for this gender conventions-bending generation.

Ironically, some divorced fathers actually discover fatherhood after the family break-up, allowing them to make amends. Before, they couldn't spare one minute to spend with their children, but now, as they spend 'quality time' alone with them, they discover they have the ability to function as engaged fathers. They also learn to make time for their children in order to make up for their absence from the family routine.

The new dedication of divorced fathers also indirectly helps the mothers, as they now can catch a break from caring for the kids and have some time for themselves.

Parental Discomfort

One would assume that this pluralistic generation would be open to family harmony and parental peace of mind. In fact, the exact opposite occurs. The expectation to be 'the perfect parents' alongside the challenges at home and the ongoing pressure by unrestrained toddlers (who can sense their parents' weaknesses and exploit them), creates parental discomfort and causes feelings of guilt. Many young parents feel as if they're not good enough. In fact, they see themselves as 'not good enough' the moment the baby first arrives.

Many young parents also develop excessive concerns and become over-protective of their children, trying to remove every obstacle out of their way, thus denying them the opportunity to have experiences and learn from their mistakes.

This generation's insecurity and discomfort as parents are also caused by their tendency to rely on 'operating instructions' and assistance in every situation rather than solving problems on their own. Even when they make decisions by themselves, they are filled with anxiety and doubts: did I do the right thing? Am I causing harm?

The media also has a hand in this. Alarming and sad reports about all sorts of family tragedies are posted almost every hour, described in detail with gruesome photos. Furthermore, these reports are followed by alerts on the dangers that lurk for our children from every direction: on school buses, the crosswalk, kindergarten and even at home with the nanny.

Passive Parenthood

Softer parental authority is the result of an ongoing evolutionary process: increased sensitivity to the child's rights and needs as a person, while restraining oppressive education. One positive result is a consistent drop in the physical and emotional abuse of helpless children. However, what started out as balancing an extreme situation has over time turned to the other extreme.

Education is essentially an ongoing process of testing and learning boundaries and options where the interests of the child and parents meet. However, this task is particularly difficult for a generation of parents who never learned how to deal with conflict. They feel uneasy at the sheer notion of any kind of tension and struggle with being decisive and assertive when necessary (when it comes to instilling healthy sleep habits, restraint, manners, eating habits, cleanliness and more).

Since many millennials lack the resilience and determination that make a strong parent, and since they tend to view any confrontation as violent behaviour, they've created a model of passive parenting. They'd rather talk to children as if they were adults, try to convince them (often going as far as begging them to answer their plea) and avoid 'taking charge'. Many also seek their children's approval for their own behaviour – making sure they didn't cross any lines with their demands.

It's common nowadays to see small children scold their (millennial) parents with no response from the parents, as well as parents who stand there helpless before their 'out of control' child. Phrases like 'dad, you have no clue, you don't understand anything', or 'mom, you're starting to annoy me', are commonplace examples. The interesting part is that such phrases aren't as jarring to the young parents' ears as they are to older generations who witness the incident. This also penetrates into TV commercials, where children are seen rudely scolding their parents, occasionally even mocking them, while the audience cheers.

The damage caused by this phenomenon goes beyond the family, as it also reaches other educational frameworks such as kindergartens and elementary school, where the new teachers are also millennials.

As a result, it's getting harder for older people who were raised on values of restraint, manners and mutual respect to spend time in crowded public spaces such as restaurants, cafés, libraries or public transportation. Small children crawl on the floor, climb chairs, shout, misbehave, cry and make noise while their parents stay quiet and even seem pleased. The passive parenting model is reflected in disregard for other people and public spaces. Young parents don't even ask themselves if their child is bothering other people. As long as it doesn't bother them it's all good.

Competing with the Smartphone

The duration of time parents spent with their children used to be a measure of the quality of the parenting. This criterion has become less relevant nowadays, as the duration itself isn't necessarily an indication of quality, namely introducing a new, destructive element: the smartphone.

Many parents spend time with their children physically, but mentally they're miles away. With one eye watching the child and one ear listening to them, the other eye and ear focus on the tiny screen.

Deep down they know it would be healthier for their children and for them if they cut off, but they lack the courage or the ability to take a digital break. A lot of them just 'peek' every now and then to catch up on things, but as we all know, the smartphone is a source of endless distraction. It's not uncommon to see a parent pushing a baby carriage with one hand and typing with the other.

This leads to 'stuttering parenting', ('sorry honey, did you say something?'). They may be able to deceive themselves, but they're definitely not fooling their kids. They understand that the smartphone is just more interesting to their parents than they are.

What kind of long-term effects will this phenomenon have on the relationship between children and their parents or on the children's emotional and social development? Time will tell. Previously, children would confront their parents about spending too much time at work and neglecting them. Perhaps in the future they will confront their parents for spending too much time with the smartphone. On the other hand, nowadays even toddlers have their heads stuck in smartphones, so both parties are disengaged.

Urgent Help Needed

Confession of Material Failure

Millennials suffer from chronic sleep deprivation. They work long hours, go out a lot, surf the web often and watch a lot of television. Taking care of the kids is another task in a long, exhausting list. Fatigue comes to many families at some point, followed by a total breakdown. In many cases it's linked to a crisis in the parents' relationship, adding to the burden of parenthood. This is also the stage where the 'new man' 'wakes up' from the equal partnership ideal and starts 'faking it' when it comes to housework and caring for the kids.

The high rate of parents who reach the point of collapse, allied to the new social legitimacy for showing weakness, have completely turned the model of ideal motherhood around. Suddenly, men aren't the only ones who can publicly admit that 'parenting isn't fun' – women can do it too (on television, in movies, in literature and on the internet). It turns out that 'motherhood isn't as great' as we were told – particularly if the mother is a millennial. The trend of 'flawed parenting' confessionals, usually performed humorously and ironically, is gaining momentum in the western world, and the debate over this phenomenon is growing more popular by the day. For instance, the *Bad Parent* section on Babble gets 1.8 million views a month, and Truu Mom has collected over 400,000 confessionals from mothers as of October 2014. Such expressions are multiplying in various media outlets in Israel as well and particularly in popular non-fiction books, blogs and social networks.

The maternal failure confession trend is tied, among other things, to a long and wide process of disillusion and demystification from myths and ideals, and to the culture of personal exposure and the loss of intimacy. Advances in feminist worldviews have also played a part in this trend, as they allow women to shed traditional roles or at least bend long-standing gender conventions. One of the sources of this phenomenon is a universal sociological principle: the creation of a new pillar of values is followed by the 'flame adjusting' stage. The ethos of parenthood was important for establishing the updated status of children and women in western culture, but when this ethos leads to moral and puritan zealotry, people start to yearn for proportion.

Some claim that this trend is also related to the common view among millennials that anyone who admits weakness should get 'a pass'. They admit they're not good parents and hope to be forgiven or at least get some help. Famed columnist and blogger Ross Douthat called this phenomenon the 'Parental Pity Party'. It would be interesting to see what millennials' offspring will have to say about these confessions in the future. Some believe the reaction will probably not be so empathetic, for sometimes you're better off not saying anything, even if you have something interesting, honest and bold to tell the world.

Outsourcing of Parenting Roles

The difficulties parents face in performing their duties and the expanding 'outsourcing' trend have led to the creation of a new market of 'parenting services' – from personal trainers and parenting instructors to nursing and sleep consultants.

The industry of parental support extends beyond the period of infancy. Roles that were once reserved for parents like teaching your kid how to ride a bicycle or roller-skating are now performed by professional instructors. The helplessness of young parents and perhaps also laziness, insecurity and fear of making mistakes and failing, have led them to send children off to private ball-kicking lessons. One could argue that a qualified trainer is always better than an amateur parent. On the other hand, this phenomenon augments parental impotence and further weakens their status in their children's eyes.

Return of Parental Authority

There have been countless articles and television programmes in recent years that try to restrain and balance the confusing parenting phenomenon, calling on parents to regain their place in the family and set clear boundaries.

Many young people are well aware of the need to set boundaries for their children, but don't exactly know how to do it and also struggle with it emotionally. This is the source of the rising popularity of parenting workshops and schools as well as television programmes that focus on wise, assertive parenting consultants turned celebs such as Michal Daliot (Israel's *Super Nanny*) and Prof. Amos Rolider.

The new authority trend can be seen in the new approach endorsed by many parenting consultants and instructors. Obviously, most of them do not recommend going back to the age of authoritarian punishment, but rather recalibrate the relationship between parents and their children with a tougher, more determined approach in regards to independence, manners, restraint and boundaries for children. For example, Prof. Amos Rolider, a child psychologist who has become a popular national figure, recommends a 'controlled, age-appropriate, situation-based punitive reaction for children who misbehave'. In his eyes, the real test here is 'withstanding the pressure of tears and responding firmly and consistently'.

'Joint Custody' with the Grandparents

One of the most common solutions for millennials' parenting crisis is bringing in their parents to help with raising the kids. A new pattern can be seen where the grandparents serve as a second pair of parents, often even actively replacing them.

This has also become common because many parents of millennials (mostly grandmothers) have taken early retirement, and they yearn for a relationship with their grandchildren. Grandparents aren't just babysitters any more, they also go to parent-teacher conferences, pay the children's tuition, buy gifts and help with homework.

Parents of millennials feel a strong need to help their children with their first steps as parents because of the helplessness the latter project. Millennials are sending out an S.O.S. to their parents. It's also easy for them to assist because there's no intergenerational tension, and everything is done in a friendly manner out of shared interests. Young people's need to get help from their parents is due to four additional reasons: first, going out is a basic necessity for them, and they can barely afford a babysitter; second, many of them work long hours, under strict employment conditions, and find it hard to spend time with their children even when they're sick. Grandma and Grandpa are called to save the day; third, the education system's incompetence requires another adult to help with schoolwork; fourth, as the divorce rate rises, more single moms require parental help. Divorced fathers also need assistance, and often share their shifts with their parents.

The phenomenon of young parents who require intensive assistance from their own parents in raising their kids is consistent with the 'un-empty nest syndrome'. You could say that we're seeing signs of a return to pre-industrial society, with the extended family living together as a tribe and helping one another. Essentially, everyone benefits: the young parents need help, the grandparents are looking for something to do and for companionship and wish to continue to make a difference and be relevant. Their dedicated care for their grandchildren is sometimes meant to make amends for their own parenting. The grandchildren benefit the most, of course. Studies show that having grandparents around has a major positive impact on the child's mental stability.

14

It's Too Long – Learning in
the Age of Google

A Degree at any Cost – The Most 'Educated' Generation

Statistics and Reality

The Israeli education system has gone through two opposing processes: progress on one hand and decadence on the other. The progress includes significantly more diverse teaching methods and study materials. Educational sciences, which have seen major developments in the past decades, continue to feed and improve the system. Awareness of learning styles, learning disabilities and of the student and teacher's general psychology has grown, creating the more democratic atmosphere in which millennials were raised.

The gaps between ethnic groups, genders and sectors have also gradually diminished. A consistently growing percentage of Israeli students graduate from high school with a diploma and pave their way into higher education. Considerable resources are invested in the field of education, by public bodies (the government, local authorities, NGOs etc.) as well as by parents. In the 1990s (millennials' adolescent years) the investments were particularly high, even when compared to other western countries. In other words, Generation Y was raised in the most highly budgeted education system in the history of Israel.

Despite this positive trend, the results did not meet expectations, and criticism for the system only grows with each passing year. Various findings show a consistent drop in quality, not just compared to other countries, but also compared to past data in Israel. Millennials are actually the first generation to go from first grade to twelfth grade in a distressed education system. They are the product of a cumbersome, conservative institution that has failed to adapt to the spirit of the time, an institution that struggles to recruit high quality teachers and delays the introduction of alternatives to obsolete methods. The few alternatives that have managed to take root are non-regional 'special schools' that are usually the product of local initiatives by caring parents who have the means and determination required. Many of these educational projects had to overcome bureaucratic and political obstacles by forcing de facto changes.

Millennials are also a generation raised under the ideology of 'putting the child at the centre' (paedocentric pedagogy). This pedagogy promotes sensitivity to the students' needs and their human dignity on one hand, while on the other hand reducing the authority credit of teachers and making it difficult for them to mark boundaries, control behaviour and to motivate their students with a high level of effort and determination.

This created a paradoxical gap between the level of this generation's formal accreditation and the actual width and depth of their real education. When it comes to official diplomas, millennials are the most educated generation in the history of mankind, particularly in western countries. In Israel, this is the first generation in which most of its secular Jewish boys and girls graduated from high school. The percentage of Bagrut (matriculation) certificates and academic degrees among this generation is also the highest in the history of Israel.

Statistics don't tell the whole story, however. What really hides behind the Bagrut certificate? Does the education system truly produce educated, curious people? What kind of intellectual and moral values do they acquire after twelve years of school? So far, no one has ever tried to answer these questions in a precise, comprehensive manner. College professors bear witness to the naked truth perhaps more than anyone else. But despite feelings of discomfort in hallway conversations and departmental seminars, the system's official response silences and represses this harsh reality.

You Wanna get Nuts? Let's get Nuts!

The general trend of softening authoritative education and putting the child at the centre instead of teachers and educators has undermined order and discipline in kindergartens and schools as early as the 1980s. However, this trend was radicalized in the 1990s to the point of partially neutralizing the education system. This happened under the auspices of laws, regulations and procedures (led by the Knesset and Ministry of Education), public and academic policy as well as media influence.

Violence in schools, which is only an extreme example of the loss of control, isn't a new phenomenon in the Israeli education field. The classroom has always been a sensitive, volatile arena, and crises between teachers and students have always been an issue. However, this previously marginal phenomenon has become a malignant disease during Generation Y's teen years.

Millennials' parents didn't just fail to mitigate the crisis in education, they actively escalated it. Many of them were aggressively demanding, disrespecting and defiant against the authority and actions of principals and teachers, often to the point of verbal as well as physical violence and excusing disobedient students. Millennials were the victims of this phenomenon, which undermined their learning environment and compromised their future.

No Effort Needed

The forgiving, lenient approach has also left its mark on the bar of educational requirements. The general approach in schools attended by millennials was and is 'let's make it easier instead of harder': let's be generous with grades, ignore tardiness, truancy, and discipline violations and bring educational requirements down to a minimum, and often far below the minimum. Also, let's praise the young students for every modicum of achievement, no matter how minor.

The 'child at the centre' worldview, the worship of statistical (and completely mechanical) success rates and the parents' pressure brought forth a general approach of 'meeting the student halfway'. This approach lowered their commitment to learn, encouraged laziness and generated ignorance.

Bored Now

The widespread chaos in schools in recent years is a product of the deep social crisis Israeli society is in and the Ministry of Education and academic establishment's ongoing, systemic failure. The reasons for this are as follows:

Unstable, Incoherent Educational Agenda based on shifting political considerations.

Dry, Boring Educational Programmes that produced pseudo-ADHD (a bored student often becomes an interrupting student). Many of these programmes include archaic texts, filled with bloated and ridiculous academic jargon.

Obsolete Teaching Environments with a blackboard and chalk, teacher in a classroom, pen and paper which are no longer suitable for the new age.

Excessive Burden on the Teachers, resulting from too many exams, meetings, seminars and red tape. This makes their professional lives miserable, and does not leave much time for the important stuff.

Over-emphasis on Theoretical Knowledge. Many students are completely unsuitable for academic learning, and any attempt to force it upon them is harmful and futile. At the same time, arts and vocational education programmes have suffered ongoing cuts.

Importing and Developing Pretentious and Reckless Educational Programmes. These programmes have compromised many skills such as mathematical and language based ones.

But above all, the education system excels in stagnation when it comes to changing the traditional outline of frontal instruction. This problem significantly escalated when cellphones entered schools. Millennials are actually the first generation to go to school with a phone in their pockets, and its influence has left its mark on their ability to pay attention and concentrate.

Out-of-Touch System

Generation Y was born into the PC revolution and developed along with it. However, this mostly took place at home rather than at school. Parents bought their children desktops, laptops and smartphones, and they acquired know-how and dexterity in the digital world on their own. Meanwhile, most classrooms stuck to the traditional learning methods, highlighting education in schools as an irrelevant desert island within a new, growing and dynamic world.

The education system also failed to adapt to millennials' daily lifestyle in the age of leisure. Many students go out in the evenings (on weekends as well as on school nights). They also surf the internet or watch TV until late at night. As a result, they have a hard time waking up in the morning. They tend to come to school tired, if they even bother showing up at all. Their parents, lacking in authority, would be inclined to give them a pass on this issue as well.

Test Score Assembly Line

Since the Bagrut certificate has always been the gateway to the world of higher education and high-paying jobs, final exam results have turned into a national psychosis. The pressure around the exams has turned from a means to the ultimate goal, and the entire system fell in line accordingly, creating a mass assembly line for exam results.

The pursuit of success in Bagrut tests shaped the education system's agenda and pushed aside its others goals – particularly imparting a wide general knowledge and good values onto the students. Focusing on the test has encouraged students to memorize spoon-fed summaries and limited their creative thinking. The education system provided the labour market with new graduates who basically learned how to follow instructions and to think inside the box.

In order to achieve the highest graduation rate, the schools and the Ministry of Education also started to cut corners. For example, by significantly raising internal test scores, lowering test levels and allowing students to take the same test over and over, with the best score being the deciding one. Local authorities applied immense pressure on principals to make it possible for every high school student to be eligible for a diploma.

The test score psychosis birthed the Mikud method focus in Hebrew, which cut the volume of study material and led to incoherent learning of fragments of information.

The race for test scores also led to an increase in incidences of test fraud. The extent of this phenomenon can be indirectly established through the increased number of tests that were disqualified by the Ministry of Education.

New Ignorance

The growing social weight given to formal education as well as the growing ethos of competition and ambition were supposed to produce the most educated generation ever. In reality, there's been an alarming decline in young people's knowledge in many fields of education, and particularly in three fields, which have served as the infrastructure of knowledge and literacy until this point: history, English and maths.

Leaving the Past Behind

It seems as if young people have never been particularly interested in history or cared enough to learn about the past, for obvious reasons: first, young people look mostly forward, because they've yet to reach a point where they can look at themselves with the perspective of time. This is why they're also not interested in the socio-historical perspective. Second, for years, most history books, and particularly ones intended for schools, have been poorly written. They dealt mostly with political agreements, conflicts and wars, and didn't deal with more engaging topics that interest people in general and young people in particular such as fashion, entertainment, food etc. For some reason, there hasn't been a systematic approach that provides students with the story of history in some sort of chronological order. Students would study an eclectic collection of events, while the reasons these particular issues were selected were not entirely clear.

Furthermore, history studies in Israel have always focused on Judaism and Zionism, and students received scarce information and commentary about global processes. The language in which the textbooks were written was often dry and devoid of illustrations such as photos or videos. Add to that the fact that students didn't like history studies because it also required them to learn information by heart and young people hate memorizing data.

In this respect, not much has changed to this day. However, the problems that all generations have faced in history studies were made even worse for millennials, due to the following reasons:

No Need to Remember. While historical information was once found almost exclusively in books, nowadays the media, mainly the internet, is packed with such information. When you can 'Google' any basic historical information, the motivation to memorize stories from the past decreases.

Tired of Stories. In the age of information explosion, people are exposed to countless human stories every day, which leads to cumulative fatigue. The media's bias also plays a role here. People prefer 'hot' stories they can immediately relate to over episodes from the distant past.

Unholy History. In the innocent age of Zionism, history books were essentially regarded as a form of sacred text. For millennials, Israeli reality is no longer perceived metaphysically and the attitude towards history is affected accordingly. Most of them see the past as a dry, long forgotten story that doesn't excite them on an emotional level.

History no Longer a Status Symbol. History is also not as intriguing to youngsters due to the consistently eroding image of the educated man. In previous generations, wide horizons (with history at its centre) was considered important human capital. These days, it is commonly believed that the key to success in life lies more in material possessions and specific professional know-how.

Studying for Grades, Not for Knowledge. Since a school's success is measured by its test scores, historical content is regarded in a functional manner. The past is seen as material one should memorize only for the exam and not as an interesting dramatic story with moral, national, literary, sociological and psychological contexts. Classes focus on memorizing materials to get the highest grade rather than on enjoyment and intellectual enrichment.

All of these factors have created the conditions where millennials lack the most basic historical knowledge, so when they begin their academic studies, they are seriously unprepared.

Broken English

As the media becomes accessible to more people, their linguistic common ground expands, and local languages weaken. The internet has vastly accelerated this process, uniting the surfers around common languages (for example Mandarin, English, French, German, Spanish, Swahili). Linguists call this process 'the fourth revolution of language', the first being the birth of spoken language, the second being the invention of writing, the third being the invention of print, and the fourth being the invention of digital technology.

In all European countries, young people speak and write in English better than their parents (on average). The most significant cause for this difference is of course their intense exposure to the internet. Awareness of the importance of fluency in English has also increased, leading it to be taught at younger ages. Moreover, young people are more mobile than their parents due to the aviation and tourism revolution. This rings even more true for young Israelis, as the annual per capita percentage of Israelis who travel abroad is probably the highest in the world.

Israeli millennials speak better English than their parents for two more reasons: first, they were exposed to American television shows more than any other generation before them, and in Israel, unlike many countries in Europe, films usually aren't dubbed (therefore you can listen to the actors speak English). Second, they've been exposed to the anglicization of the Hebrew language since childhood. English is present everywhere in everyday life: in the names of businesses and companies, brands, commercials and more. Even children's names correspond more with English nowadays.

However, since English studies in schools are subpar, and because millennials usually avoid reading long texts and due to the existence of online machine translation tools (which are basic, but keep improving over time) – young people have a limited grasp on reading and writing in English. The results are grim: while reading articles and books sounds dreadful to millennials, reading articles and books in English is more like parting the Red Sea.

The declining level of English literacy is also due to the formal as well as informal leniencies higher institutions grant students in admission standards as well as in the requirements for obtaining a degree. Many students nowadays manage to acquire an academic degree without having read a single line of text in English.

As a matter of fact, one of the criteria that students consider when ranking a course's difficulty is how much reading in English it requires. When there's a lot, the course's ratings drop (particularly in humanities and social studies). Because lecturers are aware of this consideration, and because they are concerned about their rating, many try to include as few English materials as possible in their required reading lists.

When there's no leniency, most students simply buy translations or give up on reading assignments altogether in the hope that questions about this material won't appear in the final exam, or by simply acknowledging that they would be forfeiting part of the grade.

This phenomenon lowers the degree's standards, as graduates leave without sufficient English skills (a basic necessity in the employment world), and because access to quality scientific and educational material drops (most scientific publications are in English).

Maths Escape

An increasing number of army, industry and academic leaders have voiced concerns in the recent years about the dramatic decline in mathematical knowledge among younger high school graduates. Statistical data provides an explanation for this phenomenon and point to a crisis: a plummeting rate of high school students who choose to extend their studies in this field; a drop in fluency and demand for chemistry and physics studies in high schools; a tumbling demand for maths and exact science studies in universities.

This creates a strange situation where a high percentage of high school graduates need to undergo an SAT course not just as a refresher course that improves their chances of getting accepted to desirable departments and classes, but rather in many cases simply so they could acquire the basic maths skills they never got in high school. Why did this happen? Here are some possible reasons:

Sub-Standard Maths Teachers. Few high school graduates who studied advanced maths and science choose to be teachers, if at all. Furthermore, among college students who choose to become maths teachers, many get certified in teachers' colleges rather than universities – where the level of maths studies is higher. Moreover, the shortage of maths teachers has led to a situation where a considerable portion of elementary and high school teachers lack the proper training required to teach this subject.

Computer Replaces Multiplication Table. From the moment the digital calculator and personal computer were introduced to the students' daily lives, they turned mathematical calculations into a mechanical thing, perpetuating the perception that the manual act of calculating is redundant. Information that was once considered critical has turned into disciplinary knowledge. Maths literacy has been cheapened so much, that nowadays even many junior high students don't even know the multiplication table by heart.

Why Bother? Since schools are only measured according to matriculation eligibility and not the exams' level, they encourage students who struggle with the material to transfer to a lower class, because it's easier to get a passing grade there. Furthermore, millennials were led to believe they excel in everything. This is why when they don't succeed in maths (which is common), they avoid dealing with it ('maths and I just don't mix') instead of buckling up, working hard, practising and getting better they often choose to study at a lower level.

No Corners to Cut. Because maths only has one right answer, there are no 'discounts' in the test, which drives young people away as they've grown accustomed to succeeding even without studying for the test (unlike 'soft' subjects, maths requires hard work.)

Lack of Discipline. One of the keys to solving mathematical problems are clean, orderly work habits. Therefore, a generation raised without discipline struggles to succeed in maths. This difficulty is also very discouraging. Furthermore, the digital generation that has forsaken the pen and paper, lacks practice in the different stages of the solution, which is key to understanding the logic in making calculations.

Flawed Teaching Programmes. One would expect that schools in Israel, which is famous for being a 'start-up nation', would incorporate advanced maths and science programmes. In reality, this almost didn't happen. According to the 2014 State Comptroller Report, the maths education programme for high schools hasn't been updated in 20 years! Even special programmes developed specifically in universities for excelling teens were not welcomed with open arms by the Ministry of Education.

Since maths studies not only just provide necessary basic knowledge for educated people, but also cultivate orderly and logical thinking, abstract thought, organized, clean and consistent writing, and primarily work discipline – the crisis in this field is devastating. It also has a harmful impact on science, engineering, industry and national defence. Although many have already realized the magnitude of this problem, there are still no solutions on the horizon.

Who Wants to be a Teacher?

The status of teachers in society started to crumble in the 1980s, for several reasons:

No Longer Visionaries. Expectations from teachers changed: from visionaries and educators to professional technocrats. This change served a blow to the profession's reputation, consequently downgrading its appeal as well.

Those Who Can't, Teach. As academics (scientists and lecturers) became more prestigious, the impression people got was that good teachers should work in academia, while in the past, many doctors and even professors worked as high school teachers.

Not Just Female Teachers. The third generation of Sabra women, the daughters of veteran teachers from the 'Israeli Mayflower aristocracy', went through processes of feminization. The variety and supply of interesting, luxury professions grew, and they were directed towards more male-oriented professions and higher-paying careers in the fields of law, media, medicine, computers, economics and more.

This void was filled mostly by women of the new middle class, i.e. mobile young women who climbed the professional ladder of the teaching world (by getting a matriculation certificate, teaching diploma and academic degree). Since their education came later in life, many lacked the general knowledge that make for a good teacher. The result was that millennials started their journey in the public education system with teachers who were not as broad-minded as before, which had a crucial effect on their education and on their perception of school. This also created escalating tensions between teachers and more educated parents.

Immigration from the former Soviet Union in the 1990s increased the number of high quality teachers (particularly in the science field), but many of them have had a hard time integrating into the system over time, opting to leave because of the difference in mentality. They were appalled by what they encountered in the classrooms (the undisciplined children and teenagers) and often found themselves in constant conflict with the students.

The crawling depreciation in quality of teachers has damaged the profession's reputation, further crippling talented young people's motivation to turn to a career in teaching. Besides the negative image and the rough, eroding atmosphere in schools, there are several other factors that still prevent high quality people from entering the teaching world to this day: low salaries; the non-selective nature of this profession and limited opportunities for promotion.

At the end of the day, millennials were forced to learn in an archaic, short-sighted and sinking public education system. This is a system mostly devoid of true leadership, where the power of teaching constantly wanes. The grim result is that schools produce narrowly-educated graduates with limited life skills, learning capabilities and the ability to deal with intellectual and emotional challenges. Even more worrying, the more talented members of this generation don't end up as teachers, so things only keep getting worse.

Higher Education Revolution

The growth of regional and private colleges has led to a revolution in higher education. It has had a major effect on Israeli society as a whole, but it appears that millennials, who were born into this reality and essentially created the acceleration, were affected by it most of all.

While in 1989/90, there were 21 institutions in Israel that offered academic degrees, some two decades later there were already 71 such institutions – most of which being various types of academic colleges. Meanwhile, non-academic professional colleges have also seen massive growth.

The rising percentage of higher education students was dramatic. In 2011, nearly half of the relevant age group (24-40) were admitted into higher education. This rate is almost twice what it was during the 1990s.

Generally speaking, one could say that the level of education in Israel, judging by the number of years of formal learning, has risen considerably in the past decades among all ethnic and religious groups as well as among both genders, and the gap between the veteran elite groups (high-income, male Ashkenazi Jews) and the peripheral classes has narrowed. The gender change is particularly significant. The ratio of women among college and university students has risen over the years and they have become a demographic majority in every degree. The scientific disciplines women choose to study have also been transformed, as they gradually conquer fields that were once considered to be distinctively male territory (STEM, computers, architecture, law, medicine etc).

Wholesale Degrees

The increasing number of students in higher education institutions and their share in Israeli population were joined by several historic reasons, the primary of which was the increase in matriculation certificates, both in absolute terms and as an annual percentage; the SATs industry; the development of pre-academic preparatory programmes; the growth of scholarships, foundations, loans and encouraging awards.

Since every academic institution wishes to grow and develop and since the Council for Higher Education budgets higher education institutions according to the number of students, institutions are forced to fight over students – including ones that don't belong there. This competition has produced a troubling, large-scale phenomenon: universities and colleges offer various leniencies in order to lure potential students to apply. This has generally led to a process with far less selective screening of applicants and a consistent lowering of admission standards.

The inflation of leniencies is expressed in lower admission standards as well as in lower academic requirements during the semesters: less reading material in general and in English in particular, lower attendance requirements, fewer exercises, reliefs and indulgences for students who don't meet basic requirements (additional and informal chances after failures, delayed submissions etc.) and over-grading. The main goal is to avoid annoying the students, who are perceived as privileged customers.

Even advanced (MA and PhD) degrees have seen a crawling devaluation in admission standards and requirements. More and more academic departments accept MA students based on a lower BA grade than before and rarely have additional (complimentary) requirements. Quite a few departments have arranged their curriculum into a concentrated one day or two day week. This may help students who work full-time jobs but turns classes into an exhausting journey with low educational efficacy. Whereas MA students used to also write an extensive scientific dissertation, nowadays most of them finish the degree without a thesis, and even those who do are only required to submit an increasingly thinner manuscript. Furthermore, a full Masters degree (with research) is no longer a benchmark for doctorate studies, and many students are permitted to take a 'thesis-compatible' bypass route (submission of a limited thesis that may be accounted also as a chapter in the future doctoral dissertation).

Universities and colleges maintain a conspiracy of silence when it comes to the level of students who are accepted, and few faculties dare to publicly criticize this catastrophic situation. This occurs for a number of reasons: higher education institutions are in deep economic crisis and struggling to survive; lecturers are afraid of being reprimanded by management and colleagues; and political correctness (it's not nice criticizing your students).

Everybody Wants to be a Lawyer or Business Manager

The most popular fields of study in Israel are social sciences, management and law. The highest increase in students was in business management studies, which has tripled in the past fifteen years. In 2012, there were 22,650 students studying this profession, making up some 12 per cent of all students.

The number of law students also increased by hundreds of percentages during that time. 80 per cent of them go to private colleges that aren't budgeted by the government. This has created a lawyer surplus in Israel, and many wind up unemployed or underpaid.

Israel is the country with the most lawyers (per capita) in the western world. For every 100,000 citizens in Russia there are only 44 lawyers, 123 in Jordan, 232 in England, 332 in Italy, and in Israel – 661.

A Crisis in Humanities

The number of students who major in humanities has drastically decreased in recent years all across the world. This phenomenon hasn't passed over universities in Israel: from 18.5 per cent of all students in 1999 to merely 7.5 per cent in 2013.

Many humanities courses have become extinct, including: African studies, Arab language and literature, French language and literature, musicology, bible studies and more. In some cases, whole departments were shut down. Other departments cut down on the number of faculty members, along with the variety of study fields.

Even the most prominent departments in humanities, which were once the highlight of institutions of higher education (such as history, Jewish studies and philosophy), are in a deep crisis due to the lack of demand and low-quality students.

Some consider the downfall of humanities a natural and even desirable process, paving the way to a new education world, which is more suitable to the age of fast-paced communications and the information revolution. Others see the phenomenon as another milestone in the spiritual collapse of western society.

Why are young people steering clear of the humanities? There are several possible reasons:

Low Admission Standards. Due to the desperate competition with other departments, humanities departments have set a very low bar for admission which has led to the acceptance of low-quality students. This has given departments a bad reputation that drives away good students. When good students stay away, the bad reputation only gets worse, and it's been spiralling down ever since.

'Lawn Sciences'. Few people within the academic system are willing to admit the fact that it's easier these days to be awarded a PhD in 'soft' sciences than it is with exact and natural sciences. In many disciplines it is common to come up with esoteric research ideas. Moreover, anybody can be assisted by a ghost writer, editor, translator or expert in survey analysis to compose a thesis. This has tarnished the reputation of lecturers in these fields as well as led to the growth of mediocre faculties. Whereas professors of the humanities were once viewed as giants, these titans have now been replaced by dwarves – grey 'science clerks'. This has had an effect on the quality and content of classes and has driven talented students away.

Furthermore, humanities, more than other fields of science, are less committed to a rigid educational programme and the courses mostly comprise of whatever it is that the lecturer wishes to teach. Since the quality of lecturers has consistently dropped, the courses have become less and less attractive, making these subjects generally more boring as a result.

Outside Competition. Humanities studies are no longer exclusive to academia and the many players out there who teach it know how to do it better: courses by various institutions (like Yad Ben Zvi), open lectures (like Ascolot), guided tours, online videos etc. Furthermore, many people feel that the humanities are taught in a boring, lifeless manner and have failed to compete with the world's most advanced instruction and demonstration methods. When comparing a history or art class with a gallery or museum exhibit, or rich presentations and online videos, the winner is clear. Additionally, millennials follow a purposeful approach, and are less willing to waste valuable time on sitting in classrooms, where the material is 'hammered into' their brains for long periods of time.

Popular media, including the internet, covers many issues that the study of humanities deals with. Attractive materials in the media overshadow classes at the university, which are usually performed using the traditional method of writing on the blackboard, or with some unprofessional digital presentations here and there. History departments have lost their prestige in particular, as it's become common belief that academic history studies are redundant, as anyone can study the field on their own (through Wikipedia or Ted Talks).

Preference for 'Practical' Studies. In the past few years, people have come to believe that the study of humanities is useless and offers no benefits for life. Millennials are already driven by more utilitarian motives, which is why many young people choose to study subjects that can lead to a potential job and income.

Politicized Academia. In recent years, humanities and social studies in Israel and around the world have been taken over by the 'critical' worldview. This is actually a euphemism for the politicization of these subjects, painting them as distinctively anti-Israeli and anti-Jewish. Furthermore, many lecturers from these fields use the platform they're given to politically shape the minds of their audiences, under the pretext of academic freedom and teaching critical thinking. Since most young people in Israel (contrary to western countries) lean towards right-wing politics, they've come to despise these subjects.

Moving to Colleges. From the moment academic colleges were opened (in the early 1990s), they became the default for a significant percentage of students. The emphasis there is on social studies, which are more closely tied to the world of employment.

Not Willing to Put in the Effort. Humanities put a stronger emphasis on reading and writing (in English as well) than other sciences, and many students aren't willing to put in the effort.

It's All Gibberish to Me. In recent years, humanities (as well as social studies) departments have developed pompous, condescending and inaccessible language. It makes these subjects appear ridiculous in the public's eyes (especially millennials who hate 'bullshit') and drives away potentially good students.

No One Wants to Change the World. In the past, many curious young people with a burning desire to change the world wanted to study humanities. However, this generation's intellectual curiosity is low and their urge to start revolutions has faded. Society has developed a general disdain for anything that even smells a little highbrow or deep. In the age of 'give me the bottom line', it's considered a waste of time.

The decline of humanities reflects the vulgarization of Israeli society. It seems that Israel, which has been deeply affected by American culture, is now experiencing a delayed spiritual atrophy (or 'closing of the mind').

Hard to Adjust

Most students experience some kind of adjustment crisis when entering the world of academia, but it seems this kind of crisis has become worse and particularly common among millennials. Many young people experience a shock during their first year and send out distress signals. A considerable portion drop out (the first academic term is when students are most likely to drop out) or change majors, department or institution. The reasons for this academic crisis among millennials are as follows:

High School and Academia are too Different. As mentioned before, many schools have become 'test score factories', and virtually none of them provide students with tools for independent learning, thinking and analysis. Furthermore, the requirements in many high schools are so low, if there are even any, that students have been conditioned to be spoon-fed by their teachers, and anything that isn't relevant to the test isn't even worth listening to. Many students find themselves in a situation where, for the first time in their lives, they are required to perform educational tasks (reading, writing, research) that they've never experienced or been prepared for.

Tough Learning Environment. Academic studies are held in a different learning environment than the one millennials have grown used to in school. Most of them are surprised to discover that leniencies and concessions that were acceptable in school are not as acceptable in higher education, and that in order to get a passing grade, let alone a high one, they need to put in the effort.

Parents Can't Help. Millennials are not used to studying on their own and struggle to manage without their parents' help. Their parents also can't apply pressure on the lecturers as they did with their children's teachers and the school administration, at least for the time being. Furthermore, many students come from a low socio-economic background. They were raised by parents that have no degrees and often didn't even graduate from high school. The educational gap between them and their parents denies them the emotional and intellectual safety net that educated families can offer.

Low Starting Point. Millennials also struggle in academia because they're coming from school with a massive lack of infrastructure knowledge. Recent surveys, next to the results of the Ministry of Education's Meitzav tests, which measure efficiency and growth in schools, indicate low proficiency in all fields of study.

Some gaps are closed thanks to SAT courses, but that only applies to the more literate portions (English, maths, native tongue). The lacunae in the subjects of history, politics, literature, religion and culture cannot be closed with one course.

The Age of Skimming

People of the Book?

In recent years, surveys have allegedly found that millennials, and especially the younger cohort, read more books than older generations. However, these surprising figures paint a misleading picture.

These are general statistics that hide a more complex reality. The surveys do not take into account the educational disparities between young and old within the mobile class (whose parents did not read at all and their children read a little); they do not compare the present to the past – i.e. between young adults in different historical periods (today all age groups read less, including highly educated individuals); they do not distinguish between subgroups such as males and females or immigrants and their native offspring and they do not differentiate between genres (for instance children's and adult books).

Today's young adults mostly read targeted (utilitarian) literature, namely manuals, advice and guides, professional and academic literature (the ratio of students among the Y's is greater than any former generations), lifestyle books and those which have become media events or blockbuster movies. Obviously they also consume a considerable amount of 'fast food' fiction.

They read less than previous generations (particularly within the elite tier) when it comes to nonfiction and highbrow prose and literary classics. Naturally they dislike heavy duty books. They also read fewer books on a daily basis (according to Government studies from 2014, since 1984, the percentage of 17-year-olds who are weekly readers went from 64 per cent to 40 per cent. The percentage of those who never or hardly ever read tripled during this period, from 9 per cent to 27 per cent). They prefer to read during longer intervals (such as on vacation or when they need concrete information).

In addition, books are often not read in a linear fashion ('cover to cover') but rather by flipping and hovering through the text, as is the case in today's digital reading on screens.

People have been dedicating less time to reading books since the last quarter on the twentieth century, following the development of cable and satellite TV. This trend accelerated in the first decade of the 2000s with the dramatic increase in personal computers, cellphones and internet use.

This led to an interesting yet odd paradox: while the amount of printed material has seen a nominal increase (compared to the past), the demand for printed materials and the average time dedicated to reading non-digital text have consistently fallen (digital text reading has dramatically increased). This is true mostly regarding printed texts with multiple pages and complex content, which require advanced intellectual skills. What are the reasons for the declining demand for printed materials (books as well as newspapers)? Let's name a few:

Advanced Media Outlets. The internet has created an audiovisual alternative for print, which is far more appealing and engaging than books and in most cases is also less time-consuming.

Computers Instead of Libraries. Textbooks and article collections found in libraries and archives used to be the primary source of information about our world. In the digital age, the computer provides us with access to massive databases at the click of a button in the comfort of our own home. Therefore, it's only natural that people nowadays buy fewer dictionaries, encyclopaedias, textbooks and research books. Furthermore, digital media has perfected the means of indexing and searching, saving valuable time that was once dedicated to this task in the age of print.

Self-Published Interactive Books. The old world of print was brought to the readership by 'gatekeepers', who sorted and censored manuscripts and also produced the final product (publishers and printing houses).

The digital medium offers countless options that appeal to authors/writers: producing a book independently at low costs; crowd-funding, which makes the public an active partner in the book's production; access to large audiences without the use of expensive marketing tools; longer (virtually unlimited) shelf life; feedback and dialogue with the readers; an easier way to regularly update literary texts (modular books); an easier and cheaper way to incorporate audiovisual materials.

The Triumph of Shorthand. Reading long books is less suitable for the fast and restless age where shorthand is king. Digital media isn't just quicker and more appealing than traditional books, it's also easier to browse, which saves time and energy.

The abundance and constant flow of digital information, alongside people's curiosity for catching up on new and interesting things, force us all to adapt new reading patterns, which essentially boils down to skimming. One might call this trend 'the law of diminishing marginal reading': when you have fewer pages to read you're more likely to read them all. When there are so many pages you only read the headlines and skim the rest of it. We're forced to flip through a bunch of topics instead of focusing on one, and also because we're surrounded by distractions. In other words, we're constantly exposed to more information. On the other hand, constant skimming leads to a pattern of superficiality.

They Would Rather Socialize. The younger generation desperately needs company, constant stimulation and background noises. They don't like activities that require them to to be in isolation, such as sitting perfectly still and silently reading a book.

Are We Getting Dumber?

Towards the mid-2000s, when the internet had already become an inseparable part of everyday life, numerous articles started to pop up and warn us about the internet's influence on the 'quality of culture'.

In 2008, Nicholas Carr, an author who deals with technology among other things, published an article in *The Atlantic* defiantly titled 'Is Google Making Us Stupid?: What the Internet is Doing to Our Brains'. The article attracted much attention and created polarized reactions in the media, academia and various online platforms, and was later expanded into a book titled *The Shallows: What the Internet Is Doing to Our Brains* (2011).

Carr's main argument was that surfing and reading on the internet hurts our ability to focus on one source of content as well as our ability to delve into it. Like many of us, he too noticed this phenomenon after realizing he had been struggling to read books, even ones that interested him. Reading, he claimed, became exhausting, even when it's just a few paragraphs in a blog.

Why is this happening? Mostly, he claims, because of the abundance of content available on the internet, which creates constant unrest. Digital reading is reminiscent of men who awkwardly flip through dirty magazines. It creates a pressing feeling that there's something more interesting around the corner. Add to that the multiple distractions that often come with surfing: links within the text, ads and pop-ups, whose impact have become more dramatic than ever because they're user-targeted.

Carr wasn't just claiming that our reading habits are changing. He made a far-reaching claim, which has also been backed up by empirical study: our brain is actually changing. Since the neural circuits in the 'reading brain' are designed according to the unique specifications of every written language (Chinese, for example, uses a different lobe of the brain than English), one would expect the neural circuits designed by frequent internet use to be different than the ones designed for reading books and other printed materials.

In this respect, reading on the internet has had a significant cultural as well as mental impact. Unlike reading books, which requires us to spend time in deciphering content, skimming on the internet makes us more passive. When you don't have to make an effort and think, the brain becomes lazy.

Many sided with Carr's thesis, but there were also some strong critics who made solid counter-arguments. The most substantial criticism touched on the quantitative aspect. As a matter of fact, people nowadays read more than ever before. The texts may be shorter and more concise (and often shallower) but overall, we're living in an age where everyone is knee-deep in words. Reading has even partially replaced talking on the phone. Many people (mostly youngsters) would rather text than talk. It's short, instant, practical and efficient, and also allows sending information to several people simultaneously and getting multiple responses. More importantly, it allows people to conduct 'conversations in writing' while doing other things.

In this context, one can make a counter-argument that when the dialogue between human beings becomes a series of short digital messages, it reinforces the tendency to provide information and weakens the ability to clarify matters and exchange ideas. People who can't 'chat', can't think either.

Carr's shallowness thesis has also been criticized from another direction: skimming and quickly scanning content has many advantages. For example, the ability can help to absorb more information in a short time and separate the important from the unimportant parts. Reading and typing have also become faster, while young people are immensely more skillful when it comes to typing on the computer. Furthermore, we're all adopting a state of 'continuous partial attention' and 'multi-tasking'. This phenomenon is more prominent among the younger generation, who are used to watching TV while sending texts on the phone or having face-to-face conversations while reading messages on WhatsApp.

This is a mixed blessing, though: studies have shown that people who divided their attention between multiple simultaneous tasks struggle to deal with concentration tests, tend to feel overloaded with information and become less thorough. This could partially explain millennial students' tendency to hand in sloppy papers and miss questions on exercises and tests. A senior defence force commander told us: 'my generation works slowly and thoroughly. Young people are quicker and more efficient when it comes to dealing with information. They perform several tasks simultaneously, but carelessly.'

Shallowness as a Lifestyle

Since millennials are the first generation to read short bites, digital materials rather than long, printed materials, we can focus on Carr's criticism and ask more specifically: are millennials truly more stupid or shallower than previous generations? Mark Bauerlein, a professor at Emory University, had a decisive response to this question in his 2009 book provocatively named: *The Dumbest Generation: How the Digital Age Stupefies Young Americans and Jeopardizes Our Future (Or, Don't Trust Anyone Under 30).*

Bauerlein warned of the ignorance of young people, who only care about their immediate surrounding – friends, clothes, TV and Facebook – and blamed this ignorance on the collapse of reading culture. Young people's propensity for abbreviation appeared shallow and limiting to him and anyone who attempts to get a more in-depth understanding of anything is immediately ridiculed. He agreed that the internet has made it partially redundant to store information in our memory banks, but claimed that young people have 'emptied out the entire hard drive' – although they have almost unlimited access to everything, they still lack basic knowledge of many things and skills including the ability to rank and understand hierarchies of quality.

Too Long; Didn't Read (TD;DR)

It seems that although there is a grain of truth in them, arguments like Bauerlein's completely miss the complexity of the problem, due to their provocative and one-dimensional nature. It is empirically impossible to provide a decisive answer for whether 'millennials are more ignorant than previous generations', among other things because we don't have an appropriate scale or a comparative historical metric. However, we can cautiously point at intellectual skills that have probably weakened in the most digital age in history – at least for the time being. The main skill is reading. This phenomenon also has wider scientific evidence.

Paradoxically, not only do millennials read more text than previous generations, they also write more, not just in text messages and WhatsApp. Facebook, which is mostly comprised of young users, is packed with text. Most of it is bland and pointless, but there are sparks of quality here and there. Blogs are also an important medium, where the younger generation's designated stars speak out. Their popularity almost always leans on two components: dealing with feelings and hardships (creating empathy), and stand-up comedy-like writing, i.e. texts that make fun of the trivial in life. The trend of passing on reading a long block of text has become so common that the internet spawned a unique phrase for it: TL;DR, or: Too Long; Didn't Read.

Israel is part of the global trend, but we have another typical Israeli component: young people in Israel don't just have a problem with reading long texts, but rather even when they go ahead and read it, they publicly bitch and moan about the pointless effort. They've come to believe that long texts are inherently wrong – a nuisance (hence the slang word 'hafira' or 'digging a whole in my brain'). This is why many believe that reading books is for 'bored, lifeless nerds'. Anything that feels even remotely sophisticated or profound is met with scorn. Many even boast their handicap, saying: 'got cliff notes, bro?'; 'too long... sowwy'; and 'can you sum it up in a sentence?'

The tendency to skip the text and read it without delving into it has created a bizarre phenomenon, which has caught our attention (and was later verified by colleagues): young people usually read the first part of the document, skip vital information within the body text, and only casually read the final parts, if at all. This is also true for emails or even manuals for a scanner or camera.

What Gets Lost Along the Way?

The loss of patience for in-depth reading and the habit of skimming and partial reading have several intellectual repercussions:

Loss of Important Information. Many students miss entire sections in exams and papers because they don't read all of the instructions. They just answer some of the questions and don't perform all of the tasks.

Loss of Critical Sense. The skimming habit weakens their critical thinking, i.e. the ability to tell credible, high quality sources from cheap, unreliable rubbish. When credibility is no longer a sacred value, the drive to uncover the truth also weakens.

In Constant Motion. The flow of information has turned millennials into short-distant sprinters but weak long-distance runners. Their ability to 'lose themselves' in the material has also disappeared, because when reading is mostly used for functional and immediate needs (specific information that people need), it's impossible to pause for unsettling thoughts. Consequently, they lack the ability to stop and think in quiet, focus and concentrate on one thing or try to decipher complex notions. High quality texts, which require cognitive capabilities such as poetry or nonfiction, are not read.

Living in the Moment. A generation that doesn't read books also loses the drive to change the world and would rather live in the moment, go with the flow or escape from reality rather than fight for what's right. For millennials, reading books is mostly an academic chore, a yoke around their necks, rather than an opportunity to soar.

Passive Reading. Many books require active reading, such as using one's imagination and the ability to interpret the meaning of a continuous text and find contexts and layers therein. Therefore, millennials' indifference to books weakens their curiosity and human sensitivity, which leads to apathy.

Brain 'Muscle' Atrophy. It's difficult and perhaps impossible to assertively determine what kind of information one is required to remember in the digital world. However, assuming it is important to remember basic fundamental information, it's obvious that having information available at the click of a button harms human memory as well as indirectly hurts other cognitive skills. This has possibly already created some kind of intellectual regression for the younger generation. Just like motorized transportation weakens the body, Google weakens the mind. Many young people struggle to understand why they need to memorize material for an exam, especially when that information is available online. In many cases there is no compelling argument for it, because the academic world hasn't held thorough discussions on this issue. Professors continue to teach as if search engines haven't been invented.

Hard to Analyze, Comprehend Text

It's difficult and perhaps even impossible to compare reading comprehension across different generations in Israel, as testing and measuring in this area was not conducted in the past. However, there seem to be gaps (mostly between the top deciles of Generation Y and previous generations) derived from their tendency to read short texts, inability to comprehend complex texts, inadequate basic knowledge and contempt for highbrow language, which is perceived as distancing and unappealing (also from an economic standpoint).

The tendency to skip the text without trying to understand its meaning is commonly displayed in the comment section on Facebook. Respondents often get caught up on one word or sentence in the text without understanding the full context, and occasionally even derive a completely different interpretation from what the author of the post had intended.

Inarticulate Communications

The decline of book culture has also compromised the younger generation's ability to communicate eloquently, particularly in writing. Since higher education requires students to submit exercises and seminar papers, their linguistic disability is revealed in full (particularly in humanities, social studies, education and law – fields in which articulation is key).

In our interviews with lecturers, their immense frustration from reading student papers was a recurring theme. Students tend to present poor vocabulary skills, broken syntax and complete lack of awareness of style and linguistic precision. Their papers look as if they lifted paragraphs and sentences from various sources and slapped them together with no logic or linguistic sense.

The constantly dropping quality of writing has been felt in many western countries in the past few years, though literacy experts claim that the situation in Israel is particularly bad.

Why is it so hard for millennials to express themselves? Here are some possible reasons:

The Price of Comfort. Vocabulary is acquired primarily through written rather than spoken language, and since they don't read many books they also don't acquire a rich vocabulary or the ability to develop and articulate arguments. Furthermore, before the invention of the 'Find' function, readers had to browse through the text and actually read it too. When you can skip to the word or sentence and reach it directly, even the aspect of collateral learning is eliminated.

Lower Writing Requirements. In schools, students are required to write fewer papers. The same rings true for academia. Many departments have replaced the demand for serious seminar papers with a short presentation and some lecturers even settle for classroom attendance only. Quite a few lecturers allow students to submit papers in groups, which dumps the majority of writing onto one of the co-authors.

Low Quality Teachers. Most students who choose to study teaching (including teaching Hebrew) are not at the top scale of excellence. Many of them exhibit low linguistic skills and pass the problem on to their students.

The Decline of Fine Literature Studies. Literature studies help develop linguistic sensitivity and writing abilities. Unfortunately, this field of study has been weakened and marginalized in recent years.

Leniency and Corner-Cutting. When the general response to lazy, sloppy, messy and undisciplined work is leniency, it's only natural for these traits to spread to language skills as well. Millennials' language impairment is therefore very much a reflection of their general behavioural impairments. This is also why students tend to be sloppy not just in their wording performance but also in their citations patterns.

Poor Teaching Methods. Millennials are victims of failed pedagogic ventures. For example, a method based on the pedagogy of 'natural learning' and 'guesswork' that didn't teach how to write letters in an orderly manner and disregarded punctuation. Other methods prevented correcting writing or speaking errors, in order to avoid hurting the children's self-esteem. The result is that students are unaware of their mistakes and don't learn how to take constructive criticism, so they never improve. Getting rid of dictations and recitation has also exacted a heavy price. And to add insult to injury, educators turned linguistics into a technical and irrelevant subject, which most students have grown to detest.

Lack of Dedicated Courses for Scientific Writing in Academia. Although accurate writing and expression are basic tools in science, it is surprisingly rare to find basic writing and editing courses in higher education institutions (as customary in foreign language studies and research methods). Even advanced degree students don't receive institutional assistance in writing skills. The result is that many student dissertations are so poorly written, they disgrace the author as well as the institution.

Blurred Lines between Spoken and Literary Language. The process of the written language becoming more like spoken language isn't exclusive to Israel, and started before millennials were even born. However, it seems to have escalated during their formative years, mostly due to the communications revolution. This has denied young people of the exposure to different language registers, making them blind to high forms of expression.

Superficial Dialogue. People these days pour scorn on anyone who speaks properly, as if to do so is pretentious, unnecessary, backward-looking and impractical. The use of street language is perceived as 'cool' and these days journalists, public officials and even teachers and judges use it frequently. There is nothing wrong with using street language, but sometimes it is not rich enough to convey complex messages. When you dismiss rigorous formal language you send a symbolic message of contempt for it.

Speaking in Foreign Tongues. The internet has had a hand in the decay of the Hebrew language skills, because it reinforces its anglicization. The decline of the local language can of course be seen as a natural and necessary stage in the process of social evolution. The electronic medium reorganizes the old Tower of Babel, leading to the creation of a 'digital Esperanto'. There are some who mourn the anglicization of Hebrew, while others consider it to be a welcome global trend, which helps bring foreign and distant cultures closer together.

Maybe Young Speak is More Efficient?

Some claim that criticizing the way millennials express themselves does them an injustice. Hebrew is a renewable language and through generations of young people it sheds its redundant layers. In other words, perhaps their language skills aren't poor; it's that they're just using an updated, more frugal and efficient language. Perhaps the rules of grammar are ritualistic and anachronistic, and we're better off without them. We write however we please, as long as our message gets through. It's pointless to waste valuable time on proofreading and rephrasing. Their propensity for shorthand is reflected in their tendency to meld words (e.g. Gamani instead of Gam Ani), omission of letters, use of numbers as substitutions of letters (e.g. 100 Memet), attaching nicknames to words (e.g. Mushi instead of Mushlam). It is also reflected in their frequent use of emoticons. One cartoon figure is often enough to express emotions such as joy, excitement, sadness, amazement, laughter and more.

What are we losing when people are too lazy to use language 'correctly', and when educators refrain from correcting them? It seems the price isn't about linguistics, but rather about psychology. Inarticulate linguistics encourages sloppy thinking and a general disrespect for language and rigorous meaning.

Generational ADHD

The modern education system, which developed under the industrial revolution, was based on the concept of frontal instruction. This method, in which the lecturer stands and speaks to his or her students who listen and take notes, was considered economical, didactic and symbolic. It demonstrated and exercised the professor's authority and the students' subordination (which translates into subordination in society).

Over the years, various attempts have been made to soften the traditional structure of the class, such as making the students sit in a circle, developing a class based on open dialogue, lessons that take place outside of the classroom (such as field trips) and recently, the use of digital means (Powerpoint presentations, videos, computer stations, interactive whiteboards etc.) Online learning has also gradually been introduced to the system, though not without resistance. However, most classes in high schools, universities and colleges are still based on the traditional model of frontal instruction. Although the academic world preaches openness and flexibility, it hesitates and is unable to practice what it preaches. Not only is it in no rush to change the traditional structure of courses and classes, it continues to build classrooms and auditoriums as if the internet doesn't actually exist.

Consequently, young people who came up during the digital age and are used to a dynamic, interactive, audiovisual environment, have a hard time sitting in class. They consider this medium to be long, exhausting and pointless. If only they had the power and the courage, they would flip the channel and change the boring lecturers.

In order to deal with their suffering, they surf the internet during the lecture and in many cases don't even show up in class at all (when attendance for the course isn't mandatory). In order to catch up, they help one another, i.e. take turns for taking notes or rely on notes from previous years. Since the level of many courses is low, it's not that hard to get a good grade even without attending class.

Sitting in the traditional classroom is hard for millennials for another reason: this generation is always 'on edge' and many suffer from ADHD (and therefore also take drugs such as Ritalin and Concerta in high doses). There is also an environmental effect here: they were never taught to sit still for long periods of time. Not even around the dinner table. No one has ever tried to discipline them, asked them to be quiet or forced them to listen and learn. They generally have a problem with focusing on one thing, and hate the silence and contemplation that arrives once you cut away from all the noise. Sitting in class requires self-discipline as well as the ability to listen and hold back for long periods of time. That's why the classroom is like a suffocating dungeon for young people. Fortunately for them, the smartphone, laptop and tablet exist, and they provide them with a means of escape.

Walk into a classroom or auditorium in institutions of higher education nowadays and you will immediately notice students who take notes and glance at the lecturer while watching videos, surfing on news sites and texting with their friends. Students without laptops surf on the smartphone and post updates on WhatsApp.

Charismatic lecturers still manage to get students excited here and there and make up for the anachronistic medium, but their numbers have dwindled in recent years. This creates a situation where not only is the study environment boring, so are the teachers.

Moreover, people used to sign up to university courses because it was one of the only places where one could acquire new information about the world. But in the Age of Google, you can get an answer for virtually every question, even if it's poorly phrased, with the use of search engines. In the escalating contest between lecturers and the internet, it is clear who has the upper hand (which is also the reason for the declining status of teachers in society).

Why then is the academic system sticking to a frontal instruction model and isn't rushing to implement alternative models? There are several possible reasons: first of all, the academic establishment is generally conservative and it's hard to introduce change to cumbersome non-autonomic institutions (which are under the thumb of the Council for Higher Education in Israel). Second, academic institutions are afraid they'd lose 'clients' if students were allowed not to show up on campus. Third, e-Learning is still in its infancy and it will require more time and a lot of resources to establish a mechanism to replace the old model. Fourth, a large portion of lecturers are not interested in 'changing'. The transition to unconventional teaching methods could make lecturing services obsolete and lead to massive layoffs. Moreover, alternative teaching requires a great deal of time and effort that is still not properly rewarded in academia (faculties are mostly promoted based on scientific publications rather than on developing innovative teaching methods.)

Paradoxically enough, the students themselves aren't keen on changing. Most would rather stay in their comfort zone and stick to the devil they know (frontal instruction) than learn on their own or adapt to a new model that is changing the one they have been accustomed to for years.

Expectations and Let Downs

Based on studies performed in the United States as well as our interviews with students and lecturers, we've noticed gaps between millennial students' typical expectations and the regulations and conventions of higher education institutions. These gaps produce tension within the system and undermine it from within. Let's review the main differences.

Personal Attention and Informal Atmosphere

The world of academia has for years represented the hierarchic order of the industrial revolution: the lecturer (professor) was seen as a person with knowledge and authority – hovering above his or her subordinates, like a boss, military commander or parent. This perception created a formal distance between students and lecturers. The lecturer gave assignments (reading, memorizing, solving problems) and evaluated the students' performance through questions in class, papers and tests, while the students followed these demands obediently, without question and out of respect. The good students were promoted to advanced degrees, while a selected few were appointed research and teaching assistants in service of 'the master'.

Over the years, the traditional model has been softened and the friendly and personal approach has grown stronger with each passing year. This change stems from pedagogic, technological and economic influences, which Generation Y reinforces.

Pedagogic influence. The anti-authoritarian ideology (the child in the centre) was originally developed in academia and it makes sense for it also to be implemented in higher education institutions. Furthermore, today's lecturers were raised, and are raising their own children, according to this pedagogy, and therefore try to treat their students in a similar manner. The fact that the percentage of women among the academic staff has grown supports this trend, since the female teaching style tends to be 'friendlier' and less authoritarian. Millennial students see the world of academia as a natural continuation of high school, and since their high school teachers and principals treated them with kindness and empathy, they expect the same in higher education. Several years ago, an inter-collegiate team reviewed the qualities that students attribute to 'good' lecturers. The study shows that they prefer human empathy ('likable and nice', 'nurtures a social life', 'gives fair grades') over teaching capabilities ('knows how to explain the material well').

The problem is that millennials push the familiarity envelope far beyond the lecturers' expectations. Many lecturers complain about the direct and 'overly friendly' way their students communicate with them, which often comes across as rude. For instance, they send emails like 'What's up? How are you? Everything is cool here'; 'Hi… here's the homework assignment. I went over it again, kinda funny… if only I knew what was waiting for me next.'

Technological Influence. In the past, students would come to the classroom to talk and consult with the lecturer, among other things. Nowadays, every student can contact his or her lecturer electronically. Many students take advantage of this personal medium to make inappropriate requests, such as tips and unusual leniencies, additional exam dates, rounded up grades etc. – requests that previous generations thought of as brazen and rude.

Electronic correspondence is often a trap for lecturers, as any Freudian slip or harsh statements are saved by students and later used for making spiteful complaints.

Economic Influence. A culture of threats and complaints has been building up in the world of academia because of millennials' tendency to band together and because they're aware of their economic and legal power as consumers. They haggle, organize protest groups and make complaints to the secretary, department head, dean, student body etc. This is a new, threatening power, especially for new lecturers, who are concerned about losing their jobs.

Due to the influence of American service culture as well as the financial pressures institutions of higher education are under, they've grown to view students as customers (who are always right, of course). The general atmosphere of flattery discourages lecturers from standing their ground and gives more power to the 'clients'.

Since millennials view their studies as some kind of paid service and lecturers as service providers, many lecturers find themselves trapped between the need to uphold academic standards and the need to satisfy the customers.

Teaching evaluation surveys conducted periodically by student associations and teaching improvement units in various institutions have created an official and unofficial ranking of courses and lecturers. However, it seems that under millennials, the teaching survey is more of a customer service survey than a review of the course or lecturer. Even the service's definition changes over time due to the shifting goals of the degree. As more and more young people define their academic studies as a hurdle one must cross with minimal time and effort – courses are perceived accordingly. Furthermore, when the average quality of students declines, the courses are judged by their difficulty and load, rather than their long-term pedagogic value.

The result is that boring, uninspired lecturers start getting high ratings because they're friendly towards students, while good lecturers (with high standards) who once led the academic system are faced with empty classrooms and low student evaluation results.

Since higher education institutions are afraid to lose 'customers' and lecturers are afraid to confront them, the teaching survey has essentially become a weapon that students can use against lecturers. When niceness is the most important quality a teacher can have, the level drops and academia loses its prestige and betrays its mission.

Compliments, Not Criticism, Please

Because millennials are low in resilience, can't take criticism and are naturally childish and over-sensitive to the comments made within their social environment, they expect to get praise and compliments from the lecturers. As a result, it's become harder and harder for lecturers to publicly correct students (constructive criticism) or put them in their place (e.g. for submitting a sloppy paper). Even the weakest oral presentation gets a big round of applause from their classmates, as the goal isn't just to support their friends but also to inform the lecturer that this is the correct way to respond. When the lecturer 'dares' to criticize the presenter, even in the gentlest and most subtle of ways (so he or she could learn for their mistakes), the whole classroom will respond with discontent. The mere idea of strong intellectual criticism, intended to improve the final scientific product ('playing devil's advocate', if you will) isn't favoured among millennials. For them, any personal criticism is hateful. Since they got used to getting compliments and praise for everything they did at school and at home, they are shocked and upset when they realize that they're not as smart as they have been led to believe.

I Also have Something to Say

The fact that students don't like to be personally criticized doesn't prevent them from criticizing and even bashing their lecturers. They've learned from the media that one must be assertive, opinionated and sometimes even callous and they apply this in class. It's not uncommon for students to disagree with their lecturers with a complete lack of humility and unfounded pretentiousness as if it were a private argument among friends ('I'm just as smart and knowledgeable as you'). Classes are often taken over by insensitive loud-mouthed students who feel the urge to voice their opinions time and time again, as if it were a private lesson. The result is that many courses fall into chaos, driving competent and fed up students away.

Non-Binding Schedule

Many students fail to meet their assignment deadlines, and requests for an extension have become very common (basically automatic). The reasons for this phenomenon are poor time management and a general tendency to delay commitments, knowing they are not the only ones falling behind, the (utterly justified) belief that the lecturer will 'meet them half-way' and their busy schedule (work, internet, going out etc.) in which studying isn't a top priority. Furthermore, the fact that in this era everybody is always available on our smartphones puts us all under 'attack' by unexpected tasks, forcing us to always be on the lookout.

Cooperative Learning

Higher education institutions have always served as fertile ground for meeting new people. It seems though that among millennials, academic socializing is more important than it was for previous generations, because they are not independent on one hand and very friendly on the other hand. They're used to living in packs, sharing, consulting, passing on information and relying on one another. Furthermore, this is a party generation and therefore it's only natural for university encounters to be redirected to bars, parties, cafés and restaurants.

The collaboration among millennial students has several expressions: they consult about courses and classes they should take on dedicated information sites and Facebook groups; they gather notes from classes on Facebook, as well as article summaries and test answers for every course (each student pitches in and occasionally participates in funding for translations and summaries); and they submit papers in groups of twos and threes. Incidentally, they're so used to asking for useful information and receiving it that they're even happy to help students they don't even know personally. This isn't necessarily done out of altruism, but rather out of a barter norm that presides in social media.

Shopping Season

Since many millennials perceive the academic degree as a means rather than a goal, they get furious at lecturers who have standards that they believe are too high. This rage is based, among other things, on the notion that they're paying good money and therefore are entitled to a service befitting of their expectations.

In order to avoid disappointments and confrontation, they thoroughly investigate the lecturer's assignment workload and expectations before signing up to the course. In other words, they 'price' the courses and choose the 'cheapest' ones (this is particularly true in humanities and social studies). Many come to the first lessons just to hear what the course will require of them firsthand and whether it's 'worth sticking around for' (this is during a time in which you can still cancel your registration, administratively speaking). This turns the beginning of the semester into 'shopping season'. It's not uncommon for students to tell the lecturer that his or her demands are too much as early as in the first lesson. One of the most efficient ways is conveying how heavy this course's assignments are compared to other courses. Since every lecturer has his or her own requirements (and are unaware of their colleague's requirements), the pressure to fall in line with other lecturers usually works.

Veteran lecturers with professional ethics, high self-esteem and a stable position in academia are less inclined to give their students a pass. This difference confuses the students, reinforcing their belief that the requirements are unreasonable.

Maximum Grade for Minimal Effort

Since students see academic education as a barter agreement, they're willing to negotiate in order to lower the 'ask price' as much as possible. Questions such as 'are all of these articles relevant to the test? Even the ones in English?' are common. They beg for reliefs with a rich and creative variety of arguments: 'we're very busy right now'; 'no one else demands as much as you do'; 'don't forget that I have to make a living too' etc.

Students often ask: 'is this going to be on the test?' to confirm which parts need to be summarized and which parts they can ignore (they were taught in high school to only study for the test).

Naturally, millennials expect their grades to reflect their expectations and be handed out generously. The problem is that these expectations don't necessarily match academic norms. For example, taking off points for writing that doesn't follow scientific writing rules or the lack of references (basic principles for academic writing) seems odd and baseless to many. Even taking off points for something they simply 'forgot' also seems excessive to them. Because they are used to getting high grades even for mediocre and weak papers in high school, they tend to see the low grades they got in academia as petty, mean-spirited and unjustified. They often appeal grades, even when there's no reason for the appeal other than their own disappointment, and ask for a personal meeting with the lecturer to talk about their personal difficulties and unexpected troubles, appeal to the lecturer's emotions and beg for mercy (the barrage of stories and excuses is endless). They assume it'll be hard to turn them down, and they are usually right.

One of the most common arguments for improving the grade they got is 'but I made an effort' or 'I came to all of the classes and read all of the articles'. Many believe that the main and in many cases only way to measure the quality of learning is by looking at the effort rather than the end result.

In recent years, as more and more students have realized that grades aren't as crucial for their future employment, expectations for high marks have somewhat lowered. Many young people nowadays do a cost-benefit analysis and decide to come to academia strictly for the purpose of getting a diploma. As one lecturer framed it: 'teaching is the only service that paying young people will be happy not to receive'.

Cut & Paste

One of the basic tasks in academia is outlining phenomena by extensively researching sources that relate to it from different angles and aspects and provide diverse information. Bibliographic research ('review of literature') is the foundation of academic research and its purpose is to review what's been said and done in this field so far. It is also an important tool which provides the paper's readers with material for further investigation and study. This is why lecturers require students to submit a good literature review in their papers.

Unfortunately, fewer and fewer lecturers maintain this academic requirement and less and less students fulfil it. They settle for whatever's available on Google, don't bother to patiently scan scientific databases, and submit seminar papers with poor bibliographies. Because they perform a superficial bibliographic research, their seminar papers read accordingly.

Millennials' tendency to do the bare minimum and take shortcuts is also reflected in the content of their papers. Many seem like a random string of 'cut & paste' paragraphs, not necessarily because they're actively cheating, but rather because this is what they've learned to do in school. This also has to do with their view that if you want to understand or write about something, all you have to do is fish out the right text or interview the right expert who'll do your work for you.

Spoon-Fed Learning

In the discussion on employee-employer relations, we showed that young people expect to get 'instruction manuals' for each of the employer's requirement. We've identified a similar phenomenon, for identical reasons, in their preferences in academic studies.

They need and expect clear, specific instructions from their lecturers and teaching assistants, including examples, for each requirement – the paper's length, structure, how much of it should be dedicated to each section and more – among other reasons so they can meet these requirements and only these requirements to the lecturer's satisfaction. They don't want written instructions, though, because they don't read those or only read them partially (which is also why they submit partial papers). For example, when the lecturer asks them to 'describe three problems' they will only describe two and when he or she asks to write down the 'problems and solutions' they will only list the problems.

They will often ask for hands-on support and guidance, like an insecure child. One veteran lecturer told us of a 30-year-old married student who begged her to dictate the timetables for writing the paper, i.e. how much time she should devote to each section.

Part-Time Students

Various surveys conducted in recent years have shown that many students work long hours while studying. Students from previous generations also worked during their academic studies, to pay their tuition as well as living expenses, such as rent and food. However, they focused on studying. The balance has shifted of late in favour of work (which is usually temporary). As a result, the importance of studies in students' lives has diminished.

What are the reasons for this phenomenon? Many young people only go to study as a means to an end; others already work in the field and therefore have less motivation to invest in their studies. They also often discover that work provides them with wider knowledge and skills that are more relevant to real-life applications than theoretical studies; due to the 'inflation of degrees', the degree's importance and prestige has lessened while the importance of experience in the field has grown. Thus, many try to acquire professional experience during the semesters, even at the expense of their own education; the extension of the young Israeli's pre-determined path in life ('must do') has led them to begin academic studies later in life. With age come greater financial needs and consequently the need to earn money while studying; the cost of living, and particularly rent, have gone up significantly in recent years. These are added to by new costs such as computers and cellphones; students' leisure needs have also increased and require much more money than before; many students these days are forced to pay for some or all of their tuition, which means they have to work.

Working while studying has many implications for students as well as for the institutions, for example:

Students Invest Less in their Studies. They display low attendance rates, don't read as many articles and books (opting for cliff notes instead), don't prepare as thoroughly for tests and write less in-depth papers.

Exhausted Students Lacking in Concentration. They tend to arrive late to class, yawn in the lecturer's face and often even fall asleep in their seats. It's no wonder then that many cafés across campuses also sell energy drinks like Red Bull.

Choosing Courses to Match their Work Schedule. Working for long hours forces millennials to build their semester curriculum according to their utility level, which means low demands, smiling lecturers and easy hours that don't clash with their work hours.

Long Study Days. In order to adapt to the millennials' lifestyle, institutions of higher education have begun to shove as many courses together into a limited number of days (and sometimes even one day a week).

With a 'Little' Help from my Friends

Cheating isn't a new phenomenon in schools and academia, but ever since higher education has become a natural stage in the coming of age of most young people in western countries, it has become increasingly common. Studies show that some 70 per cent of students admit they cheated in one way or another, and some scholars have gone as far as call it a plague that threatens the field's very existence.

Common expressions of cheating among students include: copying seminar papers (from classmates or other sources); copying ideas and quotes without referencing the original (plagiarism); submitting the same paper in several courses; buying or getting test questions in advance; using prohibited materials during exams; passing on information to students during exams; using Ritalin to increase concentration (by students who don't need it and don't have a prescription); submitting one paper under several authors, while only one of the co-authors actually wrote it; fabrication of data and evidence in empirical research papers; fabricating sources for the bibliography; giving lecturers false information to get reliefs (such as lying about the reason they couldn't take a test or submit a paper on time); stealing reserved reading materials from the library or tearing out pages of books and articles.

Studies have shown that students explain their cheating with a variety of typical excuses:

Fear of Failure: If I don't cheat, I'll flunk out or don't get the grades I need (the pressure is higher when their parents are paying for their tuition).

External Force Left me no Choice: The task load is too heavy; other people in this course teach and it will make me less successful by comparison; too many tests in a short period of time; I work full-time and only have a little time to dedicate to studies; I was sick and didn't have enough time to catch up; the financial support I get for studies depends on my grades; I need good grades to get accepted to a sought-after job or further studies.

The Lecturer is Unfair: This course is too hard; the lecturer's grading criteria is too strict; the lecturer's tests are unfair and designed to fail students; the course paper load is too high and impossible to meet.

Opportunity Makes a Thief: it's easy to read the tests of the students sitting next to me; the lecturer walked out of the room during the test.

Selective Morality: I only cheat in really hard courses; I'm usually honest, but sometimes you have no choice, you have to cheat; when my friends need help, I can't turn them down.

Many students allow themselves to cheat because they feel the risk is miniscule. They generally don't consider cheating to be immoral and rather view it as the result of lack of choice or momentary weakness. But above all they do it because it has become the norm: everyone's cheating, so why shouldn't I cheat too?

Many millennials arrive in academia with a rich experience of cheating in exams and papers from high school. It usually starts with copying exercises and minor homework assignments or other collaborations with students, escalating over time to more sophisticated and extreme actions. The internet and cellphone expand their options.

A study that reviewed the scope and nature of cheating in Israeli academia found that only 2 per cent of students claimed they'd never cheated on anything during their academic studies. Weaker students reported more cheating than outstanding students, and college students reported more misconducts than university students.

The study also found that the more veteran the student, the more experienced and skillful they are in cheating and getting away with it.

The most serious and troubling offence is of course the purchasing of seminar papers and even theses. It has far-reaching implications not only because this is a criminal offence that has cultivated an entire industry, but also because seminar papers and dissertations are the most important measure of a student's quality.

Next to websites that offer papers by demand, the market also sells academic papers that were submitted in the past ('firsthand' papers are sold at a higher price). This dubious service is amazingly easy to access and is not hidden. The student makes a request, gets a price offer, sends a down payment and the deal is closed. The amazing thing is that many of these service providers openly declare that this is their livelihood – with their full name and other details without any embarrassment or shame.

Other websites also offer students learning shortcuts for various courses across all academic institutions in Israel such as reconstructed secret tests – including solutions, referent presentations, full lab reports etc.

Bulletin boards in higher education institutions are also full of such services being offered for affordable prices.

What are the lecturers' reactions? Many are aware of the phenomenon and would rather just let it go, 'because this is how things are. What can I do?', 'We get subpar students that shouldn't have been accepted in the first place.' The more idealistic (some might say naïve) lecturers try to bridge the knowledge gaps students bring with them from high school by converting portions of the disciplinary course to instructions on how to write academic papers.

Some lecturers argue that they are not 'detectives'. Even when they do suspect cheating, they don't always have the ability, let alone the time or energy, to prove it. Others blame the new reality in which grades have become the forefront of academic learning. When grades are the goal rather than getting an actual education, it's no wonder that students will do anything they can to get them.

Many lecturers put the blame on the larger number of students per classroom, which makes it harder for them to get to know their students and their capabilities. It also pushes them towards low-level learning requirements.

The heads of universities and colleges are well aware of cheating but tend to deny its scope or struggle to deal with it. Students occasionally have to face a disciplinary committee (a kind of legal proceeding in which the student is on trial and liable to punishment such as a financial fine or expulsion from studies), and in many cases walk away with relatively minor punishments, if any at all.

Lecturers and teaching assistants aren't too keen on filing a claim against students who were caught cheating, because they feel the institutions (and often their compassionate colleagues) won't support them. Another reason for avoiding this is the fact that appearing before a disciplinary committee is an unpleasant experience for lecturers and involves exhausting bureaucracy as well as humiliation by militant lawyers in some cases. Most lecturers feel that it's just not worth the hassle.

'Done Studying, Now What?' – Quarter Life Crisis

The term 'Quarter Life Crisis', which describes a whole new phenomenon, was coined by two young Americans called Alexandra Robbins and Abby Wilner. They published a book of the same name in 2001, which created a great interest and led to a flood of self-help books on the subject.

This psychological phenomenon usually takes place after the conclusion of higher education. Its symptoms include a feeling of suffocation and lack of direction, pressure to get a job, get married and have kids, disappointment, regret, confusion and frustration, dissatisfaction with life, loneliness, depression, guilt, indecision and anxiety about the future. Many young people also report a feeling of premature and unexpected ageing as well as fatigue. They knew it would be hard after graduation, but didn't know just how much, and are anxious because they don't know what to do with their troubling emotions and life in general.

After completing the typical path for their age, millennials understand they need to start making decisions on their own, and they are not used to that. They become helpless and struggle to 'get out to the world' and take responsibility for their adult lives.

There are actually two disappointments here. First, they discover that nobody's going to roll out the red carpet for them. Surprisingly enough, in many cases the academic degree can even be a disadvantage in the labour market, as employers prefer people with experience rather than inexperienced college graduates.

They're also disappointed by the wages they're offered. For many years there has been a positive correlation between the level of one's education and the salary you received. However, something in this correlation has gone awry in recent years – the salary increase that education brings (the 'Delta') isn't so high, particularly in the first year after graduation. And if that's not depressing enough, the more and higher degrees you get, the weaker your degree's effect on your salary is.

What are the reasons for this quarter life crisis? Here are some potential answers:

Fear of Being Independent. The quarter life crisis is actually an ongoing coming of age crisis. Many of today's young people are children at heart, who struggle to adapt to adulthood and lack the tools for dealing with it. Since they're used to getting an 'instruction manual' for life, independence scares them. They 'feel like dying' just from thinking about the day they will be forced to make a fateful decision and won't be able to just have fun and accumulate experiences. They're terrified of the thought that soon the burden of marriage, children, livelihood and mortgage will fall upon them.

Inflated Sense of Self. Young people's self-image, which has been cultivated by parents and teachers, in many cases also creates unrealistic expectations from life. When finally reality slaps them in the face disappointment, despair and depression follow. Even when millennials realize they should lower their expectations, they're not always willing to pay the price.

Time Goes By and they're Still Alone. Young people's confusion over committed relationships nowadays certainly contributes to their quarter life crisis. As the years go by, they fear that the dream of finding 'the one' or anyone for the matter seems to be drifting farther and farther away. This is particularly stressful for women whose biological clocks are ticking and are under more pressure from their families. Suddenly, they start wondering: maybe the reason I can't get a worthy partner is because something in my life is stuck.

'We Held up our End'. According to millennials, once they agreed to study and worked hard to finish the degree, they held up their end of the social contract. Now they expect society to reward them accordingly, with the appropriate job and salary. It's possible that this also echoes the consumerist mindset they've been instilled with, or in other words: if I paid for the product (degree), I'm entitled to what it says on the box.

Furthermore, since they lack future orientation, long-term planning and patience, they tend to get disappointed rather quickly – i.e. if their expectations aren't fulfilled immediately. They are unable to understand that life is an endless battle and isn't designed to their liking.

The higher education system manipulates the naivety of young people and their families in order to wage its own war for survival. Universities and colleges give them false hope. Furthermore, the heads of academia (backed by the Government) have prevented, both directly and indirectly, the creation of realistic alternatives to academic education, such as establishing vocational secondary schools, in order to preserve their monopoly. Consequently, many get their degree without actually acquiring a profession, thus ending up right where they started.

The Illusion of a Simple, Happy Life. Teen shows, which have become very popular in recent years, paint a picture of a happy, glamorous world, the embodiment of the American dream. And even if there are problems along the way, salvation will always come from one place or another. You just need to wait patiently. Things will work out in the end. Social media, which is filled with stories and images of success, happiness and partying, amplifies this feeling. When it turns out that what you see on the screen is very detached from what you really get, then comes the crash.

The Financial Crisis. Many young people realize too late that financial independence requires painful sacrifice. You need to party less and work more. This understanding is shocking and depressing. Unfortunately, they're entering the labour market in a time of crisis. They were supposed to reap the benefits of unlimited options in the age of globalization and the internet, but ended up in a global economic slowdown, which doesn't allow them to grow at the rate their parents did. Professions which were once sufficient for making a reasonable living and a quiet life such as teaching and journalism are gradually eroding and many will disappear in the long term due to technological changes.

The fear of settling down leads many millennials to continue to study for advanced degrees (MA, PhD) so they can buy some more time as 'young students'. But 'delaying the inevitable' isn't a solution, and often only escalates the problem.

It appears that the 'quarter life crisis' isn't just a turbulent phase like the 'mid life crisis'. This is a crisis of severe disillusionment that paralyzes an entire generation. Its social implication, however, isn't restricted to this generation. This new crisis signals that the traditional model of higher education must change drastically and adapt itself to the new social needs and capabilities.

15

Who Needs Politics? –
Escapism as a Worldview

Do they have a Stance?

In the age of information flow and fast-paced communications, people's moral decisions have become less consistent and more related to specific opinions on singular events. In fact, many people create an eclectic and dynamic mixed bag of positions and worldviews. This is true for the entire population, but even more so among young people, who seem to be better at making peace with contradictions. For example, they believe that emigrating from Israel is bad for the country, but if a friend tells them they're planning to emigrate, they won't criticize him/her and accept their choice; they don't believe the Arabs want true peace but are still willing to give up territories in exchange for a reasonable agreement; they can like the settler ideology while admitting they've never been to Judea and Samaria and can't tell Ariel from Emmanuel; they're 'all for God and the People of Israel' but against religious coercion. They do not suffer particularly from cognitive dissonance and juggle their stances lightly, without going into details, while being fed partial and fleeting information.

In many cases, stances revealed in polls contradict one another, though youngsters aren't even aware of it. This generation's political inconsistency is connected among other things to the changing definitions of identity. Unlike previous generations, political outlook is not a significant aspect of millennials' self-identity, so the urge to establish a strong worldview is weaker. Furthermore, since they don't like heated arguments, they lack the passion for politics. As far as they are concerned, everyone has 'their personal truth' and if I can't convince someone, let's just change the subject.

The media in Israel encourages loud political discourse full of clichés and slogans, for the purpose of ratings mainly. The result is that millennials have been conditioned from an early age into a very simplistic and often immature grasp of the political reality. When they do exhibit something that appears to be radical ideology, it is actually just a gag rather than a structured political doctrine.

Millennials' weak political identity also stems from the era in which they were raised. This is a period where the disagreements, tensions and ideological differences in Israeli society were toned down. Rifts based on religion, ethnicity, gender, political ideology (left-right) and economic perception (most citizens hold a capitalistic worldview) no longer make up rigid opposing 'camps'. Over time, reality has shown that everyone is right and everyone is wrong (as a matter of fact, the ideological gap deepened during this period, only on the edges of the scale, i.e. extremist groups within the camps, which have become even more extreme). Thus, most young people don't associate with any political camp (most of them belong to the political centre according to their views) and refuse to be pigeon-holed.

Since the polarization between camps is overshadowed by processes of integration and mutual influence, millennials' positions on social phenomena deviate from the old political outline. For example, they can vote for a right-wing party and also support withdrawal from territories, or admire Naftali Bennett, who leads a national religious party, and still be in favour of separation of religion and state.

Patriotism without the Innocence of Youth

Strong patriotism has always been one of the trademarks of Israeli society – a sentiment that's still very dominant in all Jewish sectors and age groups. Polls have shown time and time again that Israelis feel a strong connection to their country. Most also feel lucky to have been born in Israel.

Youngsters are supposedly no different from their parents when it comes to affection for their homeland. Most of them identify with Israel and are proud to be Israelis. When they're abroad, as tourists, backpackers or temporary immigrants, they keep constant tabs on what's happening in Israel. They also love to present themselves as Israelis and get mad at anyone who 'disses' the country, much like when someone 'disses' their family (this is also one of the reasons for the distaste many feel towards political left extremists who slander Israel). Zionism still flows in their bloodstream, even though it isn't ideologically framed.

Many millennials also feel genuine concern for the country and its longevity. They've learned firsthand that Israel is surrounded by enemies who want to destroy it, and the threat has actually only grown during their lifetime, among others due to the rise of Islamic extremism.

However, millennials are not the naïve Zionist advocates and missionaries as their parents were in their youth, because the idea of 'The Jewish State' has lost its former aura. They were born into the 'post-Zionist' age, which advocates a cynical, materialistic and selfish mindset. Over the years, they've been exposed to negative headlines that didn't exist in the past, both in magnitude and in frequency, and have absorbed the general feeling that something has gone wrong with the innocent vision.

Many young people have mixed feelings about the State: on one hand, they love living in Israel and find it to be an exceptional country, with advantages they won't find anywhere else. At the same time, they're certain that this is a corrupt country, with manipulative tycoons and self-serving politicians who pull the strings of the economy. They also feel that criminals go unpunished, workers aren't properly rewarded for their work, and there's a general sense of social injustice. But they still feel very much that they belong here.

The 'Israeli' and 'Jewish' identities are still at the top of their list, but other identities appear to have climbed up the chart: friends, family, occupation, hobbies or spouses play a central role in their lives, far more than the homeland or the nation.

The Post-Ideological Age

My Truth and your Truth

The democratization of the western world has led to a shift in moral reasoning and the results can be seen in the moral values developed by millennials: they tend to replace firm moral judgement with a more lenient approach. One that looks at reality in more relative terms. Past philosophers spoke of the death of history, death of art, death of subject and object, death of the author, death of God, death of theory and the death of truth. However, that was all more within the realms of theoretical and sociological concepts. For millennials, this spirit has completely taken over their perception of reality.

Millennials have grown up without guides or role models with institutional and moral authority such as clergymen, teachers, instructors or national leaders. They came of age in a time where most myths were being shattered, including the myth of charisma. Parents became friends with their children, which has consequently stripped them of their moral high ground. Since this generation rarely reads books, they are also less exposed to models of morality that exist in the great novels. This leaves electronic media, mostly television, although most of the characters it shows are no role models. They're either shallow and miserable or intentionally manipulative and evil.

This 'post-ideological' generation has learned that the world is relative. There's no longer one nature, one border or one truth; there are mostly points of view – which are completely subjective. The revolutionary spirit and moral gravity are replaced with joviality and gleeful cynicism, with doubt gnawing away at certainty. Millennials aren't looking to redeem themselves or the world but would rather live in the moment. They don't care about the wellbeing of society as a whole, but rather about their own personal happiness.

Some claim that millennials' popular post-modernism is another expression of the downfall of the old restricting dogmas and of disillusionment with the dangers of innocence and the artificial charm of the world. Perhaps this has more to do with moral development, i.e. the transition to a more democratic and pluralistic society, where charisma is not only removed from people but also from texts and norms. Nonetheless, it seems that the post-modern expression in millennials' worldview doesn't come from a place of knowledge and education but rather from a place of ignorance and frivolity. They were told that there's no absolute truth and that absolves them from profound thinking and the sisyphean quest to find truth.

The media assists them and actually intensifies the phenomenon. It spreads populist polls and studies, which often contradict one another. Every expert opinion is followed by an opposing expert opinion, creating vast confusion. Furthermore, in a sea of reports and interviews, anything can be trivialized, marginalized or turned upside down: good becomes evil and evil becomes good. Today's media is to a great extent a travelling circus of disposable heroes, where the most important thing is to get the audience's attention by all means necessary.

Millennials see values as a fleeting, relative thing, which is reflected in their tendency to avoid being judgmental or making strong statements about controversial public issues at any cost. Unlike their parents, they don't spend time debating whether something is right or wrong, but rather focus on whether it's allowed. They see social reality as a 'relationship' and a collection of subjective emotions and interests. There's no absolute justice as far as they are concerned and therefore there's also no absolute right or wrong. Ephemeral disputes and problems can be resolved by playing it safe and taking a step back. To borrow from the legal world: they rather go for mediation than a lawsuit, and if at all possible, resolve things with a handshake. The most refined reflection of the generational gap is a phrase that's very common among youngsters: 'I stand in my truth', which semantically means that everyone has their own 'truth' and therefore there's no point in arguing.

The relativity of truth, which guides millennials, is tied among other things to the development of the ocean of online messages, where the medium is the message and the packaging is more important than actual content. Many young people don't question the messages they're exposed to or question information in order to uncover the truth. They are led by sentiment rather than by their intellect. Therefore, if you can stir up an emotional reaction within them, you'll get their sympathy and support.

Marginal Ideologies

It should be stressed the Generation Y also includes some idealistic youngsters, who yearn to learn and delve into things and commit to a variety of altruistic causes. They are found in environmental and animal rights organizations, nonprofits for the elderly and disenfranchised youth, youth movements, the security forces, various political frameworks etc. They are particularly drawn to the socialist doctrine that tries to balance out inequality and aggressive capitalism.

In fact, because of the moral and ideological vacuum, the idealistic margins actually expand and sometimes get radicalized (for example, radical civil rights groups, environmental activists or anti-consumerists). However, this phenomenon is sociologically misleading because it gives the impression that this is a wide generational phenomenon, while in reality it's a demographic minority – the exception that proves the rule.

Marginal ideologies expand and often radicalize for several reasons: first, the spiritual void creates a yearning for something deeper and more mentally rewarding. Second, physical distance is no longer an obstacle for organizing in the internet age. You can achieve a critical mass of people for a cause through the use of social media. Third, the margins often offer a home for young social rejects, i.e. those who are unable to find their place within the conformist majority.

You could say that the age of major ideologies is being replaced by the age of minor ideologies. They're minor in regards to pretension, meaning they don't aspire to abolish the old world and build a new world on top of it, but rather focus on a concrete idea, intended to improve the quality of our lives in a specific field. In many ways, the ideological lifestyle has replaced the ideological worldview.

Fed Up with Politics

Israelis are glued to the political arena. They're naturally argumentative, assertive, caring and convinced that they have the power to make a difference. The fact that Israel is under a constant existential threat also adds a high-octane element of tension, anger and drama to the 'political plot' and encourages involvement.

Online access to political information alongside the increased level of formal education, should have made citizens more interested and involved in politics. In reality, the exact opposite has happened. Polls from Israel and around the world indicate a lack of interest in politics across all demographics and particularly among younger age groups. This is reflected in a declining voter turnout, decreased interest in reading review articles and op-eds, less active protest and a reduced interest in the news.

Some say the cause is saturation. The media constantly discusses the same political crises and arguments, and people are simply sick of it all. Most people, old and young, have started to feel as if nothing ever really changes, that we're just 'treading water' and in many cases end up right back where we started. It seems that even when reality does change, it's more due to global processes rather than as a result of any local policy or leadership. There's also the sense that life has become a rehash of advertising, public relations and artificial images, and that the news is nothing more than momentary TV drama – an extreme performance to attract higher ratings.

The declining political interest and involvement is also derived from the media outrage culture, which is particularly prominent in Israel. Any public statement attracts backlash from every direction. This is a superficial, hysterical, disrespecting, offensive and inciting discourse, all orchestrated by the media, which is out for blood. This makes many people curl up into a ball, focus on their private lives and avoid dealing with important issues.

Some say the cause is ignorance. Considerable portions of the public lack a basic understanding of a variety of fields – internal and foreign relations, economics, welfare and other important issues. This ignorance is more common in youngsters, particularly because of their information sources. Previous generations have grown accustomed to consuming daily political information from newspapers and the evening news on the radio and television, while young people have come of age in a world that settles for headlines and catchy slogans. They also don't read as many books, so they're less familiar with the historical narrative that contemporary politics is based on. Being unfamiliar with the 'dry' facts and the chain of events makes it hard for them to establish a coherent political opinion. In many cases it also leads to much prejudice, particularly concerning minorities: immigrants from the former Soviet Union, Ethiopian Jews, Arabs, the ultra-orthodox and the national religious sector.

Meanwhile, some political scientists consider escapism to be a type of rational decision, albeit not necessarily a conscious one. According to this explanation, intense consumption of information about the political world takes up too much time, which would better serve other goals such as earning money or pastime activities. In this sense, young people are simply performing a 'cost-benefit' analysis and limiting their political involvement as a result.

The fact that people are fed up with the political world has also contributed to the drop in political involvement. Polls indicate that young people see politicians as corrupt and politics as a whole as something dirty. This can be found in countless posts by millennials who lash out at public officials, which get thousands of likes and shares.

Agree to Disagree

It is possible that millennials' repressed approach towards politics is heralding the beginning of a post-political or post-ideological age that's forming in western democracies – an age where instead of seeking out absolute justice, you minimize your emotional involvement. In other words, avoiding points of friction and embracing the 'female model' of acceptance and inclusion instead of reproach and authoritarianism according to the 'male model'.

In a way, this is exactly what millennials do in their everyday lives. Many have embraced the notion that you can't educate other people, teach them a lesson or have an open discussion – especially when it comes to politics. According to this approach, anger is essentially aggression and a waste of energy, and it's best to push it out of the way and 'move forward'.

It's difficult to quantify the daily incidence and volume of conflicts in society, but it seems that a systematic observation of young people's environments is enough to detect this phenomenon. Only rarely can we see them arguing passionately about anything. They usually just sit in circles, relaxed and happy, exchanging gags and opinions on issues that have a wide consensus or at the very most an insignificant controversy (who deserves to win a reality show, which country is better for travelling etc). Any member who raises an issue of some consequence is shunned as a party-pooper and is usually met with sulking faces (though no reproach, of course). Many feel that public criticism is more immoral than the deed that brought it about, because it is aggressive and insulting.

If someone or something truly bothers them, they'll step aside or remove the source of intrusion (such as 'blocking' on Facebook). Many will simply avoid confrontation or reproach upfront, even when it's a fundamental or moral issue. When people start raising their voice, someone usually throws a phrase that defuses the situation, such as 'agree to disagree'.

Escaping from personal confrontations also affects their reluctance to participate in political confrontations. Millennials avoid political arguments, which are naturally confrontational and emotional. They would rather not engage in debates where there's no possibility for compromise, in which one opinion is certain to 'win' while the other 'loses'. This is a naturally belligerent debate and they are 'uncomfortable' with it.

Voting Patterns

Low Voter Turnout

The declining political involvement and naive patriotism, alongside the rise of individualism, are expressed in lower voter turnout in the western world. For example, the United States has a voter turnout of barely 50 per cent of eligible voters. Voter turnout in Israel is 'in a good place in the middle' compared to other countries, but the general trend here is similar.

Experts attribute this trend – which is more prominent among young people – to economic, demographic, cultural, technological and institutional factors and particularly to smear campaigns that are commonplace among both parties and candidates, which affect the way voters perceive the democratic process as a whole.

Since the media tends to sensationalize the political process, news consumers tend to respond accordingly. For millennials, leaders are nothing more than forgettable reality show participants – a colosseum of entertainment in which values are far less significant.

The Effects of Charm

Many millennials around the world judge a politician based on his or her personality, charm and rhetoric rather than the political doctrine and ideology that he or she represents. This is one of the main reasons for the way Barack Obama managed to captivate young people in his country. This was also a significant part of the success of Yair Lapid (with the slogan 'we're here to make a change') and Naftali Bennett (with the slogan 'something new is starting') in the 2013 elections in Israel. Many of the people who voted for them were millennials, who were bewitched by their background and demeanour as much as by their political platform.

Protest Voting

A considerable portion of young people vote out of protest or mistrust, rather than as an act of identification. This is a comparative political worldview – they don't identify with any specific camp, but rather as opinionated individuals. This is reflected, among other things, in a slight increase in votes for small parties (in some cases these are parties that don't pass the election threshold, like in the case of Aleh Yarok), and in voting for niche parties, which come and go. The most distinct example is the Pensioner Party, which got seven seats in the 2006 elections. Surprisingly enough, many of its voters were actually young people.

Digital Protest

The generations that rose in the western world after the Second World War (in the 1950s, 60s, 70s and 80s) are considered to be the most rebellious generations in the history of mankind. They dared to change deep-rooted historical norms in almost every field. They developed youth frameworks, which provided an alternative to the closed-off traditional family, imported and embraced the anti-authoritarian humanistic approach in schools and in family life, rebelled against the military and political institutions, opened the dams of puritanism and brought the gospel of rock 'n' roll and feminism. 'Flower girls' took off their aprons and dared to develop a professional career – first in pink-collar professions (teachers, nurses etc.) followed by white-collar professions. They later liberated the media from the chains of propaganda and censorship and become hi-tech entrepreneurs who made economic and technological breakthroughs.

All of these rebellions involved personal risks and costs, which seemed worthwhile at the time. The general feeling was that they had a reason to rebel and take the risks. Millennials put out the fire of rebellion and became more adaptive and passive compared to previous generations. This is due to several reasons: first, millennials live in a world of fast changes, which prevented them from developing the urge and commitment to rebel, defy and take risks in order to create change (they assume that if they wait long enough it will happen on its own).

Second, millennials were raised in a culture that focuses on the self. In a world where the individual and not the collective is at the centre, it's hard to motivate people to do something for the common good. Third, millennials were born into a world that didn't really have someone or something to rebel against. When the parents, teachers, commanders and bosses are your friends the impulse to rebel becomes dulled. Furthermore, most rebellious and anti-establishment phenomena of the twentieth century were institutionalized, becoming part of the mainstream in western culture. In a world where abnormality is the norm, the urge to rise up against something lessens.

However, although millennials are more adaptive and passive compared to previous generations and even though they tend to avoid rebellion, the urge to protest and express one's opinions have not disappeared in this generation, and have even grown stronger.

Social networks – which are dominated by young people – have greatly amplified people's ability to express their opinions and be heard in the public space. Digital protest has several characteristics that distinguish it from traditional protests. For example, in many cases, online protests grow and spread at great speed (thousands of protestors unite in a matter of minutes), making it 'viral'.

The new media gives a voice to every protestor (the option of voicing criticism in your own words) which is why the protest is wider and louder. It also allows the surfers to assess the strength of solidarity through likes, shares and comments.

Unlike street protest, which is rare and only occurs after a cumulative crisis or extreme event, digital protest is daily and often eclectic and specific. For example, it doesn't deal exclusively with the lack of affordable housing and the high cost of living, but also with the price of cottage cheese, misconduct of a famous singer or the offensive behaviour of a bus driver.

Online protest is also less violent than the street's (its violence is purely verbal) and therefore usually doesn't lead to clashes with the police. However, in many cases it gets out of hand, and might lead to a violent verbal stoning ritual (or 'shaming').

Facebook protests are essentially 'armchair protests'. This phenomenon has received many nicknames, like 'Facebook activism' or 'Slacktivism'. Some claim this protest has a limited influence because although it may be loud, eloquent and massive, it has a short expiration time and is devoid of any real sacrifice. There may be a lively discourse on Facebook about issues on the news and young people responding to scandals and sympathizing with the cause or voicing criticism, but these more resemble spectator responses in the theatre than criticism that motivates people to actually do something. However, sometimes social media amplifies emotions, creates social pressure and provides an efficient call to protest that goes out to the streets and can even escalate to physical violence.

Actually, vibrant politics in new media – led by the younger generation – is gradually replacing old institutionalized and rusty politics. Comments, blogs and Facebook posts create a classless digital community, where everyone has the right accessible tool to express an opinion and interpretation that was once the preserve of professional commentators and experts.

Different Kind of News Consumers

Israelis have become addicted to news because of their curious and argumentative nature, their urge to criticize and change their reality as well as security threats, which force the solidarity citizen to stay vigilant and up to date. News was also considered a form of entertainment, since the news industry in Israel has always been dynamic, clever and creative, with the capability to keep millions glued to the screen.

And yet, something has changed in the past few years. This change has affected Israel as a whole but it has left a considerable mark on millennials. Whereas Israeli media was once home to few news agents, nowadays the market is saturated. The laptop, smartphone and tablet blast out the news to everyone, wherever they go. Since they can't escape or catch a break from the never-ending flow of news, people have become jaded and numb.

Attitudes towards news has also changed in the past few years because of the media's changing image. In the distant past, Israeli media was thought of as a responsible, reliable body. This image has eroded over the years and is reflected among others in journalism's negative reputation in the eyes of the public. It creates a duality: on one hand, Israelis admire prominent and influential members of the media (this is also why young people are attracted to communication studies); on the other hand, they despise the media institution for its obvious manipulation, interests, populism, exaggeration and lack of balance – particularly in political coverage and commentary.

The change in news consumption patterns is also, and perhaps mainly, a result of the digital revolution. Very few people of all generations read a daily newspaper nowadays, and the few that do mostly consume free daily newspapers and weekend editions. They mainly get their daily news from morning and evening shows on television and through online news sites.

Another source of information for young people (and a primary source for some) is social media, which offers piquant news from Israel and around the world. Friends share interesting and viral updates and information with one another. As a result, the younger generation gets a very eclectic image of the news, whether high or low, important or marginal, credible or fabricated and local or global.

Unlike previous generations who got the gist of the news as orchestrated by the headlines (with an emphasis on the economic-diplomatic-security field), the millennial news consumer is interested in Benjamin Netanyahu's policy next to the new dance moves from Korea, or a coalition crisis next to a YouTube video of a cat teasing a dog. Whereas their parents gathered in the living room to discuss the government's misguided policy or a solution for the Arab-Israeli conflict, millennials discuss Bar Refaeli's new campaign or a new imported wine with the same gravity. Some claim this is a more flexible, democratic and balanced approach, while others see it as a type of escapism and frivolousness.

Our study shows that young people usually flip through the news headlines, pictures and 'boxes', and quickly move on to the 'juicier' sections. In this respect, millennials are no different from the general population. However, there is one aspect where the difference is significant: young people are not interested in opinion journalism and are more drawn to short pieces, headlines and news updates, consumer news (shopping, entertainment, sports etc.), and light-hearted humour. In other words, millennials put an emphasis on 'updates' rather than on depth.

Another reason for the decline of traditional opinion journalism among young people is the rise of blogs and personal Facebook pages. In the age of old media, only a handful of senior journalists were deemed worthy of a platform for expressing their opinions, which gave them immense power. In the digital age, they've lost their power because anyone can be a public opinion leader, without having to ask permission from the gatekeepers. New opinion journalism isn't just more diverse and democratic, it is also more interactive, therefore more appealing to young people. Facebook and WhatsApp groups often serve as platforms for discussions, where the news is discussed in a relaxed, supportive atmosphere.

Millennials, the Holocaust and Anti-Semitism

Trip to Poland as Formative Generational Experience

The Ministry of Education-sponsored tradition of travelling to the death camps in Poland started in the 1990s, and Generation XY was the first to partake in them. Initially, only a few delegations were sent and participation was low. Over time the tradition took root, first in high schools and later in IDF as well.

Public debate over the educational importance of the trip to Poland started even before it became an inseparable part of the curriculum. Nonetheless, it appears everyone is in agreement about one thing: the trip is a powerful emotional experience for youngsters, which also affects their patriotism and commitment to enlist to IDF.

The trip also amplifies youngsters' negative feelings towards Arabs. The unmediated encounter with the worst of humanity may demonstrate how important it is to fight racism and the exclusion of others, and fight for minority rights, but at the same time, it reinforces the sense that Arabs are the embodiment of new Anti-Semitism, which once again threatens the existence of the Jewish people.

One could assume that the tradition of trips to Poland would make millennials more informed about the Holocaust than previous generations. And yet, previous studies show that the perception of the Holocaust among young people is mostly emotional and devoid of depth. The visit to the death camps illustrates to them what the 'Final Solution' was, but misses the broad sociological and philosophical discussion of genocide throughout human history. Many of them burst into tears when they witness the horrors of the death camps, but this is often due to the pleasure of shared sadness which resembles in this sense the 'candle youths' in Rabin Square (most of them didn't even know the Prime Minister's biography prior to his assassination).

Living in a Country of Mass Murderers

In July 2013 a young man called Chen Ben-ari wrote a provocative and symbolic post on Facebook. The first line stood out: 'I'm a 27-year-old grandson of a Palmach warrior who raised the mythological Ink Flag with his friends (in the War of Independence), crossed the canal with his van (in the Yom Kippur War) and founded Kibbutz Malkia, and I have decided to leave Israel. Why? Because I'm a patriot! I'm leaving Israel and I've written a farewell letter for everyone or perhaps this is a wake-up call for us all…'. The post ended with the words: 'I'm leaving Israel. I'll be back when it's normal here again! Goodbye!!!!!!!!'

As expected, most of the comments included strong criticism. But there were quite a few people, most of whom were young, who praised his honesty and supported his thesis. The post got 9,850 likes and 3,300 shares.

Ben-ari's post was followed by one from another young man called Ben Segev who posted a photograph of a receipt from a store in Berlin. He wrote in conclusion: 'Care to guess how much I paid for it? The total amount was 22.79 Euro – which is 107 shekels. How much would this purchase have cost in Israel? Twice as much? Three times as much?'

Several months later, this debate expanded and gained public momentum, following a three-part series by Channel 10's young economic correspondent Matan Hodorov on the evening news. These serial reports dealt with the poor financial state of young people in Israel: 'Pension-less Generation' – about the lousy retirement arrangements that workers under the age of 50 are expected to get in the future; 'Crazy Land' – which investigated whether it is in the

State's interest to raise housing prices for young couples; and most notable: 'The New Emigrants' – which documented the phenomenon of emigration among Israeli youths to Europe and the United States due to the high cost of living. The people who appeared in the reports were singles and married youngsters who live in large Israeli communities around the world such as New Jersey, London and, most controversially of all, Berlin. They enjoy a relaxed and enjoyable life that comes, among other things, from their ability to live comfortably off their current income. As befitting of a journalistic instant report, they didn't discuss all of the implications of uprooting from Israel, but the effect of young people who aren't apologetic about their choice, but rather accuse Israel of denying young people hope and link this to the 2011 protest, has left its mark. Hodorov didn't stop at interviews, but also conducted a poll in order to validate his findings, which revealed that no less than 51 per cent of Israelis have considered emigrating from Israel due to the high cost of living and the escalating housing crisis. Obviously, this data did not include the ones who have already done it.

The media went berserk. Even Minister of Finance Yair Lapid quickly responded: 'forgive me if I have little patience for people who are willing to throw away the only country Jews have in the world because Berlin is more comfortable'. The grumbling response by the man who was already perceived as an unfulfilled promise by major parts of the media and many youngsters, made matters even worse.

Ynet, which had already dealt with young Israeli's hardships before, hopped on the train and published a series of articles (most of which written by young emigrants) under the provocative headline 'emigrate or stay?' which led to thousands of comments and sentimental op-eds. Other media outlets also dedicated articles to the phenomenon and received a barrage of comments.

This controversy would have faded quickly, as hot topics in the media tend to do, if it wasn't for an Israeli living in Berlin who opened a Facebook group called 'Making Aliyah to Berlin' in September 2014. He also posted a photograph of a receipt with the caption: 'one of the things we miss most about Israel is "Milky" [an Israeli brand of dairy pudding]. Please note that the price of one cup of Milky in Berlin (which is also slightly bigger in Germany) is just 0.19 Euro, 80 agorot. Milky in Israel… costs a little over 3 shekels per unit.' This post, which was also quoted on *Ynet*, lit a massive media fire.

Naor Narkis, who started the latest provocation (which was covered extensively in Germany), hid behind a veil of anonymity at first which only attracted more attention. But later on, as media pressure grew, he revealed his name and face in an interview for Channel 10 News. It turned out that this young 25-year-old was the epitome of the all-Israeli boy, the 'salt of the earth'. Narkis voiced strong criticism against Prime Minister Benjamin Netanyahu, claiming that it wasn't enough to survive in Israel – his generation also expects to live a good life in Israel in order to stay.

The connection between criticism about the high cost of living, which was said in strong, subversive language, and the call of an educated young man to emigrate to Germany, added fuel to the fire. On one hand, Making Aliyah to Berlin attracted more followers (reaching over 15,000 members) and spawned more groups on the social network that encourage and assist Israelis in emigrating from Israel ('Making Aliyah to Canada', 'Making Aliyah to New York' and more). On the other hand, rage and public outcry against the open call to emigrate grew and spread. Facebook became a battleground that connected to the intense dispute between left and right, or more accurately between Netanyahu's supporters and his opponents.

At this stage, even the Minister of Finance changed course, and moments before the budget was approved and in the midst of the reignited protest about the high cost of living in Israel, he appeared in *Ynet*'s studio and said: 'these guys are right, these products should be under price control'.

No one knows for sure how many Israelis are currently living in Berlin, with estimates varying from 17,000 to 40,000. The Israeli population in the city is diverse: singles, couples (including Israelis who married Germans), artists, salaried workers, business owners, students and more. Experts estimate that a considerable portion or even the majority of Israelis living in the city are millennials.

Although this is a negligible percentage, demographically speaking, the phenomenon of emigrating to Berlin is intriguing. Needless to say, this isn't just another European city, but rather the capital of the Third Reich, with all of its historic, moral and symbolic implications. One would expect that the grandchildren and great-grandchildren of Holocaust victims would have a problem with living in such a burdening place, let alone embrace the German culture and language. Serious protests broke out in Israel just 70 years ago over the Reparations Agreement, and buying anything made in Germany was considered taboo until the 1970s, but lo and behold, despite this baggage, it seems many young Israelis leave their homeland and flock to Berlin to make a future for themselves, while many others are planning to try.

Recent polls have shown that Germany's image in the public eye in Israel has undergone an amazing metamorphosis. Most Israelis nowadays actually perceive Germany more positively (on average) than the way Germans see Israel. The generous financial and military aid to Israel, the good diplomatic relations between the heads of state, the broad, daily contact between Germans and Israelis (tourism, science, art, youth delegations etc.), the influence of market economy (German products are considered a brand of quality) and even soccer – all can explain Germany's changed image in Israelis' perceptions. And yet, there's a big difference between a positive image and Germany becoming a destination for Israeli immigrants.

Why did this happen? It appears that there are three other factors besides image at work here: a change in the Israeli value system, including attitude towards emigration; Berlin's unique position as a young European city; and the global nature of millennials who have a different outlook on the world, and emigrating from Israel in particular.

It should be noted that the German or European passport that many Israeli emigrants have, allows them to get a variety of substantial benefits from the authorities, such as scholarships, discounts, unemployment benefits etc.

Berlin is one of the most popular cities in Europe for tourists and immigrants in general and young people in particular. It has all the advantages of a major city, including efficient public transport, interesting sites, an impressive river and green parks. The cost of living in Berlin is among the lowest in western Europe, it has neighbourhoods packed with youngsters, wide artistic and intellectual activities and of course, a lively nightlife (clubs, bars, restaurants etc). Berlin is basically a global, pluralistic metropolis that welcomes tourists and immigrants alike. Emigrating to Berlin softens the move to Germany for some Israelis (symbolically as well as practically), because even though it's the capital, it may be the least 'German' city in Germany. Even Islam, which has taken over major cities in France, the UK and Scandinavia, is less dominant in German cities, which helps Israelis feel more secure (Germans are also very sensitive about the safety of Jews living in their country).

In the past few years, Berlin has also become an important arena for the hi-tech industry in general and start-ups in particular. In a country whose economy strongly depends on heavy industry, there's a need for new kinds of companies that complement the industry and adapt it to the new age.

Furthermore, young Israelis meet young Germans during the big trip to the Far East and South America, as well as during organized youth meetings in Germany and Israel. The bonds created in these meetings also make it easier to decide to emigrate to Germany.

A great many artists are drawn to Germany, because Israel is too small for them and because they have to struggle to survive financially and professionally. Radical left-wingers also find a warm home in Berlin, because Germany as a whole is a breeding place for the extreme left (including strong political criticism of Israel).

Germany also has a considerable community of Jewish immigrants from the Former Soviet Union, and their communities, alongside other Jewish organizations (such as Chabad) create Jewish niches within German space (synagogues, classes etc.), that also facilitate the immigration from Israel.

Berlin is also suitable for millennials because the German workstyle is more attentive to the balances they seek in their lives and cannot find in Israel. One young Israeli we interviewed in Berlin told us: 'the work day ends at five o'clock here. No one expects you to answer emails during the weekend. This creates a calmer life that allows me to go out with my friends. When I worked at a high-tech company in Israel we used to joke whenever someone left the office at 7 p.m. and say "taking a half-day, aye?" In Israel everything is always so intense and restless. Here we have a 20-year strategic plan and the rest is serenity.'

And still we have to wonder: doesn't it disturb millennials to live in a country where some Nazi soldiers and their descendants live? Can a Jewish person live in a city filled with memories of a terrible time – a city that was the centre of the Nazi regime where the plan to exterminate the Jews of Europe was born?

The answer lies in the worldview of millennials, which we reviewed in our research. When your main motto in life is 'follow your dreams', it's easier to separate ideological 'distractions' and self-interest. This is why immigrants, and apparently a considerable portion of their generation (who still prefer to stay in Israel) don't view immigration as something so dramatic and definitely don't view it as treason, which is how previous generations saw it. So yes, many people sacrificed a lot to make the Zionist dream come true. But that was then, and this is now. It's possible that for young people, the Holocaust is just a chapter in history, and its influence diminishes over time. They are so self-centred that they aren't even aware of the fact that emigrating to Berlin of all places is like sticking a knife in Holocaust survivors' hearts.

In our interviews with young people living in Berlin, we asked them the following questions: assuming you fall in love with a German, how will your child feel about one grandfather who's a Holocaust survivor and another grandfather who served in the Wehrmacht? Wouldn't it bother you that your son or daughter will speak German as a first language? Most of them responded that it is indeed a problem, but in the same breath said it doesn't bother them at the moment. Most of them also don't spend too much time thinking about the implications of the rise of the extreme right and Islamic extremism in Europe, which naturally has an impact on Jewish existence in this continent. They instead look at the friendly Germans and ignore the complex social reality.

Another reason that life abroad appeals to young people is that they tend to sit on the fence anyway in an endless interim period. As far as they're concerned not being involved in either Israeli politics or German politics is the ideal situation.

Political Stances

Arab-Israeli Conflict

Ever since the collapse of the Oslo Accords in the mid-1990s, the Jewish public in Israel has experienced a consistent erosion in dove-ish positions on the security situation. Most Jews in Israel feel disillusioned about the reconciliation with the Arabs in light of the cumulatively bleak experience.

Millennials are no exception to this general trend, although their right-wing tendencies are stronger (separating Israeli millennials from their counterparts in western countries who hold a more left-leaning political worldview). Most of them vote for centrist and right-wing parties, assuming that they represent pragmatism, determination and caution against major threats. This political orientation is present among youngsters of all ethnicities and educational levels in this generation.

It should be noted that right-wing orientation doesn't reflect an ideological-Messianic worldview for most young people. This is mostly a defensive outlook that relies more on analyzing the other side's motives than on ideological or theological sentiments, i.e. the rational assumption that Arab nations as well as a considerable portion of Muslims around the world would destroy the much-hated State of Israel if they only could.

In fact, most millennials have never visited the settlements beyond the green line, and most of them don't consider the territories of Judea and Samaria, let alone Gaza, to be sacred land. Like most of the secular Jewish public, young people show flexibility when it comes to the willingness to negotiate with the Palestinians and Arab nations as well as far-reaching territorial compromises in exchange for a stable and reliable agreement on ending the conflict. They don't rule out the existence of a Palestinian state alongside Israel, but think it would be impossible to establish under the current circumstances. Their conclusion is that there's no one to negotiate with at this stage. We need to be strong and wait for the rage to pass, i.e. until the other side undergoes processes of modernization and democratization.

It should be noted that these are broad brush strokes. There is a considerable minority of young millennials who identify as leftists. They are convinced that it is Israel that is unwilling to make brave concessions. They also separate political extremism from religious extremism among the Palestinians, and are convinced that Israel is isolating itself in the international arena and endangering its existence due to stubbornness, extreme nationalism, condescension and the spread of primitive, undemocratic positions (particularly towards the Arabs).

Millennials' centre-right general inclination can be ascribed to several factors: murderous terrorism and rocket fire that have been part of their lives since birth; their generally positive attitude towards religion (there's a positive correlation between traditionalism and right-wing politics); the fact that a considerable portion of this group is comprised of the offspring of families that emigrated from the former Soviet Union (most immigrants believe that hostile Islam should be handled with an iron fist); the military service which exposed many of them to violent confrontations with the Palestinian population in the Palestinian territories; their direct approach, free of masks and political correctness, has allowed them to be disillusioned in regards to the conflict. Many millennials tell themselves: on the bottom line, after all the chitchat, most Arabs outside of Israel simply don't want us here. They look beyond the border, and all they see is destruction, religious violence and ethnic cleansing, and they draw their own conclusions. The raging wave of anti-Semitism and anti-Israel sentiment around the world nowadays, which is led by Arabs and Muslims, also reinforces young people's negative opinion of the Arab world.

This is also why most young millennials (as well as most of the Israeli public) despise the extreme dogmatic left, which has become anti-national and in many cases anti-Israel (and some would say anti-Semitic). They believe it tends to rely on falsified historical claims and is slandering Israel by presenting it as a brutal, racist society which provides ammunition for false propaganda against Israel. Most of them don't see the political left as a reflection of a humane and pluralistic approach but rather as naivety and blindness at best and self-loathing and condescension at worst.

However, the right-wing worldview among a portion of this generation is dogmatic and disturbingly tempestuous, as can be seen in the frequent comments on their Facebook pages. It is driven by a simplistic perception of the geopolitical reality, which stems from superficial or partial knowledge and immaturity. This phenomenon comes into play among others in intolerant and oversimplified views on Arab citizens of Israel – who are perceived as disloyal to their country, not sympathetic enough to the hardship of the Jewish people, and ungrateful for the benefits they get from living in Israel (as seen in the polls).

Many see this phenomenon as a sign that racism has taken over the entire generation, but is it so? We believe the situation is more complex. There has surely been an increase in the number and percentage of violent, racist, right-wing extremists – a phenomenon that obviously has also expanded thanks to the lax hand of the police and law authorities. Nonetheless, most millennials aren't racist (in the sense of hating others in the name of ideology and racial supremacy). Anyone familiar with the online arenas knows that a considerable portion of spontaneous extreme remarks don't necessarily represent established racist political positions (such as racist organizations in Europe and the United States). In many cases, these are young people who found an easy, provocative way to express their rage and attract attention through aggressive posts in times of turbulence and terrorist attacks. Facebook is a new medium that allows people to express their unmediated, unrestrained and unrefined feelings. The lines between private and public are becoming blurred, and things that were once whispered or shouted in private conversations have turned into public record. This often de-contextualizes and blows things way out of proportion. Furthermore, many young people think as they type. Spoken language is transformed into text, without supplementary means of expressions (such as intonation and body language) to regulate it, and might appear much more aggressive than intended. Abusive responses to questions on polls or Facebook posts are often more of a gut reaction than a rational, reasoned worldview.

Post-Ethnic Generation

Israeli society has had four main social rifts since its inception: the rift between Arabs and Jews, between religious and secular Jews, between Mizrahi and Ashkenazi Jews and between left and right. Each rift has arrived at the centre stage of the social agenda over the course of various dramatic events and periodic crises. The Wadi Salib riots in the late 1950s, the Black Panthers crisis in the early 1970s, and the rise of Shahs in the 1990s are some prominent examples of this.

Millennials have been exposed to these major rifts, at great velocity at times, and these have shaped their political worldview accordingly. However, two rifts have become less prominent over the course of their lives: the rift between left and right (due to the general migration to the centre) and the ethnic rift.

Recent polls indicate that 'classic' social variables such as gender, ethnicity, education, income, and in many cases age and voting patterns, have consistently lost their influence on the Israeli public's positions in general and young people's positions in particular. The most influential variables nowadays are location and religious identification.

Millennials are not as driven by ethnic stereotypes than earlier generations and give less weight to the issue of ethnicity in their voting motives, because they've been exposed to far less prejudice than previous generations. This generation was born into expedited processes of integration in the fields of education, employment, politics, leisure, communications etc. They're also the least ethnically identifiable generation because many of them come from mixed families and mixed social environments. They may not be impervious to prejudice – mainly towards Arabs, immigrants, LGBT people, women and migrant workers – but in practical terms they actually have a clear tendency to accept the other. This pluralism is also common among young people in Europe and the United States.

It should be noted that stereotypes and prejudice among young people are too complex to be traced in polls. For instance, they may express negative opinions about a broad group but not towards individuals from that group. For example, they may mock 'Ethiopian' Jews but it won't prevent them from becoming friends with young Ethiopians in the army, academia or at work. Because they're insensitive to their surroundings, they don't stop to think about how a person belonging to a minority group might feel; whether they suffer or were offended. They say: if I'm laughing at someone or mocking them, it's just for kicks. The media has actually legitimized this attitude, inasmuch that a gay comedian can mock gay people (in a supposedly homophobic style) and a Yemenite comedian can crack jokes about his grandmother's traditional customs. They completely separate literal expressions from actual discrimination.

The People Demand Social Justice – In Tel Aviv

The housing and high cost of living crisis, which reached its peak in the 2011 protest, was supposed to create political passion among young people. Some of them are definitely very troubled by the economy and constantly complain about overpriced products and the greed of business owners and tycoons. This is also the reason that new parties Yesh Atid and Kulanu, which focussed on an economic agenda, received wide support among young Israelis.

Nonetheless, the economic protest didn't evolve into a mass movement of young people and most of them didn't even impose a consumer boycott on the people who exploit them on a daily basis (landlords, club owners etc.) The reasons for this phenomenon are generational passivity (they don't take charge), self-centredness and neo-ignorance. We got the impression that despite the abundance of available information, young people's understanding of economics is rather limited. They relate to economics mostly through the prices of various products and the levels of their own salaries. This makes it hard to ascribe millennials to any specific economic camp. Many of them have a mixed worldview of neo-liberal conventions (such as entrepreneurial markets and privatization) and social-democratic sensibilities. Many millennials don't even see how these two worldviews clash. They settle for a general opinion that the State isn't doing enough for the middle class – which is reflected in the unfocused slogan 'the people demand social justice'.

It should be noted that while many, and perhaps most young people in Israel believe that Israel's economy needs a deep rethink, they don't consider it to be a failure and are also aware of the relative economic advantages of living in Israel.

As a matter of fact, among most Israeli teens and youths, the ideological axis of 'left' and 'right' mostly revolves around the national issues and positions on the Arab-Israeli conflict rather than on socio-economics.

Most of them don't relate to the socialist doctrine for several reasons. First, socialism in western society has been shoehorned into the political 'social-democratic' approach while pushing aside more vehement social ideologies. In fact, updated socialism that combines collective responsibility with personal responsibility has not been established yet. The war for 'individual rights' often turned violent and replaced the reasonable and proportionate approach. This pushes people to reject socialism.

Second, the general public associates the hostile and prejudiced anti-Israel left with the social economic left. Third, many Israelis tend to associate the age of socialism and the age of Mapai (Israel's ruling Labour party in the oligarchy era), and the common associations of this age are over-centralization, minority discrimination, austerity and isolation. Fourth, young people have undergone a process of socialization for consumerism. It's hard to criticize something when you're also a part of it.

Lite Traditionalism

Most millennials are religiously observant in varying degrees. It should be noted that the attitude towards religion in Israel has always been in correlation with ethnicity (Ashkenazi-Mizrahi), i.e. the rate of traditionalists is higher among Israelis with roots of Asian and African origin rather than European and American. How does this generation's traditionalism come into play? Here are some typical components:

The Jewish God. Most of them believe in the existence of God, while their notion of divinity is usually shallow, devoid of any in-depth analysis of philosophical or theological meanings. The majority also believe in personal divine providence, associating it with Jewish mythology – God as a father figure whose chosen people are the Jews.

Selective Kashrut. A considerable portion of youngsters (most of which are likely to be of Mizrahi origin) avoid eating pork and seafood and some even avoid mixing milk and meat, in varying degrees of scrutiny. They aren't deterred by non-kosher restaurants (most don't even check if the place has an official kosher certification) but they will prefer to order dishes that aren't explicitly non-kosher.

Friday Night Dinner with the Family. The overwhelming majority don't observe the Shabbat according to orthodox Jewish laws (they drive and use electricity on Saturday), but the Sabbath eve ritual (which is held on Fridays) is beloved by youngsters and most of them never miss out on family dinner at their parents even after they are married. Many young families even light Shabbat candles and perform the Kiddush.

Traditional Tone of Holidays and Celebrations. Few millennials attend prayers at the synagogue, with the exception of major holidays like Rosh Hashanah and Yom Kippur. Most of them would also rather celebrate Passover properly (albeit while taking various shortcuts) with the extended family. Other Israeli holidays (such as Hanukkah, Purim, Shavuot) are usually celebrated according to Israeli Zionist folklore rather than any religious format. Due to the growing influence of western culture and the influence of immigrants from the former Soviet Union, more and more Israelis in general and youngsters in particular also celebrate international holidays such as New Year's Eve and Valentine's Day.

Most weddings are still performed according to Jewish tradition, but as aforementioned, the personal touch has grown stronger in recent years at the expense of the orthodox ceremony. The majority of young parents from this generation still perform circumcision and opting out is still considered taboo.

Prayers, Talismans and Blessings. A (mostly Mizrahi) minority puts on tefillin every morning or at least once in a while, and a small yet substantial percentage of them go to Rabbis for advice, mostly about how to deal with the difficulties of life (much like going to a counsellor or psychologist). Most young people put up a mezuzah at the entrance to their home.

Separation of Religion and State. Most young people respect the Jewish religion, but prefer to keep it in the individual sphere and wish it would stay out of the political and legal arena. Most of them are against religion coercion of any kind and in favour of a tolerant approach that accepts all Jewish religious movements and streams.

New Spirituality

The Charm of New Age

It's impossible to understand the positive attitude among most millennials towards religion without understanding the influence of 'new spirituality' (New Age) on their lives. In fact, this is one of the phenomena that makes this generation unique compared to previous generations. It is reflected both in the popularity of New Age worldview and lifestyle among them and in the fact that most of the people who work in fields related to this phenomenon are millennials.

New Age-related phenomena started to emerge in western culture in the 1960s, before millennials were even born, but the 'shanti' lifestyle and worldview only became an inseparable part of popular western culture in the 1990s. Signs of the appearance of New Age in Israel started to be felt in fashion, entertainment, art and the media in the 1970s in kibbutzim, Tel Aviv and Sinai beaches, it was only ahead of the 2000s, as millennials were coming of age, did the phenomenon gain momentum and become an inseparable part of youth culture. At this stage, shanti festivals already saw tens of thousands of (mostly young) participants a year, alternative medicine penetrated the mainstream, and Kabbalah and Buddhism were adjusted for recreational needs.

What are the reasons for New Age's surge in popularity?

Blessed is the Match. The elimination of sacredness, which gained momentum after the Yom Kippur War, created an identity void that sought to be filled. Secular Israelis are looking for new deep content for their lives – a beacon of existential meaning to replace the meaning that the religion of Zionism once provided. This could also be one of the reasons for the increased affinity for Jewish tradition, which has occurred in the general Israeli public and is particularly prominent among young people (Judaism fills the void). Flocking to New Age doctrines might be another way to fill it.

Praise the Lord for it is Good. Many young people were exposed to the new spirituality during their big trip to the Far East and South America. These influences gradually made their way to Israel: trance parties like the ones on the beaches of Goa and Ko Pha-ngan; street stands that sell ethnic jewelry, clothing and food; 'self-help' workshops and enrichment classes; soul music with guitars and darbukas; shabby fashion with jellabiyas, harem pants, dreadlocks, and a variety of caps, shawls and fezzes.

In this regard, and ironically enough, new spirituality is actually something of an economic phenomenon. New Age industry provides a good living, especially for young people, because it doesn't require a lot of resources or prior know-how. All you have to know is how to import and sell the right product on time (mostly cheap trinkets) and present the right image.

A significant portion of new spirituality manufacturers and consumers belong to the international age group that has broken free of the burden of survival, and can now focus on developing leisure culture, quality of life ('spiritual wellbeing') and extending life expectancy (in the sense of New Age 'mind spas' or 'vitamins' or 'spiritual food additives').

A Clockwork Orange. New spirituality is also a counter-reaction to the development of the cold, western, industrialized metropolis. In a world where everything is commercial, artificial and manipulative, people yearn for something natural and real. Thus, natural stone replaces cast concrete, mineral water replaces Coca Cola, home-cooked food replaces fast food and vintage replaces hi-tech. This is the 'rural urbanism' that's become common in bohemian neighbourhoods in major cities and community settlements.

A Taste of Spirituality for the Hungry. Some claim that in a world that has grown used to instant culture, new spirituality is also just the tip of the chopstick. This is a trend that offers the masses spiritual fast food (utterly shallow and often fallacious and based on human weakness) or alternatively, a 'sushi combo' of science, art, philosophy, religion etc.

Incidentally, this is also the root of the relative success of the Breslov and Chabad Hasidic groups among young secular Jews. They found an appealing way to market Judaism: warmth and affection, financial aid, advise and emotional support, singing and dancing, all in exchange for observing the basic mitzvahs. Put on a yarmulke, wrap yourself in tefillin, say a few blessings and you'll win a discount ticket to heaven.

Secular Piety. New spirituality is very suitable for young people who are ejected nowadays from the competitive institutionalized systems, under the false label of 'learning disabilities'. Many of them don't suffer from learning disabilities or lack motivation, but rather are actually talented people who love and can learn in other ways than their schools and universities offer (they need a more personal touch). Much like the Hasidic movement disengaged from the demanding Lithuanian yeshiva world at the time, so does the new spirituality disengage (whether consciously or not) from the competitive and demanding education world.

Anchor of Stability. The new urge for the spiritual also express a yearning for an anchor of stability, in a world where everything is temporary and ever-changing. It's the human pursuit of deep meaning beyond the concrete, immediate and fleeting. This creates a sad paradox: the alternative that New Age culture offers the western instant world is an instant product in and of itself. It's like admitting yourself to an alcohol rehab centre where you're treated with vodka.

Chill Pill. The need to disconnect and escape the stressful everyday reality is also, and perhaps mostly, derived from the growing exposure to digital stimulation and mainly to pain and disaster. An average person nowadays could be exposed over the course of one week to more disasters than a person was exposed to over the course of an entire lifetime in the ancient world. The intense exposure to death, injuries and tragedies creates an emotional overload. In Israel, the burden is particularly heavy, due to its security situation and the familial code that creates empathy even for people we don't know personally. The solution for this overload is repression, denial (escapism) and distraction – which might be the source of new spirituality's power.

Psychoanalytical Theology. Psychoanalysis has breached the borders of science and become something of a secular theology. Its influence can be seen in many fields – from therapy to art, entertainment and speech patterns.

New Age is something of a populist descendant of western psychoanalysis with a pinch of the Far East, and just like psychoanalysis the New Age preaches self-understanding, honesty, releasing repressed emotions, stress relief and self-improvement.

In order to achieve happiness, a person needs guides. Psychoanalysis offers a private conversation on the therapist's sofa while New Age spirituality offers personal training on a mattress or out in the wild. New spirituality also reflects the growing recognition of the deep role of the human psyche and particularly its effects on the body. For example, the proven link between stress and depression and chronic and malignant illnesses. This awareness has led many young people to make more of an effort to take care of their minds in order to take care of their bodies. New spirituality has a lot to offer in this respect.

Disillusionment with Ultra-Capitalism. The new spirituality isn't just the cliché of spiritual junk food and chill pills that represses and perhaps hinders illnesses. It also has an authentic and occasionally deep expression of criticism of social injustices and mainly of 'the dictatorship of capitalism'. In this sense, it's similar and as important as green ideology (environmental protection) and neo-socialism. It is also a way to neutralize the 'noises' and 'toxins' of Darwinist market economy – a system of government and worldview that have turned into a kind of economic fascism.

Rebellion of Sensitivity. New spirituality also has a feminine orientation, or more accurately an expression of the rising power of the feminine component in our world. It promotes values of sensitivity, a warm human connection, tenderness, openness, anti-aggression and aesthetic awareness, and in this regard offers an alternative to a male-dominated culture.

Therapy for a Fragile Generation. Millennials are more fragile and not as capable dealing with difficulties and crises. They also need more mental support and require means for relaxation and stress relief. New Age offers a solution to the pressure, anxieties, failures, disappointments and personal frustrations. It provides a human empathy and tolerance for people in pain and despair, and offers assistance to those who have found themselves stranded in the social jungle. It also provides an ideological comfort for those who lack the skills or abilities to succeed in the existing competitive conditions.

Some would say that we all experience these low moments, and we all become more 'spiritual' at one point or another in our lives. The market nowadays simply offers a more diverse selection of products and services than ever before. In this regard, the new spirituality doesn't necessarily reflect an increase in demand but rather a rise in supply.

16

Now What? – Intermediate Conclusions

Between Success and Failure

Victims of Circumstance

Like any generation before them, millennials are a product of the times and not of their own making. Their parents, teachers, commanders, employers and basically the entire system and cultural environment they were raised in have left them with serious issues and scars that have yet to be healed, and perhaps never will be.

Millennials were born and raised in an unstable world. They've lived through massive changes that have forced the human race to march forwards while groping in the dark. This is a transitional period, in which the old methods no longer serve the needs of the people, and there are barely any alternatives on the horizon. No social institution has been spared from the turbulence and all are expected to either fundamentally change or be eliminated. But these middle ages are running long. We still have some difficult battles ahead before the conventions change, and the youngest among us have and will continue to pay the price for this twilight period.

The price millennials pay is particularly painful because they came of age in a time of extreme social developments that have gone out of control and become destructive rather than constructive. One could say that Generation Y isn't just a product of its circumstances but also their victim.

First and foremost, millennials are a product of the free market economy. It may have brought great wealth to mankind: developing products and services, giving millions of people access to means of survival and luxuries, extending life expectancy and expanding the quality of life. But much like a thriving, efficient factory that pollutes the air and rivers, neo-liberal capitalism has started to endanger the society which it feeds. Materialism, greed, gaps and jealousy among people and groups, exploitation of natural resources, destructive competition – all of these evils and more are a product of an economic process gone awry. Israeli millennials were exposed to these toxins more than any other demographic because they were born into the age of privatization, and they lack the moral checks and balances of Zionist socialism and pioneer culture.

Millennials are also a product of the humane psychology revolution. Education in the family and in teaching institutions has come a long way since the rise of modern science, including human science. However, what started out as a way to protect our children's souls has gone out of control. Their parents wanted so desperately to understand them, protect them and make them happy that they've turned their offspring into self-centred, agitated, insecure narcissists. Society as a whole has wrapped childhood in cotton candy and the result is eternal children who struggle to grow up and take responsibility.

Millennials are also the result of the education revolution. The rate of high school graduates has increased significantly but the content has waned and the joy of learning has faded. This generation went to school during the downfall of teaching as a profession, in an anachronistic learning environment with no discipline where the institutions have been turned into test score assembly lines. The increase in the percentage of graduates in this generation is also an illusion to some extent. Making higher education more accessible to wider demographics is a positive process that broadens horizons, narrows gaps, increases democratic openness and improves qualities and skills necessary for operating and upgrading social mechanisms. Education is without a doubt the key to progress and happiness, but opening the gates of academia without setting any controls in place has led to a decrease in quality. The modern education system has turned millennials into supposed intellectuals, driven away the overachievers and tarnished the image of learning. Wholesale education has cheapened the reputation of academic degrees, which are en route to becoming completely worthless. Young people from lower class families have surpassed their parents' education, while expecting the degree to pave the way to happiness and wealth, until reality hits them in the face.

Millennials are also a product of the digital revolution. Computer technology makes life easier, brings the world closer and provides access to information and services. It also develops creativity, lifts barriers, connects people at great distances, helps people open their eyes and creates an unprecedented scope for social discourse. Millennials were raised in the age of communication abundance, which has created opportunities for them that previous generations didn't have. But this abundance comes at a price – subjugation. Human society as a whole has become addicted to digital technology, but it happened to millennials earlier and therefore the effects are also stronger. They are addicted to fast, constant stimulations and they can never find peace.

Furthermore, the open virtual market has undermined the purpose of existence because it makes it hard for the individual to create something new, be different and unique. Young people nowadays find themselves in vicious competition with hundreds of millions of people, feeling lost and helpless.

Another price that millennials and their parents paid as a result of the telecommunication revolution is constant anxiety. This generation is terrified and depressed because of incessant exposure to the 'radiation' of negative information. In order to protect themselves, millennials have had to numb their senses and wrap themselves in a cover of indifference. They focus on the present, because the future has become vague and threatening.

Millennials are also a product of changes in the labour market. Young people nowadays enter an employment world in which the personal computer and smartphone have turned on their creators. Being available around the clock enslaves the workers and violates the balance between work life and home life. Millennials are crying out about having no time for themselves, and their cries speak for us all. However, while their parents' generation learned to comply and grind their teeth, they don't even have a pension worth 'suffering a bit more' for.

Professional careers have rewarded the workers on a materialistic and spiritual level, but have taken a heavy personal toll. Millennials work more hours than their parents' generation because of the culture of exploitation and bulimic consumption. The assembly lines no longer provide basic commodities but rather exist to feed the never-ending appetite of insatiable consumers. Young people are paying the price both as producers and as consumers. They're overworked and underpaid to make them spend money on things they don't need. They're materialistic and hedonistic because they've been brainwashed since childhood to think that maximizing pleasure is the purpose of life.

Millennials are also a product of the age of abundance because wealth is disorienting and blinding. The massive variety on the shelves allows consumers to buy tailor-made products, while at the same time overloading their senses and emotions and making it hard to choose. Confusion and simulated hunger have become second nature for them, and they are no longer able to be happy with what they've got.

Above all, millennials are a product of an entirely new degree of democratic freedom. The unrestricted ability to criticize and condemn is part of the essence of democracy, but it also brings forth cynicism and nihilism. Excess democracy has weakened civility and mutual respect and has undermined social order and harmony. The edge of liberty is a breeding ground for anarchy, cruelty and violence.

In light of the above, our research isn't just a study that draws a sociological portrait, but rather an 'intelligence' report from a frontline spy who is trying to tell the indifferent rear: we're in real danger and we have to wake up, because the problems and difficulties we've identified, which are rooted in cultural changes, are endangering the very existence of society, or at least slowing down and even reverting crucial developments. It should be noted that social pollution is similar to environmental pollution. It can't always be seen by the untrained eye and has a cumulative effect, which can only be discovered over time (such as the rise in cancer and heart disease, fish disappearing from the oceans and forests that fail to regenerate).

The Strengths of Generation Y

Nonetheless, millennials aren't necessarily a generation of social failure. Their character traits are the result of tremendous social achievements and never-ending social evolution, among other things.

For the children of the digital age, the computer world is like home. Their major advantage is their quick mind and fast fingers, their natural technological savvy and uninhibited openness to new computer uses. They're also more efficient in many aspects and are always looking to trade up. This is why millennials are very good at developing services and apps that make our lives easier.

Millennials are more in touch with their feelings and more open to receive advice and share with others. This is a graceful, smiling and integrally democratic generation that has narrowed ethnic, religious and gender differences, and is open to all sexual preferences. They're much less rigid than previous generations, more mobile, less driven by their ego and more open to admit weakness. This is a societal generation that builds new bridges in every direction, and its contribution to the development of a borderless global world is immense.

Millennials are also more prepared than their parents for the age of leisure. They are showing us all the way ahead: the post-modern man no longer lives to work, but rather strives for a flexible and diverse career of hobbies and leisure. Their parents dedicated their lives to their toil, but they'd rather dedicate themselves to parties, trips and vacations. Because of their updated priorities, they will probably not experience the personal retirement crisis that their parents and grandparents have been through – when after decades of hard work, they all of a sudden find it difficult to find purpose and order in life. Millennials don't just love partying and celebrating together, they also know how to do it with astonishing passion and skill.

This generation also carries a healthy dose of criticism and skepticism, and they're less willing to accept ancient conventions and 'bullshit'. These youngsters came of age in a culture of demanding clients, and therefore have developed patterns of price comparisons and ROI. They're also more flexible and open to experimentation and change. And above all, this is the generation in which the socio-economic status gaps are the lowest in history and in this respect serves as a forerunner of a new democratic age.

The Great Cultural Crisis

Public opinion leaders and decision-makers in Israel tend to focus on three types of recurring crises: political, economic and security-related. This research implies that above all of these crises, and essentially below them as well, there's a much deeper and wider crisis that is taking place, which also affects all three of them: the cultural crisis, as aforementioned: the growth of a younger generation with a worldview and lifestyle that don't coincide with the old systems. This gap creates several secondary crises, which will only escalate in time.

The Leadership Crisis

Western society is driven by the pluralistic world view, and therefore has reduced barriers and allows access to influential positions and means. This process carries evolutionary significance, but also presents some risks, such as diminishing merit-based systems in the name of the complete equality ethos. When excellence is marginalized and elite frameworks become redundant, it's hard to produce good leaders.

The flattening process comes into play in all levels of leadership: academia, the courts, the media, economics, education and politics. The leadership problem is also the result of an ongoing perception of lower standards and expectations. In other words, even in elite frameworks that have managed to survive, the qualification process has become less demanding and therefore of reduced quality.

The political system in Israel, which is supposed to lead the other systems, doesn't appeal to young people because in order to infiltrate it, they need to go through a corrupt political party's mechanism, which they despise. Politicians' image in the media is also not very positive and there are very few public figures who receive public admiration. This reality makes expecting young, talented people to run for office unrealistic.

Regardless of the current system, millennials are inherently unfit to lead, in all areas, and are actually not all that interested in leadership to begin with. When the 'generational personality' suffers from delayed maturity, inability to take responsibility, a tendency to do the bare minimum and low mental resilience, it not only reduces the number of locomotives on the railway, but also the number of diligent engine drivers who can steer the trains to safety.

There have been many reports recently about a demographic and cultural trend with far-reaching implications: more and more previously disenfranchised groups (women, immigrants, minorities, the poor etc.) are now breaking through class barriers and gradually filling the void left behind by the disappearing elite. We might witness such a process in Israel soon, and there is actually some indication that it has already begun. For example, in scientific, medical, legal, military and economic systems, an increasing percentage of scientists, officers, doctors, lawyers and business people come from minorities and mobile groups. These young men and women are hungrier for success than the 'old aristocracy', who prefer to focus on easier, less demanding fields.

Thus, the story of Generation Y also holds a fascinating story of changing or expanding the veteran elite. On one hand, the boundaries of democracies are being stretched. More people are given the opportunity to fulfill themselves and society's talent pool has grown immensely. On the other hand, the frictional transition creates various intermediate difficulties. When the old 'dynasties' stop producing heirs, it also comes at a price.

The Labour Crisis

The economic locomotive continues to vigorously push onward, but the old railroad is creaky – the rising unemployment rates (mostly hidden unemployment in Israel), lack of motivation to work and manage, declining professional standards and productivity in organizations and institutions and the depletion of pension funds and savings – all of these phenomena and more aren't just the result of macro-economic issues but rather and perhaps mainly of generational gaps. The old economic system isn't suitable for young people's style and needs, because it exploits them and wears them down materialistically and mentally, doesn't provide them with sufficient flexibility and mobility and denies them of job security and financial stability.

The employment world in modern society was based on differential distribution of benefits and resources. In most economic organizations, the employees get paid based on their skills, ties, experience, seniority, investment and overall achievements. Everyone has a 'market value', which determines their ability to negotiate in the work market. With the development of higher education, academic degrees have become one of the main keys to economic advancement. In fact, for years, having a degree served as the barrier between blue-collar workers and white-collar workers. It separated people who perform low-paying, repetitive, (physically and mentally) difficult jobs, with no spiritual reward and limited opportunities for promotion (if at all) from people whose job is diverse, creative, dynamic and emotionally, intellectually and socially rewarding. But what happens in a world where the janitor, bus driver, waiter, store clerk and all manual labourers become college graduates? Will they or their sons and daughters wish to continue working these jobs? What will happen to the factory when all of its assembly line workers acquire an education and become engineers? The kibbutz supposedly solved this dilemma through rotation of positions and rewards according to the principle of equality. But the kibbutz's system faltered and eventually collapsed.

Millennials, who flock to universities and colleges, are turning this hypothetical question into a practical one. The sons and daughters of the exploited proletariat have opened their eyes, developed new expectations and refuse to be enslaved to the kind of jobs their parents had. This has already occurred in the work market as seen in the declining demand for manual labour and ineffective long-term employee retention. This is also one of the reasons for the rise of manpower companies, which provide temporary employment, as well as the increased demand for immigrant workers.

If the modern economy wants to survive, it will have to find a fairer and more efficient socio-economic model that isn't based on the exploitation of the proletariat by the bourgeoisie. A model in which society gives the people who do gruelling, repetitive work the conditions they need to function and survive. This doesn't just mean fair wages but also proper breaks and rest as well as job rotation. In other words, this will have to be a society where everyone gets their hands dirty and doesn't just rely on manual labourers to do the filthy jobs for them. This will also require making alterations to the safety nets to allow a proper standard of living as life expectancy only grows longer.

Though this change is very far away, it seems the rise of Generation Y foretells it or at least sets the course. Young people aren't just refusing to partake in the old, utterly exploitative economic game – they're letting us all know that work isn't the most important thing in life but rather a necessity that should be reduced to the bare minimum.

However, despite the millennial perception that hedonistic leisure is the key to happiness, they and their children will have to accept that happiness lies in the psyche: in education, research, reactivity and giving. Could this reckoning happen in the near future? Time will tell.

The Education Crisis

The education and learning method in schools and higher education institutions is no longer suitable for young people's style and needs, because it is too slow, not flexible enough, doesn't evaluate its students properly and falls behind on technological and economic developments at the front. For now, many young people still flock to universities and colleges and pay for tuition that keeps these institutions afloat, but this situation is only temporary.

It wasn't just the the growing competition in the higher education market that led to the drop in quality, but rather also the common notion that white-collar professions are the key to success in life, therefore one must strive to acquire an academic degree at all cost. Many young people who do not really need an academic degree to succeed in their lives, partly because they are talented and love technical and other jobs, are forced to attend anyway as it is the social norm.

The heads of higher education are too busy dealing with their own financial survival and refuse to look beyond the horizon. Ironically, leading professors who are supposed to serve as role models for creative thinking and open-mindedness turn out to be conservative and hesitant. They don't just struggle because such a change requires a long-term perspective, courage, honesty and willingness to make personal sacrifices, but also because it involves considerable risks. They would rather stick to the devil they know.

However, there are alternatives on the horizon, and these are destined to empty the classrooms like a stock market crash. When that happens, the academic world will change forever.

The Community Crisis

The world has become more open and accessible thanks to revolutionary technological breakthroughs (mostly the internet and mobile phones) as well as because modern society is constantly learning how to collaborate and remove obstacles and barriers between people.

Oppression, discrimination and social inequality may be far from over, but when you look at cultural norms from a historical perspective there's definitely a consistent process of increasing social harmonization.

Millennials are a product and a reflection of this positive trend. They are probably the most harmonious and least violent generation in the history of mankind. Millennials naturally flow in peaceful groups, reinforcing the utopian hope for a world with no borders.

However, the social frameworks and lifestyle that are imposed on millennials don't allow them to fully implement their inherent propensity for community life.

Millennials came of age in a world that broke its socio-economic safety nets. They live in a space with free air but shaky ground. They yearn for stability and a warm, supportive community, but don't know how to get them. Even the safety net of the nuclear family, which has provided mankind with personal and social stability throughout history, has been undermined in this generation.

Young Israelis, like many across the world, aspire to live in the big city and enjoy the liberty, abundance and stimulation they create. Tel Aviv provides them with the urban experience they so desperately need, but at the same time they find urban alienation jarring and yearn to establish rural compounds and communities within the noisy metropolis. Occasionally it comes in the form of communal bars, friendly meetings in the avenue, and neighbourhood synagogues full of young secular people on the Sabbath and holidays. And yet, the tension between urban stimulus and rural tranquility remains unresolved.

No one has yet been able to find a formula that combines both needs and fits the lifestyle and worldview of contemporary youths. The tragic result is that the periphery is losing all of its youngsters but the big cities they flock to can only receive them as temporary residents and workers (mostly due to the high cost of housing and living).

Young people yearn for the old tribal life that offers human warmth and balance, but are condemned to live a life of alienation and disquiet. They find it difficult to fulfil their aspiration for communal life, among other things because they were taught to focus on themselves and because their addiction to technology makes it harder for them to develop stable, peaceful existences.

The Security Crisis

Fundamentalist and radical Islam has birthed hatred of unprecedented magnitude, and threats that once seemed fictional have now become a reality. When even long-time allies such as the United States and several European countries lose their empathy for Israel, the danger only grows. With the addition of rising Anti-Semitism, which has penetrated power centres in western countries, it seems clear why millennials are such an anxious generation living in the present because there may not even be a tomorrow.

Israel isn't a normal society where everything is simple and peaceful. It faces significant threats because of its sheer existence and its citizens pay a heavy toll for that. Millennials are obviously not the first generation forced to live under the burden of security, though it seems this burden has increased during their lifetime. Previous generations experienced serious security crises (including some painful wars), but in historical terms, these were short periods of emergencies with long intervals between. Millennials were born into an ongoing state of emergency with constant threats of increasing magnitude and severity: terrorist bombings, violent riots, rocket fire to major cities and radicalized, well-funded Islam that performs decapitations and calls for the destruction of Jews and their country.

Whereas Israelis' anxiety used to be moderated by their blind faith in the State's military strength, moral righteousness and unity, nowadays the Jewish State has become lax, divided and destabilized. This is projected onto millennials' sense of security and peace of mind.

Ironically and tragically, millennials aren't just the victims of the lack of security but rather also one of its causes. The security system doesn't fit young Israelis' style and needs because it's based on moral injustice (about 40 per cent of the Israeli population, mostly ultra-Orthodox and Arabs, do not serve in the army under the law), excessive sacrifice (the length of military service and reserve duty), doesn't provide enough options, isn't as rewarding as it once was (in terms of salary and reputation), based on an outdated work environment, rigid masculine hierarchy, inflexible work hours and a long-term commitment to the organization.

Add this to the waning reputation of security organizations and you can understand why they're gradually losing their appeal among youngsters, especially among the descendants of the bourgeois and Yuppie Ashkenazi segment.

We have not performed a systematic review that compares changes in the manpower strength of these organizations over the years, but information we obtained vicariously has created the impression that they're losing human capital every year and struggle with recruiting manpower in general and quality manpower in particular. They particularly struggle with retaining quality personnel within the organization. Our conversations with dozens of commanders in top positions in IDF, intelligence organizations and Israel Police paint a picture of organizations in crisis and particularly of generational gaps. The young workers expose and escalate old organizational problems that have been ignored for years, creating a new set of problems, created out of the changing times.

To conclude, just when western democracy needs brazen warriors and organizational strength more than ever, it struggles to recruit the right people.

The Ideology Crisis

Millennials were born in an age that has shed the 'major ideologies'. Even the national ideology, which has led humanity in the past two centuries, has weakened. Millennials may still be patriots, but national ideology isn't such a strong cohesive for them, and it definitely doesn't provide them with a sense of purpose. Millennials are a generation born into a post-naive age in which there's no one single vision any more.

So what comes instead? Imperatives like dedicated parenting and sensitive relationships are obvious contenders. As are economic, scientific, educational, legal and artistic initiatives, which manage to provide positive energies, but whether they can serve as pillars of society is doubtful.

In such an individualistic and frantic age, it might not even be possible to produce a major long-term vision at all. In this respect, millennials are doomed to be miserable. They also fail to set high goals for themselves not just because of the zeitgeist, but also because they lack spiritual depth and were taught to be skeptical. Ideologically speaking, this is probably a 'lost generation'. Mankind will have to wait for newer generations to come of age and break the mould. In the meantime, we will unfortunately enter a long period of desperately searching for the light within the darkness of materialism, cynicism and indifference.

Between Berlin and Tel Aviv

The emigration debate has always reflected Israeli people's tendency towards hyperbole. Evidently, the ratio of emigrating Israelis and returning Israelis has only improved since 2001. 2012 saw the lowest emigration rate in forty years – only 0.7 emigrants for every 1,000 residents (such low numbers haven't been seen since the early 1970s during the Yom Kippur War). More importantly, the fact that the number of Jews who left Israel since it was founded is insignificant compared to the number of incoming immigrants.

The manufactured fear of a massive wave of deserters also doesn't coincide with the state Israel is in. Despite the high cost of living, housing crisis and considerable (internal and external) security threats, Israel is still an attractive country by international standards. It has its share of troublesome issues, but the grass is not as green on the other side either. This becomes obvious in light of rising anti-Semitism in the western world which has driven many Jews (mostly from France) to emigrate to Israel, as well as due to the economic slowdown and unemployment around Europe and the United States, which used to be desirable destinations for emigration.

The term 'emigration', which reflects uprooting from one's homeland, should probably be updated. It used to involve at least some form of social and cultural disengagement. In the global age of communications and mobility, though, the old terms are less and less relevant. Because even when people move to another country, they don't break away. The smartphone and internet allow us to get updates in real time and maintain a constant connection with family, relatives and friends, virtually anywhere and anytime. Declining airline ticket prices and frequent visits to the homeland alleviate the pain of separation. Generally speaking, emigration has become more common across the world in recent years. People leave and return for limited periods because the world has become dynamic. Many people own properties and apartments in several countries, and the rate of international marriages and of bi-national passports is rising. Borders are gradually melting and nationalities are mixing. Most of us have more than one significant affinity or identity in life. Even soccer fandom nowadays is often divided between a local team and a foreign team. This is part of human society's healthy evolution across the globe. Israel has been blessed with talented human capital, and naturally people can't always fulfil their personal potential here (due to supply and demand, budgets, experience, the size of the market and other factors). There's nothing morally wrong with people choosing to emigrate in order to fulfil their dreams, develop and make a contribution. Furthermore, the success of many Israelis abroad (scientists, doctors, business people, artists, athletes, models etc.) shows that sometimes residents that leave us to fulfil their dreams abroad can serve as excellent ambassadors for Israel and improve its reputation.

Emigrants are also a reflection of the quality of life in Israel that alerts us of what we should improve. This might force us as a society and a country to improve and become more attractive. Even people who left the kibbutzim at the time, served as an accelerator that sparked a positive change.

However, Israel still might be facing an existential danger in regards to the potential of uprooting. The emigration debate in Israel has been transformed recently, with social media taking it one step forward. For the first time in history, people are publicly speaking in favour of emigration for the purpose of self-realization. Even more importantly, more and more

Israelis feel comfortable expressing 'heretic' notions in public: perhaps Zionism has failed. Reality is hectic – rocket fire, terrorist attacks, political scandals and more. Israel may have been under threat since its inception, but the dangers are growing (particularly from the fundamentalist Islamists and the western far left) and Israel seems to be weaker and helpless. The external enemies are crueller and more equipped than ever and the potential damage is devastating (they don't hide their ultimate goal – the destruction of Israel).

Next to the feeling of purpose and vision, Israel's greatest source of attraction has always been the warm relationship and feeling of belonging to a community. This 'togetherness' has lost its edge over the years. In its first decades, the State offered its citizens something very unique and rewarding: a deep sense of purpose. This is why many citizens were willing to make sacrifices and justify just about anything. They were thinking about future generations in almost religious terms. The fall of the innocent Zionist ethos and the rise of materialism, selfishness, cynicism, vulgarity and mistrust, have eliminate the deep sense of purpose that once captivated the Israelis. If the main purpose in life is to make money and consume entertainment, there's no real reason to do it here. When the social pillars of fire weaken, one simple question remains: what's the best place for me?

Emigration isn't as hard and tormenting for millennials as it is for previous generations because their lifestyle is global. They share a language with their contemporaries abroad. They basically live the same lifestyle, use the same technologies and buy the same brands, watch the same TV shows and surf on the same websites. Operating systems are the same on all computers around the world as are the smartphone apps. We're heading towards a global language that weakens the importance of one's geographic whereabouts.

The global world's mobility and openness nowadays also increase young people's potential for meeting partners from other countries. At the moment, most marriages across the globe and particularly in Israel are endogamous, but in a world without borders, love for one's partner is stronger than love for the homeland.

The soaring demand for foreign passports and increase in the number of respondents who have admitted to positively considering the option of living abroad, indicates that we might be looking at a big wave of emigration in the future after all. Though moving abroad is more of a fantasy at the moment, like the dream of changing one's profession or workplace, when people feel less attached to their country, when human relations become contaminated and when relocating to another country becomes easier on a practical and technical level, the potential for emigration grows.

In our estimation, the greatest threat to the State of Israel is the development of a good Israeli alternative abroad. There already are 'Israeli kibbutzim' (informal Israeli communities) in California, Australia and other places across the globe. These 'kibbutzim' are inhabited by business people, scientists, artists, potheads, students and even pensioners (living in cheap places because Israel has become a tense place where it's expensive and more dangerous to grow up in). Moving to Berlin is but one symbolic example of this process.

At the moment these are tiny 'kibbutzim', but if one of them grows and turns into an Israeli town or city, it could definitely attract a mass of high quality people and thin out the minerals within the decaying body of Israel.

Israeli emigrants are no longer ashamed of leaving the country, and many of them build their own social frameworks and local facilities for the Israeli communities or cooperate with the local Jewish population.

Furthermore, leading politicians, scientists and artists often visit and entertain in major Israeli emigration centres in the United States and Canada, in an atmosphere of tolerance and mutual fondness. Many also take it upon themselves to serve as goodwill ambassadors, proudly representing Israel and protecting its image from slanderers and enemies.

Not Coming to Town Meetings

Millennials continue to grow old, at least biologically-speaking, and it begs the question: will the personality traits depicted in our study change over time? Obviously, the answer is yes, but we probably won't be seeing any sweeping changes. Psychological studies have shown that people's personalities are mostly formed by their mid-twenties, after which their core traits are either refined or radicalized.

Can this generation redeem itself as well as the rest of us? Change the system and lead a social revolution? Doubtful. Millennials aren't likely to bring the revolution, because they don't have the morals or the ambition that past generations had.

Perhaps Generation Y's weaknesses will lead to a solution in the future. Sometimes it's the 'slumping rebellion' that does the trick. This is how the kibbutz movement changed at the time. While the founders were arguing amongst themselves, the kibbutzim's youths stopped coming to town meetings and some of them quietly abandoned their roots. They figured the kibbutz would do just fine without them, which escalated the internal crisis and eventually forced the conservatives to embrace change.

A similar process is already taking place in the employment field. Young employees aren't hitting the streets holding protest banners in order to change their employment conditions (wages, hours, etc.) They simply quit and go on a new adventure. In between, they go on self-prescribed vacations and sabbaticals that allow them to catch their breath. Hence, the private rebellion, which is driven by selfish motives, becomes a silent social movement that applies more pressure on the system.

Generally speaking, millennials would rather manoeuvre and manipulate the existing rules than fight the establishment to enact change. This isn't exclusive to the employment market but often happens in other fields as well. However, the 'quiet subversion' is undermining long-standing conventions, generating an escalating crisis that will require us all to reinvent ourselves.